STOURTON BEFORE STOURHEAD

STOURTON BEFORE STOURHEAD

A History of the Parish

1550-1750

STUART A RAYMOND

THE HOBNOB PRESS

First published in the United Kingdom in 2019

by The Hobnob Press,
8 Lock Warehouse, Severn road, Gloucester GL1 2GA
www.hobnobpress.co.uk

British Library Cataloguing in Publication Data
A catalogue record for this book is available from the British Library

ISBN 978-1-906978-68-6

Typeset in Scala 11/14 pt. Typesetting and origination by John Chandler

CONTENTS

PREFACE AND ACKNOWLEDGEMENTS

As a child, I regularly visited the gardens at Stourton after church on summer Sunday evening with my family in the late 1940s and 1950s. I rarely visited for the next three decades, but in the 1990s and 2000s I began to do so occasionally whilst travelling up and down the A303 to Exeter. But it is only since moving to Trowbridge in 2010 that I have been able to visit more frequently, and to research the history of the parish.

Most historians of Stourton (with the important exceptions of Calland and Day) have concentrated their attention on the development of Stourhead. The people who actually lived in the parish (with the exception of the Hoare family) have mostly been ignored. However, the parish and its people do have a fascinating history pre-Stourhead. Its religious history is particularly interesting; there are very few places in England where a Catholic congregation has survived from the Reformation until the twentieth century. My aim in this book is to provide a history of the ordinary people of the parish in the two hundred years before Stourhead was built. Note that I have standardised many family and place-names: Davies and Jupe, for example, are both spelt in many different ways in the sources.

Most of my research has been conducted at the Wiltshire & Swindon History Centre, and I am particularly grateful to Steve Hobbs and his team for their help and advice over the last few years. Many useful documents can also be found in the National Archives. I have also used the resources of Wiltshire Archaeological and Natural History Society at Devizes, Somerset Heritage Centre in Taunton, Dorset History Centre in Dorchester, Downside Abbey, the National Trust at Stourhead, and the Bodleian Library. The librarians in Trowbridge have obtained most of the books I have needed to consult. John Chandler drew the map on p. xii, and typeset the book. My thanks too to Cathy Day, Gill Hogarth, Chris Deverill, and Rob Bonser-Wilton for their help.

ABBREVIATIONS

TNA   The National Archives
WANHS   Wiltshire Archaeological and Natural History Society
WSHC   Wiltshire and Swindon History Centre

PEDIGREES

John Cuffe (-1636) =
Joan Hill
m.1613

John (1614-14)	John (1616-32)	Richard = Selina Lewin (-1698)	Francis=Basil	William (1636-1726)	Adam (1623-75) = [?] Bayley	John (1631-)

Francis (1649-) — Richard (1715-16) — William — Basil (1662-) — Elizabeth

Martha (1672-3)

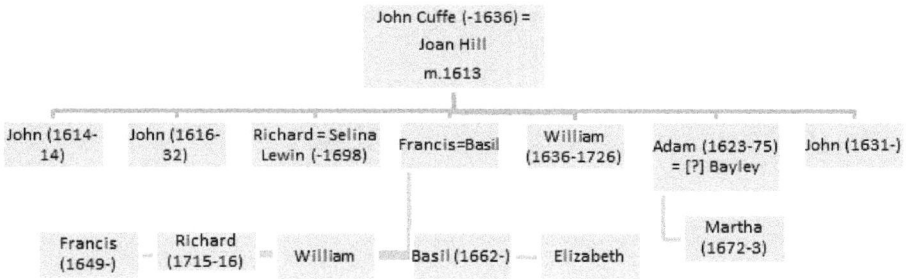

Pedigree 1: Cuffe family

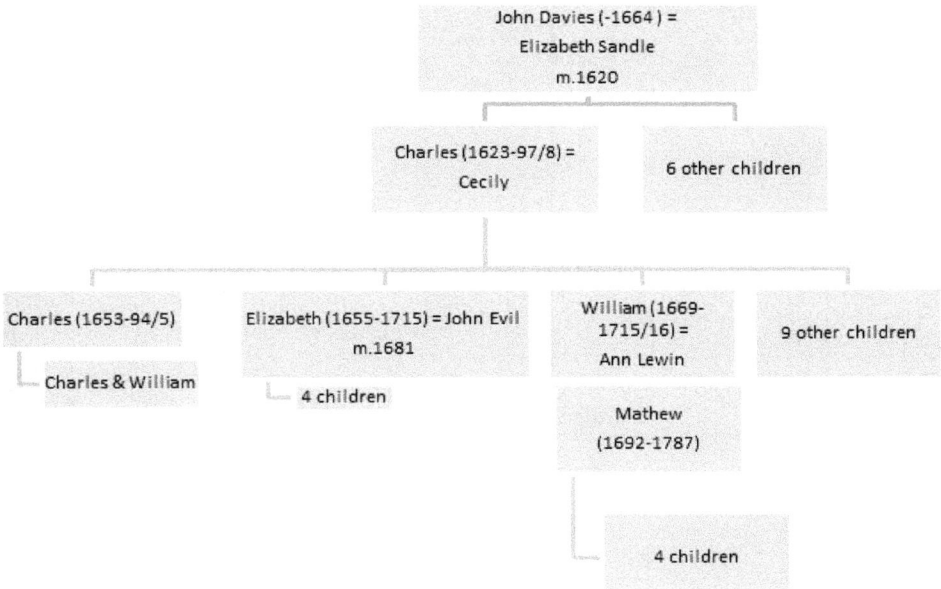

John Davies (-1664) =
Elizabeth Sandle
m.1620

Charles (1623-97/8) =
Cecily

6 other children

Charles (1653-94/5)

Charles & William

Elizabeth (1655-1715) = John Evil
m.1681

4 children

William (1669-1715/16) =
Ann Lewin

9 other children

Mathew (1692-1787)

4 children

Pedigree 2: Descendants of John Davies

John Green

Alexander (1577-1645)

Alexander

Robert (1618-87) = Alice Bryant

George (1621-) = Mary

5 other children

Edith (-1658)

George (1645-) = Elizabeth

3 other children

8 children
See separate pedigree

Robert (1674/5-)

Elizabeth (1676-)

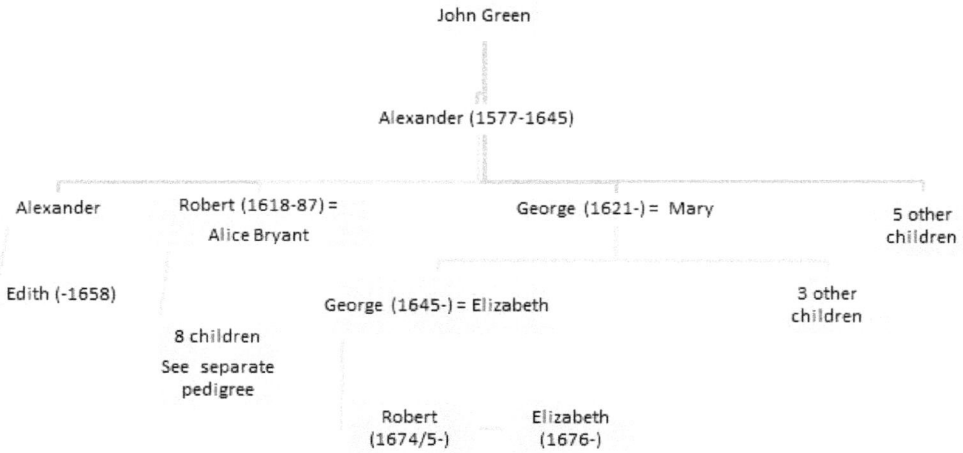

Pedigree 3: Green family, part 1

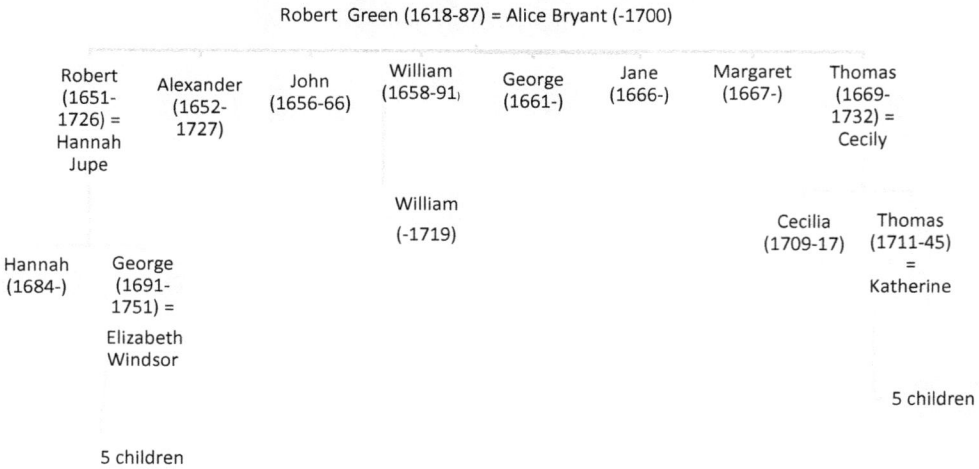

Robert Green (1618-87) = Alice Bryant (-1700)

Robert (1651-1726) = Hannah Jupe

Alexander (1652-1727)

John (1656-66)

William (1658-91)

George (1661-)

Jane (1666-)

Margaret (1667-)

Thomas (1669-1732) = Cecily

William (-1719)

Cecilia (1709-17)

Thomas (1711-45) = Katherine

Hannah (1684-)

George (1691-1751) = Elizabeth Windsor

5 children

5 children

Pedigree 4: Green family, part 2

Rinold (-1600) = Elizabeth (-1617)

John (-1638/9) = Edith Norris (-1635)
m.1578

Robert (1600-1672 =
Ann
m.1631

Francis (-1666) =
Margaret Bernard (-1649)
m.1633

4 other children

Robert (1631/2-
1675) =
Melior

See below

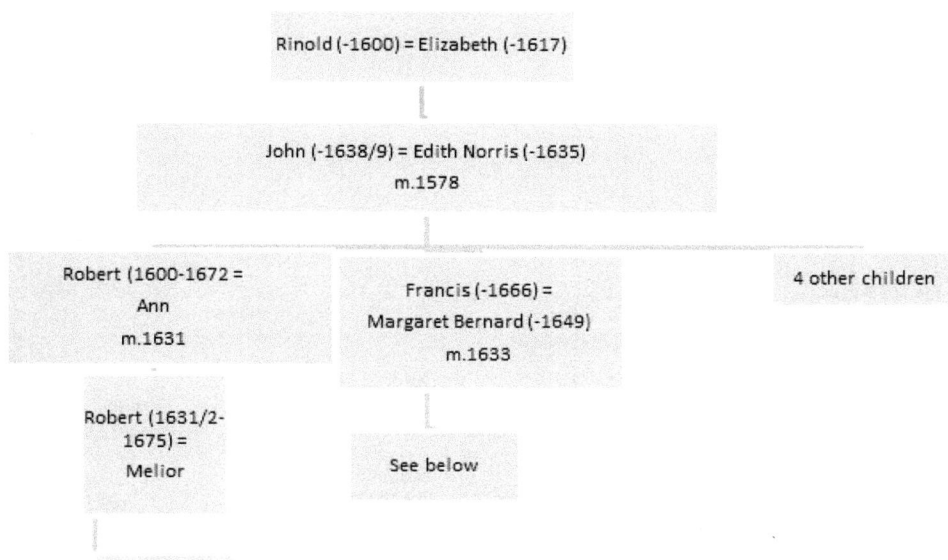

Pedigree 5: Jupe family, part 1

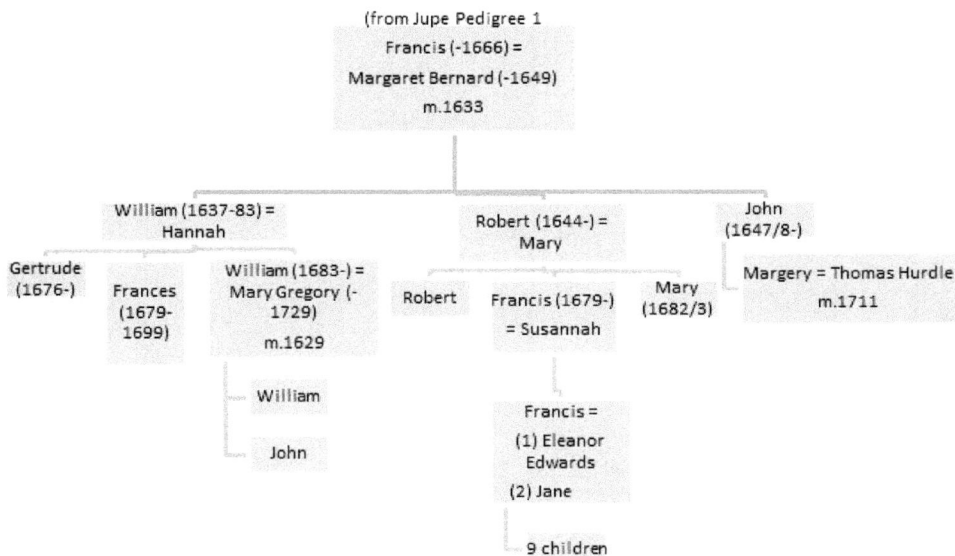

(from Jupe Pedigree 1
Francis (-1666) =
Margaret Bernard (-1649)
m.1633

William (1637-83) =
Hannah

Robert (1644-) =
Mary

John
(1647/8-)

Gertrude
(1676-)

Frances
(1679-
1699)

William (1683-) =
Mary Gregory (-
1729)
m.1629

Robert

Francis (1679-)
= Susannah

Mary
(1682/3)

Margery = Thomas Hurdle
m.1711

William

John

Francis =
(1) Eleanor
Edwards
(2) Jane

9 children

Pedigree 6: Jupe family, part 2

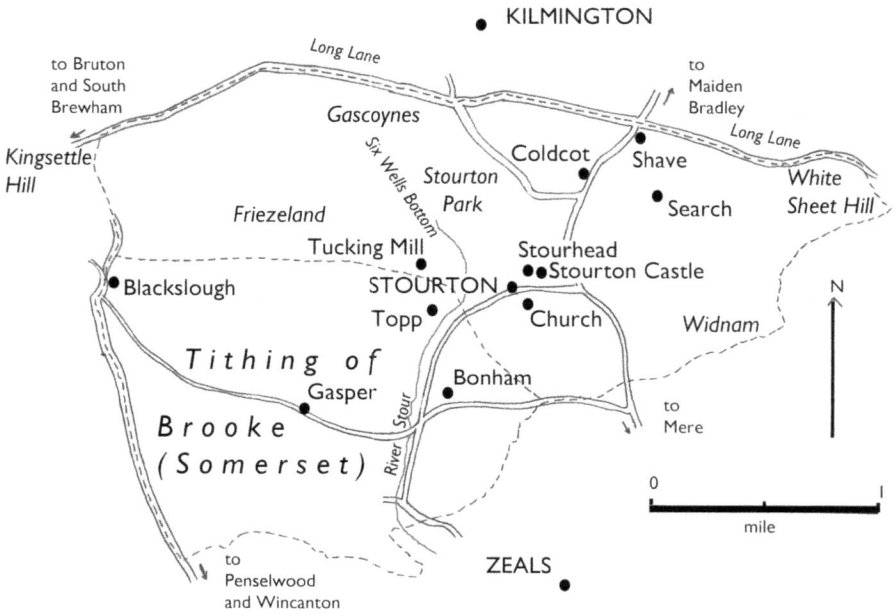

KILMINGTON

Long Lane

to Bruton
and South
Brewham

to
Maiden
Bradley

Gascoynes

Long Lane

Kingsettle
Hill

Coldcot

Shave

Stourton
Park

White
Sheet Hill

Friezeland

Search

Tucking Mill

Stourhead

Blackslough

STOURTON

Stourton Castle

N

Topp

Church

Widnam

Tithing of

Gasper

Bonham

*Brooke
(Somerset)*

to
Mere

0   1

mile

to
Penselwood
and Wincanton

ZEALS

Map of Stourton parish

I

All Horrid and Woody: Pre-Stourhead Stourton

'ALL HORRID AND WOODY'. That is how John Aubrey characterised the Stourton landscape in the early seventeenth century.[1] The fact that the land rises by 400 feet between the present Lake and Alfred's Tower would not have impressed him. But it does mean that three locally important rivers rise in the vicinity. The sources of the Brue and the Wylye are just across the parish boundary, in South Brewham and Kilmington respectively. The Brue flows to the Bristol Channel, the Wylye towards Salisbury. The Stour, from which the parish takes its name, rises in Stourton itself, and flows south to the sea at Christchurch, Dorset. In the medieval period, it was dammed just below its source in Six Wells Bottom, in order to create a number of fish-ponds. In our period, there were a number of water-mills lower down the stream, using the power of its flow to grind corn and full cloth. At the end of our period, dams created the centre-piece of the Stourhead Landscape – the Lake.[2]

Geologically, the parish mostly lies on greensand, although Whitesheet Hill is the most westerly outcrop of Salisbury Plain's chalk. The soil on the greensand is sandy; subsoil is gravel and flint in most of the parish, but changes to clay and sandstone in Gasper. There were two quarries at Search, and another at Bonham. Henry Hoare was hoping to dig a stone quarry in Little Coombe to help build Alfred's Tower in 1765.[3] The western part of the parish was described by Colt Hoare as 'adapted only to the growth of wood'.[4]

---

1 Jackson, John Edward, ed. *Wiltshire: the topographical collections of John Aubrey.* Wiltshire Archaeological & Natural History Society, 1862, p.380.
2 For a semi-fictional account of the development of the Lake, see Woodbridge, Tim. *The Choice.* Dotesio Publishing, 2017.
3 Ibid, p.197.
4 Hoare, Richard Colt. *The Modern History of South Wiltshire.* John Bowyer

Aubrey was not alone in disparaging the pre-Stourhead scenery. Mrs Powys in 1776 thought that it had been 'nothing more than naked hills and dreary vales' before Henry Hoare took the landscape in hand, and said that 'this might be discovered from the disagreeableness of the country the instant you are out of Mr Hoare's domains'.[1]

Despite the comments of Aubrey and Powys, the area is now designated an area of outstanding natural beauty. It would be almost unrecognisable to the tenants of Edward Lord Stourton, the 13th Baron. He sold the estate in 1714 to Sir Thomas Meres, having secured an act of Parliament to confirm his title.[2] Meres' son, Sir John, in turn sold it to the London banker, Henry Hoare, in 1717, although not before having a survey of the manor made.[3]

Hoare's purchase led to dramatic changes in the landscape of the parish. Developments began with the demolition of the Castle (at a cost of over £114) in 1721,[4] and the building of Stourhead. In 1704, the Castle was described as 'a noble large house in a most pleasant country'.[5] But it was probably in a poor state when Hoare purchased it, given that it had been made uninhabitable during the Civil War,[6] and that the financial woes of the Stourton family would have prevented them from spending much money on it. The Hoares, however, were not strapped for cash, and spent upwards of £20,000 on building 'a large family seat with outhousing, gardens, wood-works, water-works &c'.[7] The church, which

Nichols & John Gough Nichols, 1822, p.87.

1   Climenson, Emily, ed. *Passages from the diary of Mrs Philip Lybbe Powys of Hardwick House, Oxon., A.D.1756 to 1808*. Longmans Green & Co., 1899, p.169.

2   Mowbray, Lord. *The history of the noble house of Stourton*. Elliot Stock, 1899, p.514 & 525-6.

3   WSHC 383/348.

4   383/58, f.7.

5   WSHC 383/255. Despite the existence of a contemporary map, its exact location has not yet been discovered by the archaeologists; cf. **https://archaeologynationaltrustsw.wordpress.com/2016/10/15/stourhead-wheres-stourton-castle**

6   Firth, C.H., ed. *The Memoirs of Edmund Ludlow, Lieutenant General of the Horse in the Army of the Commonwealth of England, 1625-1672*. Clarendon Press, 1898. Vol.1, p.97; Green, Mary Anne Everett, ed. *Calendar of the proceedings of the Committee for Compounding with Delinquents &c., 1643-1660 ... cases 1643-1646*. HMSO, 1890, p.1258.

7   WSHC 212b/6265. The date of this estimate is not clear, but it was made by the son of the purchaser, perhaps after he had moved in after his mother's

had no doubt been neglected under its impecunious Roman Catholic patron, was also renovated.

Much greater alterations were commenced in the 1740s. Henry Hoare – known by his family as 'the Magnificent' – took up residence after his mother's death in 1741, and began to design a huge garden centred around a lake. He had already planted a fir walk c.1733.[1] Mrs Powys thought that not even Capability Brown could have 'executed [the design] with more taste and elegance'.[2] The amount of work involved was enormous. The lake began as a series of ponds around the springs at the Grotto and Paradise Well.[3] It finally took its full shape in 1757.[4] It was surrounded with gardens, grottoes, temples, and numerous sculptures. During the eighteenth and nineteenth centuries, the estate was replanted with new species of trees, such as beech, conifers, rhododendrons and other exotics. By 1843, there were 1,288 acres of woodland in the parish.[5] Almost all the houses on the estate were demolished and rebuilt by the Hoares.

In order to appreciate what the landscape of Stourton looked like in the seventeenth century and earlier, it is necessary to ignore the gardens, the Lake, the houses, and Stourhead itself. Apart from the church and Bonham, none of the buildings currently standing in the parish date back much further than the Hoare era. The Stour, after passing through the fishponds in Six Wells Bottom, flowed uninterrupted past the church and village, only encountering a few mills and ponds. There were many woodlands, predominantly oak, ash and elm, which also dominated the

death in 1741. Building accounts show that £10,150 10s 5d had been spent on the house alone at the time of Henry Hoare's death in 1725; cf. Hutchins, Victoria. *Messrs Hoare, bankers*. Constable, 2005, p.46.

1 McKewan, Colin. *Stourhead Lake Project 2005: Survey and Excavation of the Lakes at Stourhead House*. Nautical Archaeological Society, 2006. Online at **https://nauticalarchaeologysociety.org/sites/default/files/u9/NAS%20 Stourhead%20Master%20composite%20Report-01_sml.pdf**

2 Climenson, op cit, p.169.

3 Woodbridge, Kenneth. 'Henry Hoare's Paradise', *Arts Bulletin* 47, 1965, p.92; McKewan, Colin. *Stourhead Lake Project 2005: Survey and Excavation of the Lakes at Stourhead House*. Nautical Archaeological Society, 2006. Online at **https://nauticalarchaeologysociety.org/sites/default/files/u9/NAS%20 Stourhead%20Master%20composite%20Report-01_sml.pdf**

4 For the land purchases required for landscaping, see p.122.

5 Sandell, R.E., ed. *Abstract of Wiltshire tithe apportionments*. Wiltshire Record Society 30. 1975, p.95.

hedgerows. Alder, ash and withies grew in Friezland; there were some elms in Little Oare.[1] The poor were presented in the manorial court in 1742 and 1743 for cutting 'holleys and other sorts of wood' in the commons.[2]

Stourton lies in the far south-west corner of Wiltshire, bordering on Somerset and Dorset – a situation which may have proved useful for the parish's many Roman Catholics, who could avoid arrest by crossing county boundaries. The small manors of Bonham (350 acres) and Gasper (1240 acres) were in Somerset, and sometimes referred to as the Tithing of Brook.[3] The 1819 perambulation of the boundaries of the manor of Stourton recorded that the adjacent manors were Zeals, Mere, Norton Ferris, Kilmington, South Brewham, Gasper and Bonham.[4] The manor of Gasper was perambulated at the same time; it was found to bound South Brewham, Shepton Montague, Wincanton, Penselwood, Zeals, Bonham and Stourton.[5] The northern and western boundaries of the parish were also the boundaries of the Forest of Selwood, although it is possible that in the twelfth century the Forest had extended into Stourton.[6]

The area of the parish was measured at 3,544 acres in 1839,[7] and at 3,543 acres in 1851.[8] It was bounded on the north by Long Lane, leading towards Kingsettle Hill and Bruton. Before the turnpikes, this was a part of the main route between London and the South West.[9] There are still milestones dated 1750 on the dis-used part of this road across Whitesheet Hill.[10] Celia Fiennes travelled this way, and found it

1   WSHC 383/253.
2   WSHC 383/353.
3   Acreages of Bonham and Gasper are as given in Ellis, John Henry, ed. *The Registers of Stourton, County Wilts., from 1570 to 1800.* Harleian Society publications 12. 1887, p.viii.
4   WSHC 3117/13.
5   Ditto.
6   McGarvie, Michael. *The Bounds of Selwood: an examination.* Frome Society for Local Study, 1978, frontispiece & p.18. See also McGarvie, Michael. 'Brewcombe', *Notes & Queries for Somerset & Dorset* 32, 1986, p.517-22.
7   Sandell, R.E., ed. *Abstract of Wiltshire tithe apportionments.* Wiltshire Record Society 30. 1975, p.95.
8   Mowbray, op cit, p.1.
9   Jackson, Gwyneth F. *A tale of two manors: Zeals, a Wiltshire village.* Dickins Printers, 1999, p.15 & 18.
10 Day, Cathy. *Wiltshire marriage patterns, 1754-1914.* Cambridge Scholars, 2013, p.135.

somewhat tortuous: from Bruton 'we ascend a very high steep hill all in a narrow lane cut out of the rocks, and the way is all like stone steps; the sides are rocks on which grow trees thick, their roots runs amongst the rocks, and in many places fine clean springs buble out and run along out of the rocks'.[1] It took her an hour to ascend Kingsettle Hill in her 'chariot'.

Another fairly straight road ran from Long Lane through the middle of the parish, passing Coldcot Farm, and keeping the Glebe on the west, crossing Bonham Lane near the southern boundary. Stourton Lane led from this road towards Kilmington, also crossing Long Lane. Slightly further to the south, another road went in a westerly direction from this north-south route, passing through Stourton Town to join up with the road to Gasper on the right. On the left lay Bonham Lane, leading to Bonham, which was close to the southern boundary. The present-day road layout is not identical with this pattern; some diversions were inevitable given the dramatic changes to the landscape. By 1743, Henry Hoare had laid out 'a new made road or droveway' from Stourhead to Whitesheet Hill, and wished to plant an avenue of trees along it.[2]

The parish was characterized by small enclosures of four or five acres. There were some arable fields, but the majority of the land was used for pasture. Probate inventories reveal that there were many hay ricks dotted across the landscape. In the sixteenth and seventeenth centuries, cottages were being built (none survive), gardens were being created, and orchards planted. In 1567, William Green leased two acres 'with dwelling howse newly built upon the same'.[3] William Harding had just built a dwelling house on land 'sometime enclosed out of the common' when he was granted a lease in 1610.[4] John Cuffe was granted a lease in 1629 on consideration that he had 'at his owne cost erected a cottage or dwelling howse'.[5] In 1671, Robert Davies took a lease of a 'dwelling house' at Black Stoke, which had been 'latelie erected' on land which had recently been enclosed.[6] In 1719, Mary Hartnall was a widow living in a cottage built by

1   Morris, Christopher, ed. *The illustrated journeys of Celia Fiennes, 1685-c.1712.* Macdonald & Co., 1982, p.43-4.
2   WSHC 383/751.
3   WSHC 4314/1.
4   WSHC 4314/1.
5   WSHC 4314/1.
6   WSHC 383/109, f.75r

her father, John Jupe.[1] When Robert Alford died in April 1746, and his lease fell in, Henry Hoare took the opportunity to build a new cottage on the property before letting it again seven months later.[2]

Tenants were frequently required to plant trees. When John Shepherd leased a cottage with 'one small pasture' at Bonham in 1688, he was expected to plant one oak, ash, or elm tree every year.[3] Thomas Hurdle was required by his 1724 lease of ten acres to plant 'six good young growing oakes elmes or aishes' each year.[4] In 1742, when James Whitaker leased five acres from Henry Hoare, he was required to plant three trees of oak, ash or elm each year, until the premises were 'sufficiently replenished with trees of those kinds'.[5] A map drawn in 1722[6] shows a number of areas which may once have been open fields, but which by then were farmed in severalty.

There were a number of substantial farms in the parish, although not a great deal is known about them. The largest was the demesne at Stourhead, which constituted 569 acres at the end of our period.[7] By 1829, the boundaries of many properties had changed; the Home Farm then had 453 acres, which included 30 acres at Upper and Lower Gascoynes (formerly a separate farm). It seems that the Hoares had gradually rationalised the boundaries of farms during the eighteenth century; the printed survey of their properties made in 1829 shows the result.[8] Although the areas of properties shown in the survey differ from those in our period, nevertheless they do provide us with an overall impression of the extent of parts of the parish.

Coldcot, on the road towards Kilmington, is largely missing from the record, as it was not a part of the manor of Stourton. In 1627 86 acres of land were leased with the farmhouse.[9] In the 1829 survey, the farm covered 139 acres.[10]

Shave, on the Kilmington border, had once been a substantial farm, but leases indicate that it had been converted into a number of

1   WSHC 383/348.
2   WSHC 383/353.
3   WSHC 383/381.
4   WSHC 383/745.
5   WSHC 383/709.
6   WSHC 383/316.
7   WSHC 383/721. This included part of Stourton Park.
8   WSHC 130/76.
9   WSHC 4314/1.
10 WSHC 130/76.

small tenancies by the beginning of our period. In 1633, there were at least eight tenants at Shave; Robert Barnes was probably the most substantial, with 43 acres as well as the farmhouse.[1]

Search, at the bottom of Whitesheet Hill, was a substantial farm in 1829; it occupied 674 acres, and included Shave Cottage and garden,[2] although it is unlikely that it was farmed as one unit in our period. It included a number of fields known as Widnam or Widenham. Widenham may once have been a single farm in its own right, although there is no definite evidence of this. Some land there was described as 'parcel of Shave', and no fewer than fourteen tenants had property there in 1633.[3]

Bonham was another substantial farm; in 1829 it had 368 acres.[4] The 1829 survey also recorded some smaller farms; Gasper (39 acres), Heath Hill (83 acres), Blackslough (29 acres), Friezland (37 acres), and Mill Farm (27 acres).[5] The survey did not record farms at Rode and Topp, although these were mentioned in many other sources.

The rector's income partially depended on another substantial farm. The glebe covered 92 acres in 1608. It included an orchard and several large fields; there was also a barn, and an old cottage at Cribbes, which by 1663 had become a hop yard.[6]

The 1608 terrier records that the glebe included seven acres of 'arable in eastover in the open field'.[7] No other reference to open fields has been found, but there was a substantial deer park, common rough grazing, several other open areas, and much woodland. We know that there were fallow deer, and a warren stocked with coneys (rabbits) in the 1610s.[8] In 1428, John Stourton, esq., had been granted a licence to create a deer park of 1,000 acres.[9] A park was certainly created, lying to the north-west of Stourton Castle, although it may be doubted whether it ever reached the extent that was licenced. In 1611, in a Star Chamber case, John Symes referred to the fact that 100 acres of common had

1 WSHC 4314/1.
2 WSHC 130/76.
3 WSHC 4314/1.
4 WSHC 130/76.
5 WSHC 130/76.
6 Hobbs, Steven, ed. *Wiltshire glebe terriers 1588-1827*. Wiltshire Record Society 56. 2003, p.406-7.
7 Ditto..
8 TNA STAC8/73/13; STAC8/256/26.
9 *Calendar of Patent Rolls 6 Henry VI*, part 2, p.477.

been taken into Stourton Park by John, 9th Lord Stourton,[1] almost half a century earlier.[2]

In 1708, Stourton Park had 'some oaks growing on the west side, rows of aish planted by the Lodge, and rowes of aish by the fish ponds'. A survey commissioned in that year estimated the size of the Park at 265 acres – although such measurements have to be taken with a grain of salt. Lord Stourton actually had two separate surveys conducted, and found 'great differeings' in their measurements. His surveyors' arithmetical skills left something to be desired,[3] as one of them admitted. The map of 1722[4] suggests that much of the Park was wooded at that date.

Stourton Common, in the west of the parish, occupied 268 acres in 1722,[5] although it had been much larger in previous centuries. It served as rough pasture for the tenants' sheep, cattle, and horses. Both it, and the Park, were subjected to constant nibblings at their edges throughout our period, not to mention the enclosure of 500 acres in 1633.[6] They were bounded by the common of Norton Ferris, which was within the bounds of the ancient Forest of Selwood,[7] and in which the occupants of Rode had common rights. The Crown's rights in the Forest had fallen into desuetude by the seventeenth century, but were revived under the impecunious Charles I, who sought to benefit by disafforesting and enclosing them.

Disafforestation of Selwood commenced in 1627, although it was not completed until 1640.[8] It led, in 1631, to the enclosure of Norton Ferris common. Rights of common were held by the occupants of Rode, who consequently received allotments[9] from the commons. However, cottagers who benefited from the common, but had no legal rights in it, suffered the loss of an important supplement to their income, with no recompense. Forests might provide pasturage for a few cattle,

---

1   TNA STAC8/256/26.
2   John, the ninth lord, was the lord of the manor from 1557 until 1588.
3   WSHC 383/353.
4   WSHC 383/316.
5   WSHC 383/316.
6   TNA c2/ChasI/S89/24.
7   'Royal forests', *A History of the County of Wiltshire: Volume 4* (1959), pp. 391-433.
8   Sharp, Buchanan. *In contempt of all authority: rural artisans and riot in the West of England, 1586-1660.* University of California Press, 1980, p.243.
9   WSHC 383/719.

pannage for swine, game to be poached, and wood for fuel or building.[1] The importance of fuel from Stourton Common was acknowledged in Alexander Green's 1587 indenture, which granted him 'convenient fuwell according as other tenants have'.[2] When the widow, Susan Tyte, leased a house and an acre of land at The Moor in 1659, she was permitted 'sufficient fuel of furze and ferne without any wast or spoyle'.[3]

The attitude of Stourton cottagers towards enclosure had already been demonstrated over half a century earlier. In 1549, Lord Protector Somerset issued a proclamation restraining noblemen from enclosing open commons and converting them into parks and pasture for their own use. The poor took the law into their own hands and tore down the fences of Lord Stourton's Park.[4]

There is limited evidence for disturbance arising from the disafforestation of Selwood. We do know that many enclosures were thrown down in 1642 and 1643, following the outbreak of Civil War, and that the remaining enclosures were continually threatened in the following years.[5] Rioters levelled the fences of Sir Charles Berkeley at Kilmington, and of Lord Broghill at Maiden Bradley, during the 1650s.[6]

Disturbances following disafforestation were common, and are especially well documented in the neighbouring parish of Mere.[7] No direct evidence of any seventeenth-century Stourton 'rioters' has been found, but it is quite likely that some of the men who threw down fences and attacked the enclosures in neighbouring parishes came from Stourton.

Enclosure was also taking place in Stourton quite apart from the disafforestation of Selwood. Even before its commencement, Robert Sandle in 1611 leased a tenement 'built upon the common or wast'; his lease included three acres of land, and a wood, 'parcel of the common', which he presumably enclosed.[8] In the same year, John Symes insisted in the Star Chamber that the tenants of North Brewham had the right

1   Sharp, Buchanan. *In contempt of all authority: rural artisans and riot in the West of England, 1586-1660.* University of California Press, 1980, p.167.
2   WSHC 4314/1.
3   WSHC 383/538.
4   Mowbray. *op cit,* p.394.
5   Sharp, op cit, p.243.
6   Underdown, David. *Revel, riot and rebellion: popular politics and culture in England, 1603-1660.* Clarendon Press, 1985, p.214-5.
7   Sharp, op cit, p.151-4.
8   WSHC 4314/1.

to pasture eighty sheep on the common, which had been taken into the Park, and that the late John Lord Stourton had permitted tenants to kill the coneys in his warren to prevent them from destroying adjacent commons. Symes complained that his successor was attempting to end these practices.[1] His deposition also pointed out that Edward Lord Stourton, the 11th lord, had recently enclosed commons, outside of the Park.

The disafforestation of Selwood may have prompted Lord Stourton to consider enclosure in Stourton itself. In 1633, he set about the enclosure of about 500 acres of 'wast ground' where his warren had been. He kept a third of the land for himself; the remainder was divided between his tenants, who were given the right to kill 'coneys' who strayed on to their land, and to take the underwood, furze, and fern growing there. Thirty acres of land was reserved for poor cottagers. Whether that was enough to content them we do not know. Our evidence for the enclosure is provided by a complaint and deposition in the Court of Chancery, a collusive action designed to secure a Chancery decree giving legal title.[2]

There are many subsequent references to this enclosure, or perhaps to later ones. In 1653, Richard Cuff's lease of a tenement in the town of Stourton included land enclosed from the common.[3] Lord William Stourton's 1672 will refers to 'my newe inclosed common grounds lying neare Stourton Parke'.[4] Land had been 'lately assigned and allotted upon the division of the common', according to 1671 and 1678 leases.[5] In 1693, Charles Barnes' lease included 8 acres 'taken out of ye common'.[6] In 1706, George Harding's lease included eight acres formerly taken out of the Common.[7] In 1731, John Owen's lease of a cottage included a garden 'taken out of the Park'.[8] The strip of land beside the highway to Mere on which John Hill had 'lately erected' a dwelling house, smith's shop, and other outhouses in 1743 had formerly

1   TNASTAC8/256/26.
2   TNA C2/ChasI/S89/24.
3   WSHC 383/725.
4   TNA PROB11/339/297
5   WSHC 383/726. Lease to John Warham, gent.; 383/109,f.75r &v..
6   WSHC 383/346.
7   WSHC 383/721.
8   WSHC 383/99, p.21.

been waste.[1] In 1746, James Whitaker leased 'all that new built cottage or dwelling house & two gardens & pasture ... in Stourton Lane ... part of ye wast of ye said manor'.[2] Similarly, Mary Edwards' lease of the same year included 'a little strip of garden ground lately taken in out of ye wast'.[3]

Stourton's manorial court attempted to regulate access to the common. In 1734, the homage ordered that no tenant should sub-let his estate 'without letting his common, therewith'.[4] This order may have been intended to prevent the poor from gaining access to the four acres of land they required before they were allowed to build a cottage. Four acres was considered by statute to be the minimum amount of land required to support a family. The order did not achieve its purpose. In 1738, 1742, and 1743 a number of individuals were presented for erecting cottages on the commons, without permission.[5]

There was much woodland in the parish. A Chancery case from early in Elizabeth's reign concerned a complaint that the sub-tenant of the Rectory had 'destroyed felled wasted and cut down dyvers and sundry woods and underwoods'.[6] An Exchequer case in 1671 concerned tithe on faggots of wood cut from a coppice.[7] In 1704, the timber on the estate was said to be worth £4000.[8] In 1707, Lord Stourton was accused of having taken advantage of this. He 'felled greate quantityes of timber', sufficient to call into question the security he had given for his mortgage to Sir Thomas Meres.[9] That probably included the timber on some 25 acres in Broom Wood, which in 1708 had recently been felled and replanted; it had a 'great many young oaks & timber oaks from 10 inches square to 20 inches'. However, at the same time, another 39 acres of the same wood was 'well grown with timber oaks of 20 inches square'. There were also several coppices, and a withybed. There were 74 acres at Friezland which had 'some trees that be oake & aish stand growing & 2 fish ponds'.[10] The fields at Rode which are now at the bottom of the lake

1 WSHC 383/752.
2 WSHC 383/353; 386/736.
3 WSHC 383/353.
4 WSHC 383/353.
5 WSHC 383/353.
6 TNA 33/75/34.
7 TNA E134/23Chas2/Mich7.
8 TNA 383/255.
9 WSHC 383/366.
10 WSHC 383/254.

boasted a bank of alders which were cut down and sold every ten years.[1] Two decades later, a rental stated that 'there is timber upon this estate of considerable value'.[2]

Henry the Magnificent was responsible for transforming much of this landscape. According to Richard Colt Hoare, his successor, Henry began to think seriously of 'improving his place by plantations' when he was in his forties, at the end of our period. 'He proceeded *con spirito* upon a widely extended scale covering barren waste with woods luxuriant'. Henry's successor, however, did not approve of the mixture of firs and beeches which he planted, and condemned 'the fir tubers calling loudly for the woodman's axe'. Colt Hoare, however, did 'feel the benefit of those extensive plantations', and thought it his duty not to suffer 'a single acre of wasteland to remain unplanted'.[3] By 1829, there were no less than 1964 acres described as 'plantations, woods, and lakes'.[4]

Most of the parish was occupied by the manor of Stourton, which, in the eighteenth century, also extended slightly into South Brewham. There were two other minor manors in the parish, separately owned in our period, although gobbled up by the Hoares later in the eighteenth century. Gasper and Bonham both lay in the South-West of the parish; Bonham was topographically a part of Gasper, although legally it was a separate manor. The lord of the manor of Norton Ferris also had some minor rights in the parish.

The Town of Stourton, between Stourton Castle and the church, was the most important centre of population. There were also hamlets at Gasper and Bonham, many cottages were built on the commons, and others were scattered across the parish, although there were very few east of the Town. Houses were thatched; their roofs were timbered. Despite repeated injunctions from the manorial homage to repair houses and barns,[5] most of these buildings have been lost; they were demolished by the Hoares, who replaced them with the picturesque cottages and farm houses which can now be seen in Stourton Town and scattered across the parish.

The Hoares also replaced Stourton Castle, tearing it down and building Stourhead in the 1720s. It is quite likely that much of the

1   TNA C11/2069/28.
2   WSHC 212B/6265.
3   Stourhead House Research Room Folder *c*.1.
4   WSHC 130/76.
5   WSHC 383/353.

building Stourhead replaced had been uninhabited for some years. However, we do know that William King, the tenant of the demesne *c.*1700, occupied the northern part of the house. He had the use of the kitchen garden, and of the 'nursery' when needed. He was able to use its 'court'.[1] Some sources refer to it as Stourton House, others as Stourton Castle. It had been a remarkable building in its day. Leland,[2] writing in the mid-sixteenth century, tells us that the Stourton 'maner place hath 2 courtes. The fronte of the inner courte is magnificent, and high embatelid, castle lyke'. Leland also tell us that there was a 'goodly gate howse', built with French prize money. There was also a bowling green.[3] The barton attached to the house included a 'great barne', a waggon house, a sheep house, and a stable, some of which were jointly used by Lord Stourton and William King, his demesne tenant *c.*1700. The two men had some discussion about the erection of new barns, a dairy house, and stables when the lease came up for renewal, but it is not clear whether anything was done.[4] The entire property was demolished when Henry Hoare bought the manor.

Hoare left the medieval gate-house to the Castle for his successors, but it too was demolished at the end of the century. The present gate-house, erected by Sir Richard Colt Hoare *c.*1799 on the site of its predecessor, may have been modelled on the original.

The manor house at Bonham, and the medieval church of St. Peter, also pre-date Stourhead. At Bonham, there is evidence of fourteenth and sixteenth century work. The rebus of William 7th Lord Stourton is built into the wall, so some building must have taken place in the early sixteenth century.[5] In the 1710s, the house was adapted for use as a Roman Catholic chapel and priest's residence. St Peter's was renovated under the direction of Nathaniel Ireson, the builder of Stourhead, who served as churchwarden in 1722. Many memorials to the Hoare family have since been erected, as have most of the tombstones in the churchyard.

The liturgy that was used in St. Peters in our period may still be used there occasionally. The church calendar likewise remains much

---

1   WSHC 383/737.
2   'Leland's journey through Wiltshire', *Wiltshire archaeological magazine* 1, 1854, p.194.
3   WSHC 383/737.
4   WSHC 383/737.
5   Mowbray, op cit, vol.2, p.588.

as it was. That calendar was largely determined by the seasons and the weather, and especially by seed-time and harvest. The rhythm of life in early modern Stourton followed the agricultural calendar. School terms would have been determined by the need for young labourers in the field. We know there was a school, because a wing of the rectory became a schoolroom in 1722, and because the schoolmistress and her charges were allocated seats in church.[1]

The ecclesiastical calendar was super-imposed on the agricultural calendar, and most major events in the Stourton calendar were ecclesiastical. Easter was celebrated in the spring, and Christmas in the depths of winter. The churchwardens had the use of the Parish House for six weeks before Pentecost, so that they could 'brew and bake' for their annual 'church ale'. Until the sixteenth century, church ales had been a popular means of funding the church; however, puritan objections led to their almost complete disappearance from the calendar following the Reformation. Evidently, this aspect of the Reformation did not extend to Stourton, perhaps as a consequence of the influence of its Roman Catholic lords.

The fair on Whitesheet Hill was another annual event. Traders came from Shaftesbury and Frome, Wincanton and Hindon, Warminster and Bruton, as well as many of the surrounding villages. There were mercers and goldsmiths, glovers and milliners, bakers and butchers, and even booksellers. The fair was a major event, requiring stabling for 'three score horses',[2] and lasting for at least three days. In 1726, Thomas Spinks and Peter Davies leased the fair for a period of three years from Henry Hoare. They were to pay £10 per annum, although in the first year they were allowed £5 to erect the required stables.[3] In 1724, there were seventy-one booth and stall holders. They each paid 10s for their booths; some also paid for sporting events such as 'cudgelling' and running. Many other traders did not have booths; they 'sat up and down as they could'.[4]

Who, then, were the parishioners who cudgelled each other and ran? Who attended the church ale, and took communion at Easter (or perhaps went to the Roman Catholic chapel at Bonham)? And who lived in the many houses and cottages which have now disappeared? It is this

1   WSHC 383/744 & 928.
2   WSHC 383/746.
3   WSHC 383/746; see also 212b/6265.
4   WSHC 383/903.

author's contention that people should be the most important feature of any local history; therefore, chapter 3 will be devoted to the histories of a representative sample of Stourton families. First, however, is the question of how many people actually lived in Stourton, where did they come from, and where did they go?

2

Counting the People

LOCAL HISTORIANS RARELY have adequate sources for determining the numbers inhabiting their parishes in our period. The parish register is generally the most useful source; tax lists, the protestation oath rolls of 1641/2, militia lists, and other listings, can usually be used to supplement its information.

For Stourton, most of this evidence is not available. There is no protestation oath roll, no militia lists, and no adequate tax list covering the whole parish. We do have the parish register, but unfortunately, it cannot be used to estimate total population in our period, since it omits an indeterminate number of Roman Catholic baptisms and marriages. Its burial entries are more useful, since it is unlikely that these were seriously affected by religious differences; the great majority of Catholics would have been buried in the churchyard, if only because, at least until much later, there was nowhere else to bury them.

Most surviving tax lists for Stourton are of little demographic value. For example, the monthly assessment for the relief of Ireland collected in 1648 gives the names of only twenty tax-payers. Obviously, many others were able to evade this levy.[1] The only other levy which has any value for demographic purposes was the 1664 hearth tax, which should list all householders. Unfortunately, only the portion relating to the tithing of Brook (Gasper) survives.[2] It was in Somerset, so was separately assessed. The assessment lists thirty-nine houses. Another hearth tax listing for the tithing, dated c.1670, lists a further twenty-

1   WSHC 413/29, edited in Hurley, Beryl, ed. *Wiltshire protestation returns 1641-42 & taxation records for Warminster Division 1648.* Wiltshire Family History Society, 1997, p.54-5.
2   Holworthy, R, ed. *Hearth tax for Somerset 1664-5.* Dwelly's national records, 1. Fleet: E.Dwelly, 1916, p.95-7. Calland, Gary. *St. Peter's Stourton: a tour and history of the church.* Henry Cadogan Hoare, 2010, p.74-5.

five householders who were exempt. If we assume that there were 4.3 inhabitants in each house,[1] then the population of the tithing would have been c.275 at this date.

Fortunately, there are a number of other unique sources, which provide us with some limited information. The seating plan for the church,[2] which can be dated to the 1720s, names the occupants of 118 seats. Another nine pews are mentioned. They presumably all had room for several individuals, but no names are given. This plan should in principle list every householder, but there are demonstrable omissions – although admittedly some may have sat in the pews whose occupants are un-named. There are two other difficulties. Some pew-holders are referred to by the name of their house rather than by their surname. The plan also lists some wives – but not all. It is therefore not possible to multiply the total number of seat-holders by the average size of households in order to estimate total population.

A much more useful listing is dated just after the close of our period. It describes itself as a 'list of the inhabitants of Stourton & Gasper to Dine at Stourhead Dec 22 1751'.[3] It names heads of households, and provides a count of the numbers living in each house. It is clear, however, that some inhabitants were missing. It records 478 inhabitants altogether, living in 111 households (excluding Stourhead itself). It thus provides us with a minimum estimate of the population in 1751. Incidentally, it records an average of 4.3 inhabitants per household, which is the multiplier we have already used to estimate population from the hearth tax lists.

We also have the 1722 map of the manor of Stourton,[4] which, crucially, depicts all of the buildings on the manor. There were 69. A few of these may have been barns and other outhouses, but the vast majority were houses. It is unlikely that houses were uninhabited, and we can therefore multiply the number of houses by the average size of a household to calculate total population. The houses included Stourton Castle, which would have had a larger household than average – although at this date it was in the process of demolition. Against this we must balance the fact that a handful of the buildings may not have

1   Arkell, Tom. 'Multiplying factors for estimating population totals from the hearth tax', *Local population studies* 28, 1982, p.51-7.
2   WSHC 383/928.
3   WSHC 383/259.
4   WSHC 383/316.

been houses. If we use the multiplier of 4.3, as discussed above, we can estimate that the manorial population was 296 in 1722. This, of course, does not include the population of the tithing of Brook, which is not covered by the map. If, however, we add the estimated population of that tithing for 1665 – admittedly over half a century earlier, then we have a possible population of 571. As we will see, population was increasing towards the end of our period, so this is likely to be an under-estimate, but it does bear comparison with the number of diners at Stourhead in 1751. The available figures are not very accurate, but, broadly, it seems reasonable to suppose that the population of Stourton in our period fluctuated between 500 and 600, perhaps more by 1750.

It is probable that population increased during the early eighteenth century. That is suggested by the increasing number of entries recorded in the parish register. Burial numbers admittedly fluctuated considerably, decade by decade, although they were steady in the thirty years after 1640. Decadal figures are as follows:

1570s	35
1580s	66
1590-1639	Not available
1640s	87
1650s	83
1660s	82
1670s	118
1680s	Not available
1690s	Not available
1700s	85
1710s	124
1720s	147
1730s	91
1740s	121

Despite the fluctuations, the long-term trend was upwards. Numbers never returned to the level of the 1570s.

Using marriage entries from the registers for demographic purposes is more problematic, in view of the strength of Roman Catholicism in the parish, and the fact that most Catholics did not marry in St. Peters. We also have to discount the increasing numbers of early eighteenth-century couples who used St Peters as a marriage centre, but actually came from parishes as far away as Wherwell in Hampshire (43 miles[1]) and Shepton Mallet in Somerset (17 miles).[2]

In the seventeenth century, there were, on average, roughly fifteen marriages per decade. The discounted numbers for the succeeding period were:

1700s	21
1710s	27
1720s	17
1730s	30
1740s	31

It is clear that as in the case of burial entries, the trend was upwards. Increasing numbers of marriage and burial entries both reflected increasing population, which is also evidenced by the constant 'nibblings' at the edges of the common and Park discussed in chapter 1.

Eighteenth-century marriage entries in the parish register, unlike earlier entries, record the residences of those parties who resided outside of the parish. We can therefore gain some idea of where Stourton parties sought their marriage partners. Again, ignoring those cases where both parties came from outside of the parish, no less than 45 of the 105 marriages that took place between 1710 and 1749 included one party who was not from Stourton. They all came from local parishes. No less than nineteen were from Mere. Six came from Kilmington, and three from Horningsham. Gillingham, Longbridge Deverill, Maiden Bradley, Penselwood, and Wincanton all sent two. The rest came from a range of other local parishes; the most distant were from East Pennard and Shepton Mallet – both seventeen miles away. Interestingly, there were none from the adjacent parishes of Charlton Musgrove and Brewham: did the exceptionally steep Kingsettle Hill act as a barrier to courting in this direction?

The bonds required from couples seeking marriage licences also reveal the distance travelled by marriage partners.[3] Those for the early

---

1   Distances are as calculated by the AA **www.theaa.com/route-planner/index. jsp**

2   For Stourton as a marriage centre, see below, pp. 213-14.

3   The following paragraphs are based on Sarum Marriage Licence Bonds **www.findmypast.co.uk**. Note that the grant of a licence did not necessarily mean that a marriage took place.

eighteenth century largely corroborate the parish register entries just discussed. Seventeenth-century licences identify at least eight couples who entered bonds with partners from outside of the parish. Marriage licences were more expensive than the calling of banns, so most of the couples involved would have been relatively well off. Most of them came from no further away than five or ten miles, but one partner, Richard Batt,[1] was studying at the Inner Temple. He actually came from East Chinnock, over 30 miles distant. Another came from Salisbury, which was almost as far. Both partners from Stourton were amongst the parish elite: one, Elizabeth Field, was the daughter of the rector (who in the end did not marry her Inner Temple partner); the other described himself as a gentleman.

The marriage bonds also reveal that a number of Stourton couples elected to have their marriage ceremony away from their home parish. For example, John Bennett married Sarah Band in Warminster in 1731. Similarly, according to their 1730 bond, James Whitaker and Ann Lamb were considering marrying in Pertwood (9 miles). In fact they married in the adjoining parish of Chicklade. Two Stourton couples, both from the families of leading tenants, intended to be married in Salisbury, one (John Hurdle and Elizabeth Parsons) in the Cathedral, the other (Thomas Lampard and Mary Carey) in St Edmunds.

Parish registers from other parishes have not been searched for spouses from Stourton. However, Ellen Banister is known to have married Ralph Jukes (or Dukes) of Gillingham before 1693.[2] Mary Davies married John Anstis of Wells (23 miles) in the early eighteenth century.[3] A marriage is also recorded between John Bradden and Mary Cable, widow, in 1725; she came from Lopen, near Crewkerne[4].

Bastardy examinations from the early eighteenth century also provide information on how far potential spouses might travel. In the early eighteenth century, most fathers of bastards did not travel far to find their victims. Some were Stourton parishioners, but others came from Bayford and Kilmington, both just across the border in Somerset, and from Marston Bigot, at the other end of Selwood Forest (although

1   Inner Temple Admissions Database **www.innertemplearchives.org.uk/ detail.asp?id=14101**
2   WSHC 383/346.
3   WSHC 383/97, f.13.
4   WSHC 383/541. The manuscript reads 'Lopham'.

the grandfather lived in Stourton).[1] Mary Martyn had a different experience. She encountered Dupe Pierce, a travelling razor grinder, in Blashford (Hampshire) – nearly forty miles from Stourton – in 1741. But she was not examined until 1745, by which time she had travelled home to Stourton.[2]

Baptismal entries in the parish registers also tell us something about the horizons of local people. Few entries prior to 1700 record out of parish baptisms, but there were 54 between 1700 and 1749. Unlike marriage partners, the great majority of out of parish babies came from parishes immediately adjacent to Stourton: there were eighteen from Kilmington, ten from Zeals, seven from Mere, and five from both Bourton and Brewham – although, surprisingly, only one from Penselwood, and, again, none from Charlton Musgrove. A handful came from a little further away – three from Gillingham, two from Frome, one from Stour Provost, one from Maiden Bradley, one from East Knoyle, and another from West Knoyle. It appears likely that most parents resorted to their nearest clergyman to conduct baptisms when their own incumbent was not available.

There were fewer entries for burials of people from outside of the parish, and, again, most of them are from the last fifty years of our period. It is likely that the majority relate to people who died whilst they were visiting Stourton. Most were from neighbouring parishes, although there was one from Upton Lovell (15 miles) in 1722/3, and Joseph Windsor of Hindon (12 miles) was buried in 1717. He was the son of a Stourton resident who had moved away from the parish, but presumably died whilst visiting family who had stayed in Stourton.[3]

There were obviously a wide range of other contacts between Stourton and other parishes. We do not know why John Kerbey bequeathed small amounts to the churches of Mere and Gillingham in 1600, but he evidently had connections there.[4] Many contacts related to employment opportunities. We have already seen that the tradesmen at Whitesheet Fair came from as far as Hindon and Frome – both roughly twelve miles away. Migrants who sought settlement certificates from their home parishes in order to be allowed to settle in Stourton legally came from roughly the same area - two came from Mere, two

1   WSHC 1240/28.
2   WSHC 1240/29.
3   WSHC P2/W/701.
4   WSHC P2/K/72.

from Horningsham, others from Warminster, Fonthill Gifford, West Knoyle, Bruton, and Stour Provost. Others came from a little further away – Quarley in Hampshire (34 miles), Bincombe in Dorset (42 miles), Chitterne (18 miles).[1] Conversely, in 1715, one family obtained a certificate from the Stourton overseers to reside in Maiden Bradley .[2]

Apprenticeship also meant migration. We know of at least one adolescent who came from a distance to serve an apprenticeship in Stourton; Thomas Landock came from Wool in Dorset (37 miles) in 1735.[3] No doubt many others travelled similar distances.

Stourton boys also travelled to take up apprenticeships.[4] We know of several who served in London (109 miles), and one in Dulverton, Somerset (77 miles). Pauper apprentices did not travel quite so far. Four are known to have served their apprenticeships in Mells; several others in parishes neighbouring Stourton.

Settlement examinations and removal orders reveal the distances that some paupers travelled.[5] Henry Cooper, his wife, and four children, only had to remove his family from Stourton to Kilmington in 1738.[6] A few years later, in 1743, the Kilmington overseers obtained a removal order to send Michael Brimson, with his wife and daughter, back to Stourton.[7] In 1746, Mary Rea and her young son was removed from Gasper to Maiden Bradley[8] .

In the same year, William Evil, also a native of Stourton, stated that he had served John Bradden of Gasper for a year when he was aged thirteen, before going into service with a clergyman in Bruton for three years, thus giving him a settlement in Bruton. Thomas Evil, probably a relative, travelled a little further; he was apprenticed in Heytesbury[9] (13 miles), and married a girl from Tisbury (13 miles) in Fovant (15 miles), before returning to Stourton, where his wife had a baby and he claimed relief in 1752[10] . William Lapham, a labourer, was in service in

---

1   WSHC 1240/20. Certificates survive for 1703 onwards
2   WSHC 482/49/B.
3   TNA IR1/14, f.98.
4   For apprentices, see below, pp. 169-72
5   WSHC 1240/21.
6   WSHC A1/130.
7   Somerset Heritage Centre Q/SR/311/77.
8   Somerset Heritage Centre Q/SR/314/164.
9   Hatchbury in mss.
10 WSHC 1240/21. He was actually licenced to marry in Swallowcliffe, a couple of miles away; cf Sarum Marriage Licences **www.findmypast.co.uk**

Hill Deverill, East Knoyle, and Wylye, before returning to Stourton in 1752.[1] It is likely that some migrants came out of the Forest of Selwood; this area provided Wiltshire with a substantial proportion of its vagrants in the early seventeenth century.[2]

Others travelled much further. William Smart, whose legal settlement was in Stourton, was removed from Carisbrooke on the Isle of Wight (70 miles) in 1730. Mary Markey, born in Stourton, 'travelled around'. Her master moved from Maiden Bradley to Tavistock (Devon), and took her with him. She then had his illegitimate child in Plymouth (109 miles), and two years later married a soldier there. In 1746 she was claiming relief in Stourton.[3]

Paupers who travelled long distances, such as Mary Markey, were regarded with great suspicion. The examination of Roger Snow by Sir Edward Hext, JP, in 1606 demonstrates why. Snow described how he fell in with thieves near Stourton, and stayed overnight in the house of Philip Tryvett, where stolen goods could be sold. He then travelled on towards London seeking service, which he actually found near Oxford. But he left his master without leave, and travelled to Wilton, where he met John Bacon (probably of Stourton). The two then broke into a house, and returned to Tryvett's house to dispose of their ill-gotten gain. However, they kept a gold ring and a few other items – which were found on them when they were subsequently apprehended near Brewham. They were committed to Ilchester gaol. Snow implicated Bacon in several other robberies, noting that he had once been apprehended in Shaftesbury, and imprisoned in Dorchester gaol. He was also able to reveal the names of the receivers of stolen goods in Cole and Lottisham in Somerset. Although Snow was apprehended, criminals who moved around could easily escape punishment.[4]

The travels of two other paupers may have had something to do with the fact that Chideock (49 miles) was a seat of the recusant Lords Arundel, and consequently the centre of Dorset Catholicism. Catherine Hurden was removed from Chideock to Stourton in 1729; William

1   WSHC 1240/21.
2   Beier, A.L. *Masterless men: the Vagrancy Problem in England 1560-1640*. Methuen, 1987, p.37.
3   WSHC 1240/21.
4   Cunnington, B.Howard, ed. *Records of the County of Wilts, being extracts from the Quarter Sessions Great Rolls of the Seventeenth Century*. Devizes: B.Simpson & Co., 1932, p.16-17

Torteshall, examined in 1751, stated that he had been born there, and indeed had subsequently served the Lords Arundel and Castlehaven, at Wardour Castle (15 miles) and Tisbury (13 miles) respectively.

The career of Richard Williams, another pauper, may also have been affected by the gentry. He was examined by Henry Hoare in 1745, and found to have his legal settlement in Quarley, Hampshire (35 miles) – where the examining Justice was himself lord of the manor, and had spent his early life.[1] One wonders if Hoare himself had brought Williams to Stourton to work on his new gardens. Williams had a settlement certificate from the overseers of Quarley accepting their liability to relieve him.[2]

There can be little doubt that the greatest draw for new families in Stourton was the building of Stourhead, and the employment offered by building work and the new gardens. Many labourers and tradesmen were recruited in the surrounding parishes. John Edwards, the glazier, for example, came from Maiden Bradley, although from 1719 he held a small tenement in Stourton.[3] The more skilled, such as Nathaniel Ireson and Francis Faugoin, were recruited from much further afield. Ireson came from Warwickshire to supervise the building of the house, although he subsequently moved on to Wincanton. The Faugoin family, who arrived in Stourton in 1747, were originally Huguenot refugees; Francis Faugoin was born in Northamptonshire, but worked for connections of the Hoare family in Grateley and Quarley before marrying and being appointed as steward at Stourton.[4] His wife, Mary Swetnam, worked for the Hoare family in London. She was probably recruited by the Hoares for their London house from Stourton, as there was a family of that name in the parish. The name was mentioned in the Hoare family's accounts as early as 1739, and perhaps earlier.[5] When the manorial lords wanted legal expertise, they looked first to their stewards, who did not necessarily live in Stourton. In 1678, for example, George

---

1 There is a settlement certificate from Quarley acknowledging their liability for poor relief; WSHC 1240/20.
2 WSHC 1240/20.
3 WSHC 383/97, f.9; 383/99, p.4.
4 Mottershaw, Julia. Francis Faugoin – Steward to Henry Hoare II at Stourhead: Who Was He?
www.merehistoricalsociety.org.uk/PDFs/MHSNewsletterFeb2017.pdf page=22
5 WSHC 383/61.

Hussey lived in Marnhull.[1] In the late seventeenth century, the Knipe family of Semley provided several stewards .[2]

The lords of the manor had wide contacts outside of the parish. Both the Stourtons and the Hoares acted on the national stage, and regularly travelled between Stourton, London, and their various other properties scattered around the country. When William, 12th Lord Stourton died in 1685, his heir, Edward, was not only a minor, but he was also in France; he was aged twenty, and perhaps visiting his brothers at Douai.[3] Many members of the family entered, or at least visited, Catholic institutions on the continent.[4] The wills of the Stourton family reveal some of their personal connections; for example, when Thomas Stourton, gent., made his will in 1688 he left John Beale of Reading, Berkshire, £25, which he was owed by Francis Coventry, esq., of Carshalton .[5] The Stourton family was closely allied with the Welds of Lulworth (41 miles); Mary, the daughter of William, the 11th Lord, married Sir John Weld in 1648,[6] and deeds record the Weld family frequently acting as trustees for the Stourtons.[7]

One survey of the manor of Stourton captures Lord Stourton receiving a fine for the renewal of a lease 'att his goeing to London' in 1688.[8] The lords took with them their personal servants, such as Mary Swetnam, so some of the lower orders in Stourton would have been quite used to travelling the Great West Road, or taking messages between different places. 'Mr Barnes's boy', for example, was paid 2s 6d in 1728 for 'bringing his horse from Shaston' (Shaftesbury).[9] It is quite likely that some tenants from Stourton moved to properties elsewhere on their estates, for example, in Stourton Caundle, or in Quarley. Lord Stourton bequeathed his servant Henry Barnes the reversion of property in Buckhorn Weston when he died in 1548[10]; it was probably the same property that his descendant, Walter Barnes, still held when he died in 1698/9.[11]

1   WSHC 383/729.
2   See below, pp. 162-3.
3   TNA C22/708/55.
4   See below, pp. 237-9.
5   TNA PROB11/393.
6   Dorset History Centre D-WLC/T/8.
7   See, for example, WSHC 383/723, deeds of 1720 (referring back to 1661).
8   WSHC 383/109, f.118B.
9   WSHC 383/58.
10 TNA PROB 11/32/258.
11 TNA PROB4/3909.

The lords of the manor were not the only leading figures in Stourton to have contacts elsewhere. Successive rectors – and especially the Kings and the Fields – were also well connected. Indeed, Nicholas King, son of the rector, was a merchant in Seville when he died in 1649.[1] George Drew, who may have been related to a later rector, was baptised in Stourton 21st February 1708/9, and was serving as a soldier aboard HMS Namur when he died in 1749. His executor was in Portsmouth (70 miles).[2] The Barnes family owned the Three Swans in Shaftesbury (11 miles) and other property in Dorset[3]; one of them took up residence there as an apothecary after completing his Dulverton apprenticeship. Another member of the family experienced imprisonment in Ilchester gaol, and subsequently spent much of his time in London.[4] And a relation made his will in Claverdon, Warwickshire (140 miles) in 1689.[5]

Land in Stourton was available for purchase, and might be owned by non-parishioners. When Robert Tabor of Kilmington made his will in 1610, he mentioned that he had purchased land at Bonham, and that he had a lease of 'Topphowse', presumably referring to Topp in Stourton.[6] This may be the property that another Robert Tabor sold to John Coake of Iwerne Courtney, Dorset (18 miles) in 1717.[7] William Lamb of Mere bequeathed his land in Gasper to his nephew, William Lamb of Stourton, in 1691.[8] A Coffin, from Bradworthy in Devon (114 miles), married a daughter of the Barnes family, and purchased Stourton property.[9] Other members of the Coffin family remained in Bradworthy[10]. In 1694, Alexander Dyer from Martock (26 miles) purchased a house in Gasper for his youngest son.[11] Thomas Davies of Stour Provost, Dorset (10 miles), tenanted a couple of acres in Bonham, which he was sub-letting in 1717.[12] A portion of the manor of Gasper was purchased by Sir

1   TNA PROB11/209/163
2   TNA PROB11/776/410.
3   TNA PROB11/451/253.
4   WSHC 383/740.
5   WSHC 383/570.
6   TNA PROB11/117/442.
7   WSHC 383/726.
8   TNA PROB11/409/442.
9   See below, p. 39.
10 See below, p. 39.
11 WSHC 383/536.
12 Somerset Heritage Centre Q/RRp/1/18.

Isaac Rebow of Colchester, Essex (182 miles), in 1719.[1] Robert Merefield of Shaftesbury purchased land at Bonham in 1729.[2]

New tenants frequently came from outside of Stourton. For example, in 1663, Robert Gapper moved from Cheriton (ten miles) to lease a tenement.[3] Edmund Wadlow was described as 'of Moore Cruchell' (Moor Crichel, Dorset – 25 miles) when he leased Pound Close in 1688, although he already had connections in Stourton. One of the lives in his lease was Sarah Wadlow of Frome (Somerset), which was ten miles in the opposite direction.[4] Another member of the family lived in Winterbourne Stoke.[5] In the 1720s, John Humphreys moved some thirty miles, from Hermitage (Dorset), to rent a property at Blackslough in Stourton; he had previously lived at Lulworth. His landlord, Mr. Hiscocks, lived in Bristol.[6] In the early eighteenth century, successive lessees of lands in Bonham came from Stour Provost (10 miles) and Shaftesbury respectively.[7] In 1707, William Reynolds of Kilmington, yeoman, purchased the reversion of a tenement at Shave.[8] There was also movement out of the parish; Katherine Green was said to be 'of Kilmington' when she surrendered her husband's lease of a blacksmith's shop in 1745.[9] Another member of the family owned a leasehold estate in Shepton Montague when he died in 1732.[10] Roger Open similarly had leasehold property in Shepton Montague on his death in 1656.[11] Robert Leigh of Wincanton sold his part of a lease of Upper Broom Hayes in 1714.[12] James Moulton of Kilmington assigned his interest in land at Shave to Henry Hoare in 1742.[13] Valentine Bradden, who was a life in

1 Ellis, John Henry, ed. *The Registers of Stourton, County Wilts., from 1570 to 1800.* Harleian Society publications 12. 1887, p.viii. Somerset Heritage Centre DD/BR/gf2.
2 WSHC 383/719.
3 WSHC 383/721.
4 WSHC 383/720.
5 TNA PROB 11/606/58.
6 Somerset Heritage Centre Q/SR/303/26.
7 WSHC 383/381.
8 WSHC 383/721, 723 & 739.
9 WSHC 383/721.
10 WSHC 383/723; TNA PROB11/659/92.
11 PROB11/259/61.
12 WSHC 383/721.
13 WSHC 383/742.

the lease of his brother's tenement, was said to be 'beyond sea' in 1722.[1] Also 'beyond sea' was James Stourton, a scion of the former lords, who had been granted a copyhold tenement in 1701, but was thought to be living in Jersey in 1717.[2]

Some Stourton families owned property in other parishes. The estates of the Lords Stourton were scattered throughout Wiltshire, Dorset and Somerset. Many smaller landowners also owned property in other parishes. Dorothy Barnes recorded the property at Buckhorn Weston mentioned above in the 1717 register of Papists estates, but made no mention of other property bequeathed to her in her husband's will, namely, the Three Swans and other property at Shaftesbury, and land at Stavordale, just across the county boundary in Somerset.[3] Joseph Stone, a linen weaver, sold half a cottage in Bourton to William Woodley, another linen weaver, in 1715-16.[4] In 1713, Walter Sparrow, a humble carpenter, bequeathed his property at Marlins Ground in Brewham to his son James, who incidentally lived in Penselwood.[5] Henry Wall seems to have lived in Stourton, but did not record any Stourton property in the 1717 register of papists estates, although he did record property in Corfe Castle (Dorset), Rockhampton (Gloucestershire), East Camel (Somerset)[6]; the bulk of his estate was in Rockhampton.

Many other Stourton families had relatives and friends in other parishes. In 1734, for example, Ruth Jupe of Zeals was named as a life in a lease of Topp; she was probably related to the lessee, Richard Arnold.[7] Similarly, George Weston of Barwick St James (22 miles) was a life in a lease of Widenham taken out by Edmund Wadley in 1723. Support for economic activities sometimes came from outside; for example, in 1737, Joseph Sharp of Bourton stood bond for £10 when Dulce Trimby, widow, applied for an alehouse licence.[8]

1   WSHC 383/97, f.36. 'Bratton' in mss, but Bradden elsewhere.
2   WSHC 383/348, p.1.
3   Estcourt, Edgar E., & Payne, John Orlebar. *The English Catholic non-jurors of 1715, being a summary of their estates* ... Burns & Oates, 1885, p.43; TNA PROB11/451/253.
4   Dorset History Centre D-1216/1/8.
5   WSHC P2/S/1163
6   Estcourt, op cit, p.43, 70, & 228. For his house at Corfe Castle, see also Dorset History Centre, D/BOC/889/54/2.
7   WSHC 383/747.
8   WSHC A1/325/1.

Many residents of Stourton had relatives and friends in other parishes. In 1598, Reginald Spencer of Templecombe was the next of kin of Robert Spencer.[1] John Best's brother Thomas lived in Dilton in 1672.[2] In 1698, William Moores' grandson lived with his father, a woollen draper, in Wells.[3] Edward Jefferies of Bourton, a kinsman of Alice Green, widow, was named as executor in her will.[4] William Cuffe left £5 to his kinsman, Edward Bernard of Mere, in 1725.[5] John Searle of Gillingham was described as the father in law of James Stroud when, in 1693/4. He was bound as the administrator of Stroud's estate, and as the 'curator', that is, guardian, of his daughter; his two sureties were also Searles, both from Silton.[6] Daniel Wiles of Shaftesbury was the brother in law of John Humphreys, and acted as administrator of his estate when he died in 1694.[7] George Knipe of Semley was described by Robert Barnes as 'my loving kinsman' in 1672, and asked to act as trustee for some property.[8] Another Robert Barnes had an uncle in Sparkford in 1728.[9] Thomas Cox of Melbury (13 miles) was described as one of William Poor's 'friends' in his 1682 will.[10]

It is a mistake to assume that the seventeenth and eighteenth century inhabitants of a parish like Stourton confined themselves to their own parish. In fact, many were very mobile, although it may be the case that small husbandmen and yeomen were more inclined to stay put than their pauper and gentry neighbours. Their leases and copyholds gave them a stake in their community; they had no need to travel, except perhaps when ecclesiastical visitations or Quarter Sessions required them to make presentments in places like Warminster and Salisbury, when they went to market in Mere or Wincanton, or when they had wills to prove in places such as Wylye and Longbridge Deverill. The poor, by contrast, needed to travel in order to find work – although if they failed to find it, they were liable to be removed back to their parish of origin. The lords of the manor similarly needed to travel, but for a

1   WSHC P2/S/88; P2/7Reg/26A.
2   TNA PROB11/341/161.
3   WSHC P2/M/770.
4   TNA PROB11/506
5   WSHC P2/C/1076.
6   WSHC P2/S/1000.
7   WSHC P1/H/570.
8   TNA PROB11/341/162
9   WSHC P1/B/976.
10 WSHC P2/P/560.

different reason: their substantial estates and business interests had to be administered, and politics sometimes demanded their presence in London and elsewhere.

It is impossible to be certain of the size of Stourton's population before 1751, but it is possible to re-constitute many families, and to examine relationships in greater depth than the parish register alone would permit. Many wills proved in the Consistory court, and in the Salisbury Archdeaconry court, are available in the Wiltshire & Swindon History Centre. More are available amongst the archives of the Prerogative Court of Canterbury. Copies of a few can also be found in the Stourhead Archive.[1] The latter is, however, far more important for the innumerable deeds, and, especially, leases for lives, which have been preserved. The manorial court book also survives from 1719.[2] Most of the estate archives post-date the Civil War; it may be surmised that they suffered when Stourton Castle was attacked by Parliamentary forces in 1644. Estate archives, probate records, and a variety of other miscellaneous sources, provide a great deal of information, and enable us to trace the history of many Stourton families.

1   WSHC 383.
2   WSHC 383/353.

3
The Families of Stourton[1]

Introduction

THIS BOOK IS primarily about the people of Stourton, rather than their lords. However, the roles of the Lords Stourton, and, subsequently, the Hoares, in the lives of their neighbours, cannot be ignored, and must be considered here first. The influence of the rectors and their curates, most of whom were not from local families was also important. The clerical dynasties from whence they came are considered in chapter 10, together with the priests of Stourton's Catholic Mission.

The rest of this chapter tells the stories of a number of randomly selected local families. It would be possible to fill the entire book with family histories; those selected here help us to tell the story of the parish from a variety of different perspectives. The stories of Roman Catholics, yeomen, blacksmiths, mercers, churchwardens, millers, weavers, cottagers, etc., can all enlighten us as to the way of life of local people in early modern Stourton. Those families chosen for consideration here include Alford, Barnes, Bradden, Brickle, Coffin, Cuffe, Davey or Davies, Evil, Frith, Green, Hill, Hurdle, Ireson, Jupe, Lamb, Lampard, Markey, Rodway, Sandle, Shepherd, Target, Wadlow, and Windsor.

1 Dates of baptisms, marriages and burials mentioned in this chapter are generally taken from the parish register; cf. Ellis, John Henry, ed. *The Registers of Stourton, County Wilts., from 1570 to 1800*. Harleian Society publications 12. 1887. Much other genealogical information is taken from 'Stourton, Kilmington and Mere Genealogies' **http://wiltshire.anu.edu.au**.

The Stourton Family

The Stourtons had been at Stourton since time immemorial.[1] There are many sixteenth- and seventeenth-century memorials to the family in the church.[2] They were ennobled in 1448, and by the mid-sixteenth century were at the height of their power and influence. The 7th Lord Stourton was the Deputy of Newhaven when he died in 1548; despite continuing to be a practising Catholic, he had 'reported a Carthusian of Witham to Cromwell for seditious speeches',[3] administered the oath denying Papal authority in England to the Witham monks,[4] and was able to purchase much formerly monastic property after the dissolution of the monasteries.[5] His son, the 8th Lord, was an ardent Catholic, even going so far as to write a *Treatise on the Sacrament*, effectively declaring his loyalty to Princess Mary, the future queen. When she ascended the throne, he became Lord Lieutenant of Wiltshire, Somerset and Dorset. He foolishly threw it all away when he murdered his father's steward, William Hartgill, and was executed.[6] His widow subsequently married Sir John Arundel; a Jesuit was arrested in her house in 1592.[7] But Queen Elizabeth herself personally intervened to stay proceedings against Lady Anne in 1601.[8]

The family's loyalty to Roman Catholicism, and, during the Civil War, to the Crown, resulted in a steady erosion of their fortunes, and, eventually, the sale of their eponymous manor. The 9th Lord was imprisoned and heavily fined after the Gunpowder plot. His brother in law, Thomas Tresham, was one of the plotters.[9] Nevertheless, he was

1   Most of the following paragraphs are based on Calland, Gary. *St. Peter's Stourton: a tour and history of the church.* Henry Cadogan Hoare, 2010, *passim.*
2   For inscriptions, see Ellis, op cit, p.viii-x.
3   Williams, J. Anthony. *Catholic recusancy in Wiltshire 1660-1791.* Catholic Record Society, 1968, p.209; Thompson, E. Margaret. *A history of the Somerset Carthusians.* John Hodges, 1895, p.134-7.
4   Thompson, op cit, p.138.
5   Brett, Colin J., ed. *Crown revenues from Somerset and Dorset, 1605.* Somerset Record Society96, 2012, p.43.
6   Jackson, J.E. 'Charles, Lord Stourton and the murder of the Hartgills', *Wiltshire Archaeological and Natural History Magazine* 8, 1864, p.243-341.
7   Historical Manuscripts Commission. *Calendar of Manuscripts of the ... Marquis of Salisbury ..., pt.IV.* HMSO, 1902, p.510-11.
8   *Acts of the Privy Council of England. Vol. 32, 1601-1604.* H.M.S.O., 1907, p.28.
9   Oliver, George. *Collections illustrating the history of the Catholic religion in in the counties of Cornwall, Devon, Dorset, Somerset, Wilts., and Gloucester.* Charles Dolman, 1857, p.95. Fraser, Antonia. *The Gunpowder Plot: Terror and*

subsequently able to regain some influence at the highest level. In 1629, Charles I personally ordered the Attorney General 'to spare ye Lord Sturton from being convicted of recusancy this session'.[1] During the Civil War, Stourton Castle was besieged, and Ludlow's forces 'ravaged the building', rendering it uninhabitable.[2] The 'garrison' probably consisted of the family and a few retainers, who fled through the back door into the Park.

Lord Stourton himself took refuge in the royalist garrison at Oxford.[3] He did not fight, but nevertheless suffered sequestration; in 1645 he complained that 'all my estate is sequestered, and my wife, children and grandchildren have not beds to lie on'. He petitioned to compound in 1646.[4] His brother Thomas was also hit by recusancy fines; he paid out no less than £256 13s 4d for his Bonham estate during the Interregnum.[5] Edward Stourton, the 11th Lord's eldest son, was killed in the King's garrison during the siege of Bristol in 1644. Another son, William, was 'fox-hunting' with a party of armed gentlemen immediately before Penruddock's rising in 1656.[6]

Despite his losses, two years after compounding Lord Stourton was able to find no less than £6000 for a marriage alliance with one of Dorset's leading Catholic families. His daughter Mary's marriage to Sir John Weld sadly only lasted for two years, as she died giving birth to a daughter, but her son William eventually inherited the Weld estate.[7]

The Stourtons were restored to their estates after the Restoration in 1660, and by 1670 Lord Stourton was just solvent.[8] When James II

   Faith in 1605. Weidenfeld & Nicolson, 1996, p.145 & 274.

1 Mowbray, op cit, p.452.

2 Mowbray, op cit, p.495. See also Firth, C.H., ed. *The Memoirs of Edmund Ludlow, Lieutenant General of the Horse in the Army of the Commonwealth of England, 1625-1672.* Clarendon Press, 1898. Vol.1, p.97. The house was, however, occupied again before Stourhead House was built in the eighteenth century; see above, p.13.

3 The jurors of Stourton Hundred in mid-1644 thought he had gone to Bristol; cf. WSHC A1/110/T1644, 20.

4 Mowbray, op cit, p.493.

5 Williams, J. Anthony. *Catholic recusancy in Wiltshire 1660-1791.* Catholic Record Society, 1968, p.211.

6 Ibid, p.210. See also Ravenhill, W.W. 'Records of the rising in the West, A.D.1655', *Wiltshire Archaeological & Natural History magazine* 13, 1872, p.178.

7 Berkeley, Joan. *Lulworth and the Welds.* Blackmore Press, 1971, p.84-5.

8 Aveling, J.C.H. *The Handle and the Axe: the Catholic recusants in England*

ascended the throne in 1685 there was a momentary hope that Catholics would experience better treatment. But Lord Stourton did not receive high office even from James II.[1] Nevertheless, he accompanied his king into exile in France, where he remained until his death in 1720. During his exile, financial persecution continued, debts accumulated, and income from the estate was too low to sustain his position. In 1714, he was forced to sell the manor of Stourton to Sir Thomas Meres, a Lincolnshire Member of Parliament. After all his debts had been met, he was left with a mere £775 19s 9d.[2]

After the sale, his brother Thomas (who subsequently succeeded as the 13th Lord) continued to hold the manor of Bonham, where he erected a Catholic chapel and priest's residence. It was apparently equipped with a tunnel, presumably to allow priests to escape if the authorities sought to arrest them.[3] In 1717, when the manor was registered as a recusant property, its value was stated to be £74 3s 4d.[4] Bonham continued to be the residence of the Lords Stourton until the 1740s,[5] but it was not until 1785 that the manor (excluding the chapel) was sold.[6]

The Hoare Family

Sir John Meres, the son of Sir Thomas, sold the manor of Stourton to Henry Hoare in 1717.[7] Hoare was an extremely wealthy banker, who had done well out of the South Sea Bubble. He viewed his purchase as

from Reformation to Emancipation. Blond & Briggs, 1978, p.187.

1   Aveling, op cit, p.237.
2   Mowbray, op cit, p.514.
3   I am indebted for this information to Chris Deverill.
4   Estcourt, Edgar E., & Payne, John Orlebar. *The English Catholic non-jurors of 1715, being a summary of their estates* ... Burns & Oates, 1885, p.228; Somerset Heritage Centre Q/RRp/1/14. The estates of the 12th Lord Stourton were not registered. However, those of Hon. Charles Stourton, who subsequently succeeded Thomas as the 14th Baron, were valued at £23 10s; they included land at Buckhorn Weston, together with his wife's annuity of £20 from her uncle; cf. Estcourt & Orlebar, p.42.
5   Deverill, Chris & Penny. 'St. Benedict's Bonham: the two earliest registers, 1767-1801, *South Western Catholic History* 10, 1992, p.2.
6   Hoare, Richard Colt. *The Modern History of South Wiltshire.* John Bowyer Nichols & John Gough Nichols, 1822, p.89.
7   WSHC 212b/6267. The following paragraphs on the Hoare family are based on Hutchings, Victoria. *Messrs Hoare, bankers.* Constable, 2005, passim, and on the entry in the *Oxford dictionary of national biography* **www.oxforddnb. com.**

both a good investment, and a route into the landed gentry. Politically, he was a Tory, and was described as an 'intimate friend' of Francis Atterbury, the Pretender's closest ally in England. He was not, however, prepared to join the Jacobite cause. In contrast to the Stourtons, he was a devout Anglican, known to his family as 'Henry the Good' for his many contributions to charity. He was, for example, a major force behind the construction of Westminster Hospital, and sat on the Commission for Building Fifty New Churches established by Parliament in 1710. He and his son, Henry 'the Magnificent' oversaw unprecedented changes for the parish and its people. The landscape was transformed, as has already been seen. The building of Stourhead was accompanied by the renovation of the church, followed, in the succeeding century, by the replacement of virtually all the houses on the estate.

Although he was buried at Stourton, Henry the Good never actually lived at Stourhead. The house was unfinished when he died, although he had spent over £10,000 on it. His widow, Jane, received the property as her jointure, and took up residence immediately after his death. A further £10,000 was spent on building between 1726 and 1734. When Jane died in 1741, her son Henry, 'the Magnificent', took up residence, beginning to plan his gardens and landscaping after his wife died in 1743. Like his father, he continued to pay close attention to his London banking business, which provided the wealth on which his plans depended. The attention to detail shared by both father and son is evident in the Stourhead archive, upon which this book draws heavily.

Both Henries took their paternalistic responsibilities seriously. So did Jane, Henry the Good's widow. They established a school for the village children, and a workhouse for the poor. They acted as trustees for village charities, such as that established by the will of Edmund Wadlow in 1725.[1] They paid the rector to preach regular sermons. In 1751, the whole parish was invited to dinner just before Christmas. We have already discussed the list of those invited.[2]

Local Families

As in most parishes, there was a solid core of families who remained in Stourton and its neighbourhood for centuries. There were also many who came and went. Amongst the former were the families of

1   TNA PROB 11/606/58.
2   See chapter 2, & WSHC 383/259.

Barnes, Cuffe, Davies, Green, and Jupe. The latter included many poor transients – but it also included a number of entrepreneurial families such as the Kings (unrelated to the clerical dynasty) and the Lampards, who both tenanted the home farm for relatively short periods, and were the most substantial farmers in the parish. The Ireson family's stay was very brief, but had an important impact on the parish. Clergy families also came and went, although most rectors died in office.

The Alford Family

The Alfords of Stourton were closely linked with the Alfords of Mere, and the family may not have resided in Stourton continually during our period. The earliest mention of the family in the parish is in the late 1620s, when James Alford was living in the tithing of Brook.[1] The Alford's family historian merely notes that the Stourton Alfords 'fell into poor circumstances'.[2] They descended from Thomas Alford of Mere; Richard of Stourton was his son.[3] In Richard's 1577 will[4] he made his widow, Johane, his executor and only legatee. He evidently had no surviving children. He did, however, have a nephew, Thomas Alford, who was living in Stourton in 1637.[5] The family of Thomas's son, James, are recorded in the parish register.

James married three times, but only two children are known; one died aged 11 in 1616. He was described as a pedlar in 1640, when he and his daughter Mary were cited to appear before the Salisbury Archdeaconry court, presumably for recusancy.[6] Mary was probably the mother of an illegitimate child, also named Mary, baptised in 1644.

James had a cousin, William, who probably lived in Mere. One of his sons, Christopher, purchased a reversionary lease of 28 acres at Gascoynes in 1696/7.[7] He never enjoyed the property; the tenant then in possession, Charles Barnes, outlived him (he died in 1723), and Christopher's son Samuel, by then a clothier living in Frome, sold the lease in 1707.[8]

1   Somerset Heritage Centre DD\S\WI/32.
2   Alford, Josiah George. *Alford family notes, ancient and modern,* ed.W.P.W.Phillimore. Phillimore & Co., 1908, p.57.
3   Ibid, p.62. See Thomas's 1551 will, TNA PROB 11/34/384
4   WSHC P2/B/15.
5   Alford, op cit, p.62.
6   WSHC D2/5/1/3.
7   WSHC 383/97, f.5. See also 383/256.
8   WSHC 383/726.

It may be presumed that Robert Alford was related to this family, although the exact relationship is not clear. Robert married Elizabeth Evil[1] in 1708/9, and the couple had six children (including twins) between 1709 and 1721. In 1719, he too purchased a reversionary lease of property occupied by Charles Barnes, which he took possession of on the latter's death. The property concerned was a cottage in Stourton Lane, with 20 acres of land (presumably arable) and 18 acres of common.[2] Robert was presumably a husbandman. He may have had other interests; we know that he paid ten shillings for a booth at the fair on Whitesheet Hill in 1726.[3] He also paid 2s 6d towards supporting the sport that accompanied the fair. It is probable that all of his children died before their father; when he died in 1746 there was no-one to take over the lease of his cottage.[4]

The Barnes Family

The Barnes were one of the oldest Stourton families; they had been there since at least the end of the fifteenth century.[5] In our period, they traced their pedigree through six generations. They were amongst the most prominent minor gentry in the parish, although they never held parish office, as they were recusants. They probably owed their gentility to the fact that they had been 'gentlemen' of the Lords Stourton; one of them served as steward of their estate during the Interregnum. They retained their links with the Stourton family, and with the Roman Catholic church, throughout our period, although at the beginning of the eighteenth century Walter Barnes's faith seems to have been dubious.[6] They purchased the property at Rode in 1603, and leased various other properties in the parish, probably residing at Shave. They also had property in Shaftesbury, where some of them also resided; the last head of the family in our period, another Walter Barnes,

---

1   Walter Alford witnessed the will of Charles Evil in 1748, but we do not know whether there was a relationship between Charles and Elizabeth, or between Walter and Robert. Cf. WSHC P2/E/341.
2   WSHC 383/734. See also 383/97, 383/98, p,14, 383/348,p.4, & 383/99.
3   WSHC 383/903.
4   WSHC 383/353.
5   This paragraph is based on Raymond, Stuart A. 'Barnes: a Catholic family on the borders of Wiltshire and Somerset, c.1548- c.1750', *Genealogists magazine*, 32(9), 2018, p.340-48.
6   Raymond, Stuart A. 'Walter Barnes of Stourton (c.1680-1758): his Family, his Debts, and his Religion', *Notes & Queries for Somerset & Dorset*, 38(388), 2018, p.337-48.

practised surgery in Shaftesbury, having completed his apprenticeship in Dulverton (Somerset).

The Bradden Family

In the seventeenth and early eighteenth centuries, the Bradden family became increasingly prominent in Stourton. John Bradden married Joan Pickford in 1614; the couple had three children, and at least twelve grand-children, most of whom survived to adulthood. Their son Valentine exceeded his allotted three score years and ten, was a copyholder of a few acres in the manor of Stourton,[1] and was suspected of royalism in 1655.[2] The Braddens were yeomen, and tenants of various small properties in the manors of both Stourton and Bonham. One of them played a role in the collusive Chancery case concerning the enclosure of Stourton common in 1635[3]; another testified in Lord Stourton's case against his steward, George Knipe in 1695.[4] Members of the family served as churchwardens in 1673, 1684,[5] 1709, 1714 and 1720-21.[6] After 1729, and until the end of our period, there were only a few years when one of them was not in office.[7] We do not have a list of parish constables, but it is likely that a Bradden served in that office in 1736.[8] In the early and mid-eighteenth century, two John Braddens, father and son, succeeded each other serving on the Stourton manorial homage[9] One of them served as hayward in 1721.[10]

The Brickle Family

The Brickle family's appearances in the Stourton historical record are brief, although it is clear that they were resident in Stourton for at least the final century of our period. William Brickle died in 1648, leaving bequests to his wife Edith, and making his son John his executor.[11] Edith,

---

1   WSHC 383/109, f.49r & 119v; 383/721 (copy dated 1684)
2   British Library Add. Mss. 34012.
3   TNA C2/ChasI/S89/24.
4   TNA C22/708/55.
5   WSHC D2/13/1; D2/13/3.
6   WSHC D1/54/21/4; D1/54/24/5; D2/11/2-3
7   WSHC 497/6.
8   WSHC 497/6.
9   WSHC 383/353; 497/6.
10 WSHC 383/345.
11 TNA PROB11/281.

in 1633, had already leased a cottage, paying a fine of £18.[1] In 1670, his son John leased a cottage, which he still held in 1693[2]. He was described as a yeoman when he acted as a witness in Lord Stourton's Chancery case against his steward in 1695.[3] In 1700/1, his estate was valued at just under £17.[4] His two cows, two horses, and lease, together were worth £14. Alice, his widow, took a long time to obtain a grant of probate. She was presented as 'possessor' of her husband's estate in 1701,[5] but did not obtain a grant of administration until 1709/10,[6] shortly before she also died in 1711/12. John and his wife Alice were both presented as recusants in 1662.[7] It may be suspected that other members of the family were also recusants; no baptisms are recorded after 1632, although there were seven Brickle burials between 1700 and 1738.

The Coffin Family

We have already discussed the Barnes family. They were recusants, and sought recusant spouses for their children. In one instance, they had to travel over a hundred miles to do so. Richard Coffin was a native of the remote North Devon parish of Bradworthy. He married Mary Barnes in the late seventeenth century,[8] and came to live in Stourton. He is mentioned in the recusant rolls of 1678-9, 1681-2 and 1683-4.[9] Other members of the Coffin family remained in Bradworthy; several were listed in the 1706 diocesan returns.[10]

As the Coffins were Roman Catholics, their baptisms and marriages are not entered in Stourton parish register. Only their burials are mentioned. In 1706, the return of papists recorded Mr Coffin, his

---

1 WSHC 4314/1.
2 WSHC 383/109, f.73v; 383/346 & 352.
3 TNA C22/708/55.
4 WSHC P2/B/1288
5 WSHC D1/54/17/5.
6 WSHC P2/B/1288.
7 TNA WSHC D1/54/1/4.
8 Richard Coffin is described as 'of Bradworthy' in his 1695 lease of seven acres at Shave; WSHC 383/723.
9 TNA E377/73, 76 &78. See Williams, J.A. 'Wiltshire Catholicism in the early eighteenth century: the diocesan returns of 1706', *Recusant history* 7, 1963, p.30.
10 The 1705 Catholic census recorded John Coffin of Bradworthy, his wife, and four children, as 'poor'; cf. MacGrath, Kevin. 'Devon and Cornwall Catholics in 1705', *Buckfast Chronicle* 32(1), 1962, p.25.

wife, his son, and three daughters.[1] Despite their Catholicism, the family were allocated seats when the parish church was re-pewed, c.1723. Mr Coffin 'for Gibbs' was seated in pew no 2, widow Coffin 'for Bisses' in no.10, Mr Coffin, again 'for Bisses', in no.21, and William Coffin 'for Gibbs' in no.23.[2]

In 1689 Richard secured his future by purchasing the reversion of his wife's copyhold.[3] In the following years, he leased a number of other small properties,[4] although he had to mortgage his wife's property at Shave in 1699 to do so.[5] In 1707, he was a member of the manorial homage.[6]

Richard was buried 30th September 1712. In 1717, his widow, Mary entered the property she had inherited from her father in Stourton in the newly established Register of Papists' estates; it was said to be worth £50.[7] She also refused to take the oath of allegiance to George I.[8] Her 1727 will shows that she was the 'administratrix of Richard Coffin gent my deceased husband',[9] and had four children.

Richard, her son, leased some property from Lord Stourton before his parents died.[10] He was not, however, able to renew the family's tenancy of Shave; Henry Hoare, when he inherited the estate in 1725, had determined not to renew any leases.

Richard and Mary also had three daughters, Mary, Margaret, and Bridget. Mary and Margaret married Richard Pike[11] and Henry White respectively. When they died, in 1770 and 1780, both were described in the parish register as 'Papists'. Bridget never married, but the reversion of thirteen acres at Road Green fell to her just before her mother died.

1   WSHC D1/9/1/2.
2   WSHC 383/928.
3   WSHIC 383/109, f.123r.
4   WSHC 383/723; 383/97, f.20, 24, 31-2; 383/98, p.4; 383/99, p.12.
5   WSHC 383/720. Deed 5th March 1717.
6   WSHC 383/345.
7   Estcourt, Edgar E., & Payne, John Orlebar. *The English Catholic non-jurors of 1715, being a summary of their estates* ... Burns & Oates, 1885, p.286; WSHC 383/720; A1/310/1; TNA FEC1/1294.
8   *The names of the Roman Catholics, Nonjurors, and others who refus'd to take the oaths to his late Majest King George* ... . J. Robinson, 1745. Reprinted John Russell Smith, 1862, p.128.
9   WSHC P2/C/1088.
10 WSHC 383/97, f.32.
11 WSHC 383/97, f.31.

Her death was presented by the manorial court in 1732.[1]

The Cuffe Family[2]

Three generations of the Cuffe family can be traced from the marriage of John Cuffe and Joan Hill in 1613. Most were not well off, although one was referred to as 'Mr', and another was a yeoman. Two were tailors; several merely occupied cottages and perhaps a couple of acres.

In 1629, John Cuffe leased a plot of ground where he had already 'at his owne coste erected a cottage or dwelling howse'. He paid 16d rent per annum. The lives in the lease were those of his sons Richard and Francis.[3] His wife Joan witnessed the will of her brother Walter Hill (a yeoman) in 1634/5.[4] John was buried in 1656/7; Joan a decade later, in 1667/8.

Seven children were born to this marriage between 1614 and 1631. These included three named John, one of whom died when he was a few days old, another when he was sixteen. Three sons married, although none of the marriages are recorded in the parish register.

Richard, the eldest of John's son to survive childhood, married Selina.[5] He was cited to appear at the Archdeaconry Court, presumably for recusancy, in 1670 .[6] The couple were presented for recusancy in 1686.[7] Selina's sister, Ann Davies, was also a recusant.[8] Despite these accusations, Richard actually served as churchwarden in 1695, and again in 1708! [9] In 1654 Richard was granted the reversion of his mother's copyhold tenement.[10] In 1657, he was described as a tailor when he leased a house next to that of Walter Barnes.[11] In 1663 he was granted a copyhold tenement at Rode, with 38 acres, which his widow held in

---

1   WSHC 383/353. She was described as a spinster.
2   Pedigree 1.
3   WSHC 4314/1
4   WSHC P1/H/214.
5   According to his will, TNA PROB11/39.
6   WSHC D2/1/5/8.
7   WSHC D1/54/11/5. They had previously been presented in 1683, but Selina was not given her forename on that occasion; cf. D1/54/10/5.
8   WSHC D1/9/1/2.
9   WSHC D1/50/5; D1/54/21/4.
10 WSHC 383/346.
11 WSHC 383/725.

1692,[1] and which his nephew William still held in 1722.[2] His 1688/9 will describes him as a yeoman. The inventory[3] is badly damaged, but he did have 'five cows five young beasts & a bull valued at £3, together with two horses, two pigs, a 'wheat rick' worth £5, and oates & barley in ye barn valued at £3. Selina died in 1698; in her will she identified Henry Lewin as her brother,[4] and also mentioned her 'kinswoman', Ann Davies. Richard and Selina had no children, and the reversion of the lease of their house was granted to Richard's brother Adam (see below) in 1674.[5]

Francis, Richard's brother, was also a tailor.[6] He served on the Mere Hundred jury in 1652.[7] Two years later, he was accused of selling beer without licence.[8] His marriage to Basil is not mentioned in the parish register. In 1654, he was the lessee of a tenement at Springs, and of four acres in Widenham.[9] In 1665, he was assessed to the hearth tax on one hearth.[10] His widow, Basil, was still living at Springs in 1694.[11]

Francis and Basil had four sons baptised between 1649 and 1662, one of whom probably died young. The second son, Richard was a husbandman leasing an acre and a half in Bonham in 1689.[12] He served as churchwarden in 1685 (probably),[13] 1695[14] and 1708.[15] He served as Mere Hundred constable in 1700, and was listed in 1712 as a potential member of the Grand Jury at Quarter Sessions in 1712.[16] His 1715/16 probate inventory[17] describes him as a substantial yeoman; his goods

1 WSHC 383/352, p.5; 383/346, f.2.
2 WSHC 383/97, f.38.
3 TNA PROB4/25439.
4 TNA PROB11/446
5 WSHC 383/109, f.82.
6 John Cuffe's administration bond, WSHC P2/C/587
7 WSHC A1/110/T1652, 222.
8 WSHC A1/110/T1654, 152.
9 WSHC 383/109, f.188r.
10 TNA E179/256/16, Ppt.18; cf. Holworthy, R., ed. *Dwelly's national records, vol.1. Hearth tax for Somerset 1664-5.* E.Dwelly, 1916, p.97.
11 WSHC 383/352.
12 WSHC 383/382.
13 WSHC D2/13/3. This could have been his uncle, but in view of the latter's recusancy it seems more likely to have been the nephew.
14 WSHC D1/50/5.
15 WSHC D1/54/21/4.
16 WSHC A1/265/2.
17 WSHC P2/C/1004.

were valued at £225. But he had no children; his estate was administered by his siblings, William and Basil. Francis and Basil had two daughters, Basil and Elizabeth. Basil was baptised in 1662, and died unmarried in 1725.[1] She was confirmed in the Church of England in 1703.[2] Elizabeth's name is only recorded in a 1694/5 lease, which states she was William's sister.[3]

William was John's third son, baptised in 1636, and buried in 1726. He was confirmed in the Church of England in 1702.[4] His tenancy of Rode in 1722 has already been noted. He was also tenant of a meadow at Harweth in the manor of Bonham, for which he paid 1s per annum.[5] He also had a 5½ acre copyhold tenement at Widenham, which had been granted to him in 1695[6]; he surrendered it in 1724.[7] The surviving court rolls from 1719 until his death show that he regularly served on the manorial homage.[8] In 1723, he was one of those complaining about the damage the rabbits in the Park did to his crop. On his death, his remaining copyhold tenement was granted to Bridget Coffin.

Adam, John's fourth son, was baptised 3rd February 1623. In his father's 1668/9 administration bond he was described as a tailor.[9] He was of sufficient status to serve as a member of the Wiltshire Grand Jury in 1669.[10] He probably married a sister of Richard Bayley, who described Adam's daughter Martha as his 'kinswoman and neece' in his will[11]. Martha, baptised at Mere in 1672/3,[12] never married. She was described as a spinster in 1694, when she was paying rent of 4s for a tenement and

1 For her administration bond, which names her brother William as administrator, see WSCH P2/C/1064.
2 Hobbs, Steven, ed., *Gleanings from Wiltshire parish registers*. Wiltshire Record Society 63. 2010, p.225..
3 WSHC 383/99, p.8. This William could alternatively have been John's son..
4 Hobbs, Steven, ed., *Gleanings from Wiltshire parish registers*. Wiltshire Record Society 63. 2010, p.225.
5 Somerset Heritage Centre Q/RRp/1/14.
6 WSHC 383/97, f.39; 383/348, p.1; 383/98, f.1; 383/99, f.8
7 WSHC 383/353.
8 WSHC 383/353.
9 WSHC P2/C/587. Adam took eleven years to apply for probate.
10 WSHC A1/110/T1669, 62.
11 WSHC P2/B/1164.
12 *The Bishop's Transcripts and Parish Registers of Mere: indexed transcripts of baptisms and burials 1561-1837*. Wiltshire Family History Society, 2011, p.72

garden next to the Court House.[1] She was living with her Aunt Selina when the latter died in 1698.[2]

Davies Family[3]

John Davies, a Welshman, yeoman, and personal servant of Charles Lord Stourton, was probably amongst those executed for the Hartgill murder in 1556/7.[4] He may have been the forebear of a prolific Stourton family. Fifty-eight Davies baptisms were recorded before 1710, although none after this date. However, only one male Davies marriage is recorded in Stourton. There are two sixteenth century wills. Alexander Davies, a husbandman, named six children in his 1560/1 will, and gave them all a cow and other legacies.[5] Edmund Davies' 1590 will named four children; his inventory, valued at just over £20, suggests husbandman status.[6] We learn, too, that one Thomas Davies served as Stourton's tithingman c.1580.[7] The 1633 survey of the manor[8] identifies Charles Davies as lessee of the Church House (from 1607) and Pool Close (from 1605). He served as a witness in Lord Stourton's collusive Chancery case in 1635.[9]

There is insufficient evidence to trace the history of the extended Davies family throughout our period. However, two lines can be traced through several generations

The John Davies Line[10]

John Davies was poor; his widow, Elizabeth, was exempt from the hearth tax imposed soon after his death in 1664.[11] The couple had at least seven children, three of whom also had children. The most prolific was Charles, baptised in 1623, buried in 1697/8, who had no

1   WSHC 383/352.
2   TNA PROB11/4746.
3   The surname has many variants, eg Davy, Davis, Daveys, etc.
4   Mowbray, Baron. *The History of the Noble House of Stourton, of Stourton, in the County of Wilts.* 1899,p.393.
5   WSHC P2/4Reg/70C.
6   WSHC P2/D/41.
7   TNA LR11/34/463.
8   WSHC 4314/1,
9   TNA C2/ChasI/S89/24.
10 Pedigree 2.
11 TNA E179/256/16, pt.18; cf Holworthy, R., ed. *Dwelly's national records, vol.1. Hearth tax for Somerset, 1664-5.* E.Dwelly, 1916, p.96.

less than twelve children between 1653 and 1677/8. Edward, 13th Lord Stourton paid Charles 'for noursing or boarding' his brother William when he was a minor.[1] According to his will, Charles also had thirteen grand-children, one of whom was given his house.[2] Their baptisms are not recorded in Stourton's parish register. His lease of a 'tenement with a garden backside and ye paricke' was valued at £12. This was presumably the three acres beside the Tucking Mill, which he leased in 1687.[3] He had 'working tooles and instruments' valued at 2s, but we do not know his occupation. A cow and a calf, valued at £3 10s, constituted his only livestock; he also had 'a little stacke of hay in ye said paricke' worth 2s 6d.

Charles's eldest son died just before his father, in 1694/5. His second son, William, baptised in 1669, evidently succeeded to his father's 1687 lease, renewing it in 1699,[4] and again in 1707[5] when he added the name of his wife, Ann Lewin (the sister of Selina Cuffe). Ann is named on the 1706 return of papists as the wife of William Davies.[6] We do not know whether there were recusants in the family before their marriage, but we do know that William and Ann's son, Mathew was brought up as a Catholic. His baptism was not recorded in the parish register, presumably because he was baptised by a Catholic priest. He was identified as a Papist in the 1767 return.[7] Despite his Catholicism, he was allocated a seat in St. Peters, c.1723.[8]

Mathew succeeded his father in 1715/16, and frequently appeared as a homager in the manorial court, despite the fact that he was described as a labourer in 1767.[9] He was ordered to repair his house in 1723, and complained about the damage he suffered from rabbits in the Park in the same year.[10] He was one of those who dined at Stourhead in 1751.[11] He lived to the great age of 95, being buried in 1787.

1   TNA C22/708/55.
2   WSHC P2/D/414.
3   WSHC 383/346.
4   WSHC 383/97, f.14.
5   WSHC 383/540.
6   WSHC D1/9/1/2.
7   Stourton Kilmington & Mere Genealogies **http://wiltshire.anu.edu.au**
8   WSHC 383/928; cf. Hurley, Beryl, ed. *Wiltshire pew lists*. Wiltshire Family History Society, 1994.
9   Stourton Kilmington & Mere Genealogies **http://wiltshire.anu.edu.au**
10 WSHC 383/353.
11 WSHC 383/259.

Like their father, Mathew's children were not recorded in the parish register. However, their names do appear in other sources. William and Robert are named as lives in 1744 lease.[1] Their brother, James, was born c.1729; he too was identified in the 1767 Papist survey, described as Stourton 'born & bred', and aged 38.[2] Mathew's daughter's name is not recorded, but we know that she too was a Papist; the 1767 survey notes that she married James Kaines or Keen(s). The couple had four children before 1750; like their mother and grandfather, none of them are listed in the parish register.[3]

The Alexander Davies line

The line of Alexander Davies, who was buried in 1638/9, can also be traced for several generations.[4] He paid the subsidy on goods valued at £5 in 1598.[5] Alexander renewed his lease of two closes, containing three acres, in 1620, naming his sons Robert and Alexander as lives.[6] He had three other sons: two named Thomas (presumably one died in infancy), and Alexander. No further information about them has been traced.

Robert was baptised in 1607/8, and buried in 1667. His inventory[7] records 'two leases containing 7 acres' valued at £30. In 1654, he had renewed leases of fifteen acres of pasture in Shave, plus a few acres elsewhere in the manor, which had previously been granted on the lives of himself and his brother.[8] He paid 2s towards the monthly assessment for the relief of Ireland in 1648.[9] His livestock included 21 sheep, a few cattle, a mare, and two colts.

Robert's will[10] named his wife, Katherine, and his daughters Katherine, Joan, and Basell. He also had a son – another Alexander –

1   WSHC 383/735; 383/97; 383/99, p.22; 383/540; 383/353.
2   Stourton Kilmington & Mere Genealogies **http://wiltshire.anu.edu.au**
3   Stourton Kilmington & Mere Genealogies **http://wiltshire.anu.edu.au**
4   There was at least one other Alexander at this date, the son of Robert Davies, baptised 1602.
5   TNA E179/198/275.
6   WSHC 4314/1.
7   WSHC P2/D/265.
8   WSHC 383/721; 383/109, f.198v.
9   WSHC 413/29; edited in Hurley, Beryl, ed. *Wiltshire protestation returns 1641-2, and taxation records for Warminster Division 1648*. Wiltshire Family History Society, 1997.
10 WSHC P2/D/265.

who died in 1643/4 aged just 8 months. He had been named after his uncle Alexander. Little is known about the latter, except that he was cited to answer a charge of fornication in 1640,[1] and that he paid 2s 2d when the grant of £400,000 was levied in 1642

Robert's daughter Katherine married John Smart,[2] and inherited the lease of her father's house; at least two of her children received bequests from their grandfather. In 1693, it was noted that her husband had paid a heriot for her.[3]

Joan married John Shepherd in 1668/9, shortly after her father's death. She inherited her father's second lease, which her husband renewed in 1675.[4] It had named her sister Basell as a life. Basell too had married, in 1663/4; her husband was John Carrier, but the surname was not mentioned in Robert's will. Robert did, however, mention his grandchildren Alce and John, without their surnames. Perhaps they were Basell's children.

The Evil Family

The Evil family (whose name was altered to Keevil by a nineteenth-century rector!) was another very prolific Stourton family, with almost fifty baptisms in our period. Many died in infancy. John Evil was a servant of Edward, 10th Lord Stourton, and was mentioned in his 1632 will.[5] The earliest member of the family mentioned in the parish register was his son George, who was baptised in 1638 and buried in 1639. Most Evil families in the ensuing century were descended from John, who had at least six other children. At least three of them married and had children, William with eight (two of whom produced at least fifteen grandchildren), John with five, and Richard with four. Thirteen members of the family (from five separate households) were invited to dine at Stourhead in 1751.[6] There were still Evils in Stourton in 1831.[7]

In surviving records, Charles Evil, the son of William, occupies the most prominent place. In 1729, he leased a dwelling house and

1   WSHC D2/5/1/3; D2/4/1/16, f.147.
2   WSHC 383/346
3   WSHC 383/ 346. The date of death is not noted.
4   WSHC 383/109, f.89r; 383/723.
5   TNA PROB11/163/663.
6   WSHC 383/259.
7   Hurley, Beryl, ed. *Miscellaneous censuses, 1695-1887, part II*. Wiltshire Family History Society, 1994, p.42.

an acre of arable, which had formerly been copyhold land.[1] He was a member of the homage in the manorial court throughout the early eighteenth century, and served as hayward in the 1730s and 1740s.[2] His son, another Charles, was apprenticed to a joiner in Gillingham in 1725; the premium paid to the master was £10.[3] Charles died in 1750, leaving a will which mentions his 'bed at Stairhead', ie Stourhead.[4] Was he, like his grand-father, a servant of the manorial lord?

Other members of the family are also mentioned as tenants. An earlier William Evil held the reversion of a copyhold tenement in 1603, which he still held in 1633.[5] Another William Evil, yeoman, purchased a lease of newly enclosed meadow land in Gasper in 1648,[6] and surrendered a part of his copyhold in 1651.[7] In 1711, Elizabeth Evil, probably Charles's uncle John's widow, held a house and plot for three lives.[8] Another uncle, Richard Evil, who was described as a husbandman, took a lease of a newly built house near the Tucking Mill in 1706.[9] Richard's son, another Charles, was identified as Stourton's 'innholder' when he was named as administrator of his son William's estate in 1749.[10]

The role of family members in the probate process reflects their status. William Evil, was named overseer in the will of John Jupe in 1638.[11] John Evil, grandson of Lord Stourton's servant, praised the inventory of William Perman in 1690[12]; he had served as churchwarden in 1680.[13] Mary Evil, probably a grand-daughter, witnessed Joan Target's will in 1728.[14] Dorothy Evil administered her husband Charles's estate when he died in 1750.[15]

1   WSHC 383/97, f.29.
2   WSHC 383/353.
3   TNA IR1/13, f.94.
4   WSHC P2/E/341.
5   WSHC 4314/1.
6   WSHC 383/536.
7   WSHC 383/109, f.180r.
8   WSHC 383/347.
9   WSSHC 383/735.
10 WSHC P2/E/340
11 TNA PROB11/180/368.
12 WSHC P2/P/626
13 WSHC D2/13/2.
14 WSHC P1/T/345.
15 WSHC P2/E/341.

Not all members of the family were prosperous. When John Evil, Charles's brother, tried to move to Kilmington with his wife, Mary, and daughters Hannah and Ann, in 1728, and presumably claimed poor relief, the overseers challenged their settlement and had them removed back to Stourton.[1] William Evil, perhaps another son of Charles, was examined in 1752, presumably because he wished to claim poor relief after being in service for several years in Bruton.[2] He was probably sent back to Bruton.

The Frith Family

We know very little about the Frith family in Stourton, except that they were legally 'settled' in Stourton in the early eighteenth century, since William and Edith Frith claimed poor relief, and four of their children were apprenticed by the overseers.[3] When William was buried in 1765, he was described as 'from the workhouse' in the parish register burial entry.

The Green Family[4]

There were many Green families in Stourton and its vicinity. It is possible to trace one of them through seven generations in our period. Alexander, the son of John Green, was baptised in Horningsham in 1577; he or his son Alexander was an 'innholder' in 1620,[5] and paid 1s 3d towards the grant of £400,000 to Charles I in 1642.[6] In 1633, one of them was a tenant of the manor of Stourton, and took part in a collusive Chancery case concerning the enclosure of Lord Stourton's waste.[7]

The older Alexander had eight children, who were all baptised in Stourton between 1604 and 1624. As far as can be traced, only three of them married. Alexander's daughter Edith died in 1658, but there is no evidence of her baptism, or of her father's marriage. George married Mary; their four children were baptised between 1635 and 1645. Robert married Alice Bryant, and had another eight children between 1651 and 1669. A little more is known about his family.

1 WSHC 1240/26.
2 WSHC 1240/21.
3 See below, p.172.
4 Pedigrees 3 and 4.
5 Williams, N.J., ed. *Tradesmen of early Stuart Wiltshire: a miscellany.* Wiltshire Archaeological & Natural History Society Records Branch 15. 1960, p.18.
6 TNA E179/259/25.
7 TNA C2/ChasI/S89/24. See below, p.81.

Robert Green was a moderately prosperous blacksmith. His house, and the blacksmith's shop next door, had been in the possession of William Green (perhaps Robert's brother) when Robert added his son Robert's name to the lease in 1658.[1] He served as churchwarden in 1675,[2] and again in 1682.[3] Robert's inventory was valued at just over £88 when he died in 1687. His seven surviving children: Robert, Alexander, William, George, Jane, Margaret and Thomas – are all mentioned in his will.[4] He was the lessee of various different properties, identified in his will. He left his dwelling house jointly to his wife, his brother William, and his son Thomas. Thomas was also given his 'Over Greens Ground'. The blacksmith's shop, which was probably attached to the house, went to Alexander. William was given the 'Lower Greens Ground'. Robert was to be paid an annuity by his brothers, and George was bequeathed another tenement.

'Over Greens' and 'Lower Greens' may have been the twelve acres of land in Shave which Robert had leased in 1673 for the lives of William, Thomas and Jane.[5] In c.1690, the property was in the joint tenancy of William and Thomas[6]; Thomas renewed the lease in 1723.[7] It may, however, be that the bequest to Thomas was of the 1678 lease of a mead and a few acres of common.[8]

In 1692, Thomas leased another seven acres.[9] In 1719, he also leased the house at Shandlowshay, together with the smith's shop which his father had given to Alexander.[10] In 1717, Alexander was in possession of the property leased by their father in 1673, which, as noted above, had descended to Thomas; it may be that the brothers had exchanged their property.[11]

---

1   WSHC 383/109.
2   WSHC D2/13/1.
3   WSHC A1/110/t1682, 81.
4   WSHC P2/G/518.
5   WSHC 383/721.
6   WSHC 383/352. The catalogue gives the date of this survey as c.1694, but William died in 1691.
7   WSHC 383/721.
8   WSHC 383/97, f.21.
9   WSHC 383/346, minit 2.
10 WSHC 383/97, f.16. The lease had previously been renewed by George Green, in 1699, when it was said to have been in the occupation of William Green – perhaps Robert's nephew; cf. WSHC 383/720.
11 WSHC 383/348.

Another brother, Robert, leased the Court House (also known as the Parish House) in 1689.[1] As lessee, he was required to permit its use for both manorial and parish business.[2] A plot of ground called the 'Tennice Court' was attached to this property.[3] It also had a shop in 1693.[4]

Robert's marriage to Hannah Jupe brought him the tenancy of ten acres at Upper Broom Hayes.[5] She brought with her a lease of ten acres at Upper Broom Hayes, which Robert renewed in 1698,[6] with the intention of assigning it to his son George.[7]

The 1717 survey records that Alexander, Thomas, and William were still leaseholders of the manor of Stourton.[8] In addition to the leases mentioned above, 1702 William leased three acres of pasture in 1702.[9] The Court House was not mentioned in the survey, but it was still in the family; in 1719, the reversion of the property was granted to George, the son of Robert.[10] It eventually passed to James Helliker, George's son-in-law.[11]

Alexander had no children, so when he died in 1727 his brother Thomas inherited much of his estate, including various parcels of land.[12] That included Mount Shears, which had been bequeathed to Alexander in their mother's will.[13] When Thomas died in 1732, he left his estates in Stourton, Shepton Montague, and Cole, to his son Thomas, although some of them were to be occupied by his wife Cecily for life.[14]

The family home at Shandlowshay remained in the family until the end of our period. In 1743, Thomas's son Thomas renewed his father's lease.[15] He was then 'of Kilmington', and described as a yeoman

1   WSHC 383/97, f.17; 383/109, f.106r; 383/346, minit 6a.
2   WSHC 383/99, p.23; 383/346.
3   WSHC 383/97, f.17.
4   WSHC 383/346.
5   WSHC 383.346
6   WSHC 383/721.
7   WSHC 383/97, f.7.
8   WSHC 383/348.
9   See also 383/348.
10 WSHC 383/97, f.17.
11 WSHC 383/99, p.23.
12 PROB11/615/485.
13 TNA PROB11/458/186.
14 TNA PROB11/659/92.
15 WSHC 383/726.

(although the transcript of the lease in the manorial court book describes him as a gentleman[1]). Two years later, his widow Katherine renewed the lease again, to include the name of their one-year old son William.[2]

The Green's also held property in the manor of Bonham. A copy of its court roll survives showing that Alexander Green was granted an acre of arable in the field of Norton Ferris called Harweth in 1698.[3] The same property seems to have been leased to George Green in 1725, although it was then described as being in the occupation of Nicholas Barnes.[4] One of the lives in this lease was Elizabeth Windsor, whom George subsequently married; the lease was presumably her dowry. The property adjoined the workhouse. When Henry Hoare wished to extend its willowbed, he paid George £12 for an assignment of the lease.[5]

The Green family was regularly mentioned in the early eighteenth century manorial court book for Stourton.[6] Various members of the family served on the homage; the earliest extant reference is for 1707, when Alexander served.[7] Failure to put in an appearance meant a fine; George Green was amerced one shilling in 1742, and again in 1744 and 1745. He was appointed Hayward in 1747, 1748 and 1749.

We have already noted that Robert Green was described as a blacksmith in his 1688 inventory; he had some new anvills & bellows and some hammers worth just over £1. He left monys due upon shop book to his daughters Jane and Margaret, but 'all my estate in the said shop; also my great bellows & my new anvill' went to his son Alexander. William, Robert's brother, and Thomas, his son, were also blacksmiths. William, in his 1691 will, left his 'cousin', that is, his nephew, Thomas 'my anvill in ye shop if continues to make use of his trade'; otherwise it was to remain in the shop for Alexander.[8]

The Greens supplied a number of Stourton churchwardens. Robert held office in 1675.[9] Richard, who was a linen weaver, and perhaps

1 WSHC 383/353.
2 WSHC 383/721.
3 WSHC 383/382.
4 WSHC 383/384.
5 WSHC 383/384.
6 WSHC 383/353.
7 WSHC 383/345.
8 WSHC P2/G/535
9 WSHC D2/13/1.

the son of John, served in 1679.[1] Thomas (or perhaps his son Thomas) served in 1704, and again in 1724, 1726 and 1727; George served in 1730 and 1731.[2] Thomas and George also served as trustees of a parish charity. They were named in a deed of 1723 as trustees of the charity of Thomas Fitzherbert.[3]

One member of the family was presented at Visitation by the churchwardens: Elizabeth Green, the grand-daughter of Robert's brother George, was said to be 'living incontinently' in 1714, with William Shepherd.[4] She had already borne an illegitimate child (also named Elizabeth) in 1703 – perhaps that was why she remained unmarried.

The family did not confine its activities to Stourton. Alexander Green, the first member of the family to live in the parish, was baptised in Horningsham in 1577. In the early eighteenth century, his grandson Thomas had his children baptised in Kilmington. Several of Robert's sons had properties in other parishes: George was bequeathed land at Silton in his brother Alexander's will.[5] Their brother William was described as 'of Kilmington' in Alexander Green's copy of the Bonham court roll mentioned above.[6] In the 1743 lease of the blacksmith's shop mentioned above, Thomas Green, the lessee, is described as a yeoman 'of Kilmington'.

Some members of the family, however, remained in Stourton. In c.1723, seats in the parish church were allocated to three members of the family, ie Thomas, George, and another George, presumably acknowledging their property rights.[7] In 1751, there were only two Green family households living in the parish. Elizabeth Green's household had six members, and John Green's two: all were invited to dine at Stourhead.[8]

The Hill Family
There were several of this name in Stourton, including, in the

1 WSHC D2/13/2.
2 D1/54; D2/11.
3 WSHC 383/706.
4 WSHC D1/54/24/5.
5 TNA PROB11/615/485.
6 WSHC 383/382.
7 WSHC 383/928.
8 WSHC 383/259.

early eighteenth century, the rector's family.[1] It is not clear whether the rector, John Hill, was related to Stourton's other John Hill, who was a blacksmith, before the latter married Grace, the rector's eldest daughter, in 1746.

The rector's son-in-law was the son of John Hill of Gasper, who made his will in 1711, and who described himself as a yeoman.[2] He owned a dwelling house and tenements in Gasper, together with fields in Bonham. His inventory demonstrates that he was a mercer: it lists his 'shop goods': casks of brandy, various textiles and buttons, glass bottles, 'inkle and tape', quires of paper, and thread. He also possessed over £135 'in mortgages bonds bills and book debts', and had over £20 in cash. His involvement in agriculture was limited: he had a cow and calf, a few sheep, two mares and two colts. The total value of his inventory was £381, making him one of the wealthiest parishioners in Stourton below the gentry.

John Hill was evidently well-respected in the parish. He served as administrator of the estate of Ruth Welsh in 1694,[3] and appraised the inventories of John Humphreys in 1694,[4] and John Brickle in 1701/2.[5] In 1710-11, the year before his death, he served as churchwarden.[6] He made his wife Ruth his executrix. She was bequeathed his house and lands for her widowhood, or until she remarried. Their three sons, John, William, and Richard, were bequeathed cash: £60 to John, £30 to the other two. Payment was not, however to be immediate; it was to be made over a period of time, partly dependant on the death or re-marriage of their mother, partly on their attaining the age of majority. William was also bequeathed two houses, which were to be his when his mother's tenure ended.

In fact, the sons' inheritances came when their mother re-married. By 1717, she had married William Jupe.[7] A Bonham deed dated 1729 identifies John Hill and his mother, Ruth Jupe, as lives in a lease then still in force.[8] She was probably the Ruth Jupe, wife of William Jupe of

---

1   See below, pp.211-12.
2   WSHC P2/H/1092.
3   WSHC P2/W/720.
4   WSHC P1/H/570,
5   WSHC P2/B/1288.
6   WSHC D1/50/7.
7   Somerset Heritage Centre Q/RRp/15.
8   WSHC 383/719.

Zeals, who was buried in 1739.

Nothing more is known of Ruth's son, William Hill, and only a little more of his brother Richard, who was buried at the age of thirty in 1729. We know that he was confirmed in 1711,[1] and was allocated two seats in church when the pews were re-ordered in 1722/3,[2] probably because his inheritance included two dwelling houses (his brother John was only allocated one seat).

The eldest son, however, is relatively well documented. John the younger had two wives. In 1720 he married Mary Burden. In 1722, he leased a small plot of ground close to the road from Stourton to Mere,[3] and regularly served as a homager in Stourton's manorial court after 1724. He was a blacksmith, and was regularly paid for work in the church in the 1730s and 1740s. In 1746, he signed the churchwardens' accounts, perhaps as poor law overseer.[4] His wife, Mary, died in the same year. As has been seen, he subsequently married the rector's daughter, Grace Hill.

He had already renewed the lease of his house and smiths' shop in 1743, naming himself, his wife Mary, and Samuel Edwards as lives.[5] The inclusion of Samuel is curious. He was said to be aged 22 in 1743, but had in fact been baptised on 2nd February 1718/19. He was the son of John and Mary Edwards, and the likelihood is that he was John Hill's apprentice. When the lease was renewed again in 1749, his name was left out; the new lives were John's second wife, Grace, and James Hill of Warminster, a cabinet maker, and probably a relative.[6] In 1750, John Hill stood surety when Mary Edwards, probably a relative of his apprentice (but not his mother) obtained a licence to marry John Wadlow.[7]

The Hurdle Family

Thomas Hurdle was a native of Kingston Deverill, who migrated

1   Hobbs, Steven, ed., *Gleanings from Wiltshire parish registers*. Wiltshire Record Society 63. 2010, p.226.
2   Calland, Gary. *St. Peter's Stourton: a tour and history of the church*. Henry Cadogan Hoare, 2010, p.72-3.
3   WSHC 383/97, F.2.
4   WSHC 497/6.
5   WSHC 383/353.
6   WSHC 383/99, p.27.
7   Sarum Marriage Licence Bonds **www.findmypast.co.uk**

to Stourton when he married Margery Jupe in 1711. His wife brought with her a 1684 lease of a property at Widenham, and a ten acre property formerly tenanted by Thomas's father-in-law.[1] He had to pay a heriot on the death of his wife in 1743.[2]

In 1724, Thomas took out a lease on another ten acres at Widenham.[3] By the 1740s, he tenanted farms at both Shave and Coldcot; the rent he paid varied, but in 1744/5 he paid £95 for Shave, and £23 for a half year at Coldcot.[4] Payment was not always by cash; in 1747, he supplied Mr Hoare with 23 quarters of oats, fourteen sacks of seed wheat, sixty store sheep, and sixty ewes, against his rent. Nor was payment always on time: at Michaelmas 1749 he owed arrears of over £170. Hurdle also occupied 22½ acres of land called Adams's, presumably as under-tenant of the Powell brothers.[5]

Hurdle served in the manorial court as a homager from at least 1719 until the end of our period; he sometimes also served as an aferror. In 1731, and again in 1738, the manorial court[6] ordered him to repair his barn. When, in 1739, he failed to comply with the order, he was fined twenty shillings, and threatened with a further fine of forty shillings. He still failed to comply, and had to pay up again in 1740, but the order does not re-appear. Hoare's accounts for 1740 reveals why: on 1st April 1740, John Green, carpenter, was paid twelve guineas 'for repairing Thos Hurdle's barn'.[7] The matter of who should pay for the repairs had evidently been a matter of dispute between the landlord and his tenant, eventually settled in the tenant's favour.

Hurdle served several stints as churchwarden: in 1714,[8] 1728,[9] 1729,[10] and 1733. Whilst he was serving in 1728, he installed a new bell in the church; his name is inscribed on it.[11] In 1736, he signed the

1   WSHC/383/97, f.41 & 43.
2   WSHC 383/353.
3   WSHC 383/745; See also 383/98, p.13.
4   WSHC 383/30. See also 383.29.
5   WSHC 383/98, p.8. The lease gives 22 ½ acres, but the 1745 survey says 28 acres WSHC 383/99, f.26.
6   For the following paragraph, see WSHC 383/353.
7   WSHC 383/61, f.5.
8   WSHC D1/54/24/5.
9   WSHC D1/50/12.
10 WSHC D1/54/31/5.
11 Walters, H.B. *The church bells of Wiltshire.* 1929 (reprinted Kingsmead Reprints, 1969), p.208.

churchwardens' accounts; in 1744 and 1745 he nominated the new churchwardens.[1] He sat on the relatively prestigious third pew from the front in church, together with other leading farmers..[2]

He also served as overseer in 1738, and possibly on other occasions.[3] Between 1731 and 1742 (when Henry Hoare himself took on the role) he was regularly named as liable to serve as a juror at Quarter Sessions.[4] Less public duties included standing surety for a labourer, Richard Clement, when the latter sought a marriage licence in 1750,[5] acting as guarantor for Edmund Ryall's widow when she administered her husband's estate in 1713,[6] and administering his father-in-law's estate, also in 1713.[7] Curiously, his name was absent from the list of those who dined at Stourhead in 1751.[8]

Thomas and his wife had three children between 1713 and 1718/19: Basil, John, and Luce. Luce died aged three months. John married Elizabeth Parsons,[9] and also had three children: Henry, Susanna and John were all born between 1748/9 and 1755. Margery, his wife, died in 1742/3.[10] Thomas himself died in 1774 at the great age of 88.

The Ireson Family

The Iresons had a very brief residence in the parish. Nathaniel Ireson was the Warwickshire mason employed to build Stourhead.[11] In July 1720, Henry Hoare sent a messenger 'to find out Mr Ireson to send him to Stourton'.[12] Accounts record Hoare's frequent payments to him; in February 1720/21, for example, he was paid £30.[13] In 1722, he served as churchwarden,[14] and was responsible for renovating the

1 WSHC 497/6.
2 WSHC 383/928.
3 WSHC 1240/23.
4 WSHC a1/265/4-13.
5 Sarum Mariage Licence Bonds **www.findmypast.co.uk**.
6 WSHC P2/R/507.
7 WSHC P2/IJ/237.
8 WSHC 383/259.
9 Sarum Marriage Licence Bonds **www.findmypast.co.uk**.
10 WSHC 383/97, f.8.
11 For his biography, see Fitzgerald, Peter. *Nathaniel Ireson of Wincanton: architect, master builder, & potter*. Dovecote Press, 2016.
12 WSHC 383/58, p.19.
13 ditto
14 WSHC D2/13/4. See below, pp.84-5 for his activities as churchwarden. He

church. He probably prepared the pew list of c.1723 (although he did not allocate himself a seat).[1] The following year, he was responsible for summoning tenants to the manorial court baron.[2] In c.1726, he bought Windmill Farm at Wincanton, and ceased to reside in Stourton; however, he continued to do work for Henry Hoare, at least until 1744, when the latter complained that Ireson was being 'unreasonable in his demand'.[3] But he also accepted architectural commissions from a wide variety of other customers in the South-West, and probably had more than enough work on hand – which may explain his 'unreasonableness'.

Ireson brought three children with him to Stourton, and had four baptised in Stourton; one was buried there, and has her memorial in the church. John Ireson, whose daughters Mary and Abigail were baptised in 1724 and 1726/7 respectively, was his brother; he died in 1729.[4] Another John Ireson was mentioned in Nathaniel's will.[5] The master mason's daughter, Susannah, was a life in a lease granted to William Smith in 1730,[6] suggesting a long-term relationship of some kind, although there is no direct evidence of a marriage. Nathaniel himself died in 1768, a resident of Wincanton.[7] Many buildings in the town, and elsewhere in the region, are the work of his hands, and his statue (possibly the work of his own hands) still stands in Wincanton churchyard.

The Jupe[8] Family[9]

The Jupes were one of the most prolific families in Stourton and its neighbourhood. In our period, almost 60 Jupe baptisms are recorded in the parish register between its commencement and 1750, the earliest

also served as churchwarden in Wincanton, one of the few men to serve in the office in two different parishes; cf. Fitzgerald, op cit, p.9.
1   WSHC 383/928.
2   WSHC 383/345.
3   Woodbridge, Kenneth. *Landscape and antiquity: aspects of English culture at Stourhead 1718 to 1838.* Clarendon Press, 1970, p.27.
4   Fitzgerald, op cit, p.11.
5   Colvin, H.M. *A biographical dictionary of British architects, 1600-1840.* Yale University Press, 1995, p.529.
6   WSHC 383/97, f.6; 383/98, p.5; 383/99, p.17.
7   For his will, see TNA PROB 11/949/134.
8   Variously spelt Jupp, Jupe, Joop, Joup, etc. I have standardised as Jupe.
9   Pedigrees 5 and 6.

dating from 1578. There are also numerous marriages and baptisms. Seven generations can be traced.

Most Stourton Jupes were descended from Rinold Jupe, who wrote his will in 1600,[1] or from the six children of his brother John. Here, the focus is on Rinold's descendants. He only had one son, another John – but this John had ten children, several of whom also had large families.

Rinold Jupe was probably a husbandman. In 1587, he leased eight acres in Shave.[2] A year later, he leased four acres at Pound Close.[3] In 1591, he leased a cottage with an orchard and four virgates of land.[4] At his death, he had a mare and colt, a few cattle, and thirty sheep; the total value of his inventory was just over £26. His wife, Elizabeth, was his executrix, and continued his farming activities; her 1617 inventory revealed a similar number of stock, and a total value of almost £25.[5]

Rinold's son John was perhaps able to rise up the social scale; he described himself as a yeoman in his will, which was proved in the Prerogative Court of Canterbury.[6] He was his mother's executor, and probably inherited his father's leases. In 1622, he was assessed to pay 3s to the subsidy – one of only six Stourton inhabitants to be assessed.[7] He valued the inventory of Richard Britten in 1626.[8] In 1630, just before he died, he took out two leases of land at Little and Upper Broom Hayes, paying entry fines totalling £30.[9] In his 1638/9 will,[10] he was able to leave his daughter Mary £60, to which he added another £12 in a codicil. This was in addition to a variety of other legacies, including some land. Bennetts Meadow went to his son Robert, and Mary also received an acre of wheat growing at Shortlands, in 'Zeales field' (in the adjoining parish).

John married Edith Norris in 1578. They were married for 57 years. Edith died just over two years before her husband; she was buried 29th November 1635, he on 10th January 1638/9. The couple were the parents of at least eight children, two of them probably twins. When

1   WSHC P2/IJ/37.
2   WSHC 4314/1.
3   WSHC 4314/1.
4   WSHC 4314/1.
5   WSHC P2/IJ/68.
6   TNA PROB11/180/368.
7   TNA E179/199/367.
8   WSHC P2/B/469
9   WSHC 4314/1.
10 TNA PROB11/180/368.

John's father died in 1600, they had four daughters and two sons.[1] By the time his mother made her will in 1607,[2] she had eight grandchildren. Elizabeth made bequests to all of them, to two great-grandchildren, and to her daughter-in-law, Edith.

John, Robert, William, Francis, and Margaret, John and Edith's children, all had children (although Margaret's son William, baptised in 1668, was illegitimate). Our comments here must be restricted to the families of Robert and Francis. Robert was the third son, baptised in 1600. He married Ann in 1631, and had six children. He was a tenant of the manor of Stourton, and played a role in the collusive Chancery case of 1633.[3] In 1642, he paid 4s 8d towards the grant of £400,000, double the amounts paid by his brothers Francis and John.[4] In 1657, he served as overseer[5]; in 1659 he was tithingman.[6] He held a copyhold tenement, but, in 1671, attempted to replace it with a lease for the lives of his sons Robert and Francis.[7] However, he died in the following year, without paying his entry fine. His son Robert died three years later, in 1675, but his widow, Melior, was able to lease her father-in-law's tenement, naming her son, another Robert, as a life.[8] In 1692, she was said to be sixty years old, and he was described as 'of Shaftesbury'.[9]

Francis, Robert the elder's brother, was a substantial yeoman.[10] With his brother William, he jointly leased Upper Broom Hayes, taking a fresh lease in 1654. At the same time, he also renewed a lease of Little Broom Hayes. He paid the substantial sum of five shillings towards the monthly pay in 1648,[11] and served as a trustee for Nicholas King's charity.[12] He had four children baptised between 1637 amd 1647/8. His

1   WSHC P2/IJ/37.
2   WSHC P2/IJ/68. She made her will ten years before she died, but added a codicil just before death.
3   TNA C2/ChasI/S89/24.
4   TNA E179/259/25, pt.1, rot.2.
5   WSHC A1/110/T1657, 94.
6   WSHC A1/110/T1659, f.125.
7   WSHC 383/109, f.76.
8   WSHC 383/109, f.76.
9   WSHC 383/352.
10 WSHC 383/109, f.187v.
11 Hurley, Beryl, ed. *Wiltshire protestation returns 1641-2, and taxation records for Warminster Division 1648.* Wiltshire Family History Society, 1997, p.55. See also WSHC 413/29.
12 WSHC 497/6. See below, p.222

wife was buried in 1649. He was buried 30th September 1666

Several of Francis's children married and had children. We have already mentioned the marriage of Thomas Hurdle to Margery Jupe; she was Francis's grand-daughter by his son John, and inherited her father's 1683 lease of a tenement at Widenham,[1] which lay next to a property leased by her great uncle Robert in 1684.

Francis's sons, William and Robert, also continued the Jupe line. William had three children between 1676 and 1682/3: Gertrude, Francis (who died as an infant), and William. William senior inherited his father's lease at Upper Broom Hayes, surrendering it in 1677 in order to take out a fresh lease for the lives of his wife and daughter.[2] In his inventory,[3] his lease of ten acres at Widenham (Upper Broom Hayes was in Widenham) was valued at £50; he also had a lease of a dwelling house valued at £20. He had 6 head of 'rother cattle', valued at £12, with three horses, one colt, and a pig. His 'corne upon the ground' was worth £12. The total value of his inventory was just over £113. He served as churchwarden in 1679.[4]

William died in 1683, soon after his last child was born. He left no will, but his widow, Hannah, was named as administrator of his estate (and presented at the ecclesiastical visitation for failing to take out the administration[5]). His son William continued the line. But first we must look at William's brother Robert.

Robert married Mary; the couple had three children, Robert (who probably died young), Francis and Mary, the latter two baptised in 1679 and 1682/3. In 1684, the year after his brother died, Robert took a lease of a house and thirteen acres of land at Upper Broom Hayes, in Widenham.[6] In 1684, like his brother, Robert served as churchwarden,.[7] In 1698 he witnessed the will of Selina Cuffe.[8]

Nothing is known of Robert's daughter Mary. His son, Francis, married Susannah and had six children between 1706 and 1720. He became a copyhold tenant of the manor of Stourton in 1729, on his

---

1   WSHC/383/97, f.41 & 43.
2   WSHC 383/723. The lease was assigned to George Green in 1714 (WSHC 383/97, f.7, & 383/721).
3   WSHC P2/IJ/181.
4   WSHC D2/13/2.
5   WSHC D1/54/10/5.
6   WSHC 383/109, f.105v; 383/346.
7   WSHC D2/13/3.
8   TNA PROB11/446.

mother's death.[1] Thereafter, he is frequently mentioned in the court rolls. as a homager, and as hayward in 1730. He also tenanted Rode, taking a thirteen year lease from Walter Barnes in 1722, although paying his rent of £40 per annum to Henry Hoare when Barnes mortgaged the property.[2] Barnes had a low opinion of him, writing to Hoare's steward that 'I will not be wrong'd by such a logerhead'. Admittedly, he could not write, and had to make his mark when he witnessed Jerome Parfitt's will in 1714.[3] But Barnes's reputation was not that great either!

Francis's son Francis married Eleanor Edwards of Kilmington, in 1730, and had four children by his first marriage: they were baptised between 1732 and 1741. When Eleanor died, Francis re-married; Jane, who he married in 1750, gave him another five children, and there were perhaps two more children from a third marriage contracted in 1759. That, however, is beyond our period.

Francis senior's uncle William was born a few months before his father died. He married Mary Gregory of Bruton in 1698. She was buried in 1729. William and Mary had two sons. William, baptised in 1706 at Longbridge Deverill, and John, baptised at Stourton in 1714.

Their father held a tenement, garden and four acres.[4] He regularly served as a homager in the manorial court between 1719 (and probably earlier) and his death. He also served as churchwarden in 1711 and 1722.[5] In 1737 he (or perhaps his son) was paid for carriage of lead to the church.[6] William was buried 17th November 1747.

William had two sons, William and John. Both married (John twice) and had several children in the 1630s and 1640s. It was probably John, his second wife, Dorothy (who had also previously been married), and her step-daughter Mary, plus a servant, who were invited to dine at Stourhead in 1751.[7] Given the number of Jupe entries in the parish register, it is surprising that there were so few – but the likelihood is that many Jupes were living in neighbouring parishes.

---

1   WSHC 383/353.
2   TNA 383/740. See also Raymond, 'Walter Barnes ...', op cit.
3   TNA PROB11/43/190.
4   According to the homage when his death was presented in 1747; cf. WSHC 383/353.
5   WSHC D1/50/7, & D2/13/4. On the latter occasion, he served with another William Jupe!
6   WSHC 497/6.
7   WSHC 383/259.

The Lamb Family

The Lamb family of Stourton were probably all related to, if not descended from, William Lamb the elder, who was buried 20th February 1571/2. Shortly after his death, at least two sons of another William Lamb – probably the elder's son – were baptised, Valentine in 1573/4 (he was buried in 1575) and John, in 1576. Several other Lamb baptisms occurred in the 1570s: Ann (1579) William, (1572), another William, (1577), another John, (1582), and perhaps Thomasin (who married Thomas Cayford in 1606/7, and whose son John was baptised in 1607/8).

It is possible that these were all William's children, although unfortunately at this date the parish register does not give parents' names. The fact that two of the children were named John suggests that one of them had a different father – perhaps another son of William the elder. One of them was buried 2nd March 1614/15, but the other not until 23rd October 1665. The latter John was probably responsible for selling a quarter of the manor of Gasper in the early seventeenth century.[1] His wife, Avis, was receiving an annuity of £4 from a tenement near the Tucking Mill in 1655.[2] John's apparently childless brother Andrew, a husbandman whose estate was valued at £35, made him executor of his will in 1677 (Andrew also had a wife named Avis).[3] The will tells us that the two brothers also had a sister, Mary, who had three young children.

Between 1619 and 1633/4, seven children were described as the children of John Lamb in the baptismal register. We know nothing of three of them beyond their baptism. The other four, however, had relatively long lives: John died aged 75, Andrew at 52, and Samuel at 83. It was probably this John who appraised the inventories of John Bradden in 1680,[4] William Poor in 1682,[5] Mary Poor in 1683,[6] Robert Sandle in 1686,[7] and Robert Jaques in 1688/9.[8] His sister, Mary, was

---

1 WSHC 383/535.
2 WSHC 383/109, f.206v.
3 WSHC P1/L/185.
4 WSHC P2/B/959.
5 WSHC P2/P/560.
6 WSHC P2/P/565.
7 WSHC P2/S/932.
8 WSHC P2/IJ/196.

mentioned in Andrew's will, which noted that she had three young children.[1]

John and Mary's brother Samuel also married; he had four children. All four of them were baptised in Mere, which suggests that his family were living there in the 1670s and 1680s. Mary and John were baptised in 1673 and 1688/9 respectively; nothing more is known of them. William, baptised 1670/1, married Rebecca, and had two children, William (1709) and Rebecca (1712). They too disappear from the historical record. Samuel, baptised in 1684, married Ann Maidment in 1706, and had four children. Only Ann (baptised 1707) married; her husband was James Whitaker. They married by licence, at Chicklade, 14th May 1730. Whitaker was one of Henry Hoare's leading tenants in the mid-eighteenth century, as we will see.

The brothers John and Samuel Lamb were both allocated multiple seats when the new pews were installed in the church in c.1723.[2] Several were allocated to Samuel for 'Presleys', which was presumably his tenement. 1723 was one of the few years of the early eighteenth century when neither brother was serving as churchwarden. Samuel briefly served in 1716[3] and 1728;,[4] John almost continuously from 1719 until 1746.[5] John also served as overseer at least in 1728 and 1737; we do not have a complete list of office-holders.[6] He appraised the inventory of Basil Cuffe in 1725,[7] and witnessed the administration bond of John Bradden in 1732.[8] His brother Samuel (or perhaps their father Samuel) similarly appraised the inventories of Robert Trouk in 1701,[9] Richard Green in 1704,[10] and William Maidment in 1724.[11]

Samuel the younger was living in West Bourton in 1735, when he described himself as a linen weaver, and as 'late of Gasper'.[12] In 1760, however, he was still occupying property in Gasper, which he

1   WSHC P1/L/185.
2   WSHC 383/928.
3   WSHC D1/50/8.
4   WSHC D1/50/12.
5   WSHC D1/50; D1/54; D2/11
6   WSHC 1240/19, 28 & 33.
7   WSHC P2/C/1064.
8   WSHC P2/5/1518.
9   WSHC P2/T/408.
10 WSHC P1/G/333.
11 WSHC P2/M/925.
12 TNA C11/2182/25.

sold by lease and release to William Smart, a leather cutter, also of West Bourton.[1] Following this sale, the Lamb family name died out in Stourton, although another Lamb family migrated from Compton Denham (Somerset) in the early nineteenth century.

The Lampard Family

The Lampards were another family who only arrived in the parish after Henry Hoare had purchased the manor. The earliest mention of 'Farmer Lampard' that has been traced was in 1727, when he paid Henry Hoare £2 for 'wintering of sheep'.[2] Joseph Lampard was the leading tenant in the 1730s and 1740s. In 1743, he agreed to renew his lease of Stourton Farm for twelve years.[3] He also rented Coldcot Farm; in 1745, he paid rent amounting to £386 per annum. In that year he gave up Coldcot to Thomas Hurdle, and his rent was reduced to £357.[4]

As the leading tenant, Joseph Lampard served as churchwarden almost continuously in the late 1730s and 1740s. In 1742, he gained the support of the manorial homage, who objected to the tenants of cottages in Stourton Lane 'treading down the fences and going across the grounds of Farmer Joseph Lampart' in order to reach their homes.[5] Curiously, despite being the leading tenant, he was not invited to dine at Stourhead in 1751.[6] And in 1756, Farmer Heale made serious complaints about the 'unhusbandlike' manner in which Lampard conducted his farming operations.[7] He may not have been well-liked.

Joseph's wife Catherine died in 1746; they had probably married at East Knoyle in 1709, and their children were not baptised in Stourton. However, Joseph stood surety in Thomas Lampard's marriage bond in 1745; it is probable that they were father and son. Thomas married Mary Helliker at Hill Deverill, and his son John was baptised at Stourton in 1745/6. Mary died soon after her son was born, and Thomas married again. He celebrated his wedding to Mary Carey at Salisbury in 1749; the couple had at least eight children, all baptised in Stourton. He had had other liaisons before his first marriage. In 1739 he obtained a marriage

1   WSHC 383/535.
2   WSHC 383/59.
3   WSHC 383/751.
4   WSHC 383/29.
5   WSHC 383/353.
6   WSHC 383/259.
7   WSHC 383/721.

licence to marry Elizabeth Rooles of Steeple Langford, but it is clear that the marriage did not take place.[1]

We may also presume that John Lampard was a relative; Joseph, as churchwarden, paid him 2s 6d in 1734 for 15 dozen sparrows heads.[2] In 1743, he was paying a rent of 12s 6d.[3]

The Markey Family

The Markey family were newcomers to Stourton in the early eighteenth century. Several were paupers, although one was a poor law overseer, and another was a presumably prosperous blacksmith. It has only been possible to trace one tenancy in Stourton for several branches of the family, and that was probably merely a cottage. It is therefore no surprise that this was a mobile family. East Pennard, Kilmington, Mere, and Plymouth were amongst the places where members of the family lived.

The Markeys are first mentioned in Stourton when Edward Markey married Grace Garret in 1711. John of East Pennard subsequently married Rebecca Garret in 1713. Were these marriages those of two brothers marrying two sisters? It has not proved possible to trace the parentage of either family; there are no baptismal entries for the Garret family in the parish register, although six marriages are recorded between 1610 and 1735. Only one baptism is mentioned for these two marriages, that of Anne, daughter of John, in 1714/15. John was a tenant in the manor of Stourton in the early 1730s, probably a mere cottager, paying a rent of 1s 1d.[4]

It is not clear whether Edward mentioned above was the blacksmith of Kilmington who stood bound in the administration bonds for William Banister and his wife Eleanor in 1733 and 1739/40 respectively.[5] If he was, he was Eleanor's son. She must therefore have been married to a Markey before she married William Banister.

A third Markey marriage took place in 1717, when William Markey married Mary Meaden. This marriage led to seven baptisms, although there were also three unbaptised children who were buried. One of the children, John, was apprenticed as a pauper in 1736; the 'trade' was

1   Sarum Marriage Licence Bonds **www.findmypast.co.uk**.
2   WSHC 497/6.
3   WSHC 383/345.
4   WSHC 383/345.
5   WSHC P2/B/1524; P2/B/1582.

husbandry.[1] Unusually for a pauper, the indenture mentioned his father William, who was described as a labourer. John's master, or, rather, mistress, was Rebecca Markey, widow, of Kilmington. It seems likely that she was her apprentice's aunt, and his father's sister. The indenture was witnessed by John Markey, who was probably another relation, and presumably not the apprentice himself.

Mary, another daughter of William, was also a pauper. She was examined by Henry Hoare, the lord of the manor, and Richard Willoughby, in 1746.[2] Their examination revealed that she had 'travelled around'.[3] She had served John Mitchell in Maiden Bradley, and then in Tavistock (Devon) for several years, but left him when she found herself carrying his child. The child was born in Plymouth. Two years later, she married James Rea, an Irish mariner on HMS Surprise. When he left her, she returned to Stourton, presumably to seek help from her family.

James Markey, William's eldest son, seems to have avoided applying for relief to the overseers. Instead, he himself actually served as one of Stourton's overseers in 1753.[4] He had married Elizabeth Tabor in 1739, but had no known children.

William had three other sons. William married Mary Edwards in 1750; he was described as 'of Mere' in the parish register. Philip married Grace Kellaway of Mere in 1747/8, and had a son John baptised in 1750. Nothing is known of Thomas, the youngest.

Rodway Family

Richard Rodway was the earliest member of the family to be mentioned in Stourton; his will was proved in 1556.[5] In it he left 'every of my childerne' two sheep each, but only named his daughter Alice, who received a brass pot. His descendants cannot be traced, but it is likely that he was related to John Rodway of Kilmington, who was buried at Kilmington in 1595. John's son John married Alice Davies, probably at Kilmington, and had eight children. Four of them died in infancy. The eldest (probably) was Ann, who was baptised at Kilmington in 1640. Soon after her birth, the family moved to Stourton, where the rest of the

---

1   WSHC 1240/19.
2   WSHC 1240/21.
3   WSHC 1240/21.
4   WSHC 1240/28. This information is taken from the bastardy bond of Mary Whitaker.
5   WSHC P2/1Reg/85C

children were baptised.[1] In 1654, John Rodway took a lease of 'one little park adioyning to the new lane' in Stourton, which had previously been in the possession of Charles Davies (perhaps his wife's father), for the lives of his daughters Ann, Eleanor and Edith[2] – all of whom survived and married.[3] Four years later, he secured a lease of a cottage at New Lane, together with a meadow called Pool Close. Presumably it adjoined his 'little park'.[4] However, the only life named in it was that of Edith. When he made his will in 1686/7, John bequeathed this lease to her jointly with her sister Eleanor[5]; eventually, as will be seen, it passed to her husband John Shepherd. The other lease passed to her brother John, who held it in 1693.[6]

Some members of the family were Roman Catholics. John Rodway had his children baptised in the parish church, but he and his wife Alice were both cited to appear before the Archdeaconry Court in 1670.[7] Alice was presented as a 'papist' in 1683.[8] Two of her daughters, Eleanor and Elizabeth, are listed in the recusant roll in the same year.[9] Eleanor and her brother John are mentioned in the 1706 return of Papists.[10]

John was the only son of John the elder to survive into adulthood. He was baptised in 1657, buried in 1733, and does not seem to have married. The family name was therefore not carried on in Stourton. No Rodway's are mentioned in the list of those invited to dine at Stourhead in 1751,[11] although it is possible that there were descendants of John Rodway's three daughters who married.

The Sandle Family

There were several Sandle[12] households in Stourton during our period, probably all related. Husbandry was probably important to all

---

1   No baptism can be traced for Francis, who was buried in 1643.
2   The mss says Elizabeth, but this is probably a mistake for Edith, who is named in her father's will.
3   WSHC 383/109, f.188v.
4   WSHC 383/109, f.49r.
5   WSHC P2/R/418
6   WSHC 383/346.
7   WSHC D2/5/1/8.
8   WSHC D1/54/10/5.
9   TNA E377/73.
10 WSHC D1/9/1/2.
11 WSHC 383/259.
12 Variously spelt Sandal, Sandel, and Sandell.

of them. Some were lessees: in February, 1611/12, Robert Sandle leased a tenement 'built upon the common', together with three acres, and a wood.[1] In 1664, another Robert (probably) was taxed on a house of two hearths.[2] This may have been included in the 'one small chattle lease', worth £6, recorded in his 1686 probate records. At that date, he also had 'my meade which lyeth between Milmore & Westover', and 'my aker of ground att Bonham Mill'. Half a century later, in 1733, another Sandle, Thomas, was a yeoman, with a tenement in Topp.[3]

Other Sandles were poor: John Sandle's house in Gasper was exempt from the hearth tax in 1670 for this reason. Peter Sandle's estate was valued at a mere £4 1s 8d in 1666.[4] Several members of the family were tradesmen. In 1633, the baptismal entry for Francis Sandle notes that his father, John, was a weaver.[5] When Peter Sandle's step-father, Anthony Newman, died in 1638, he bequeathed the tools he used as a turner to his step-son.[6] Robert Sandle's 1686 probate records reveal that he both tanned leather, and made shoes from them.[7] They also reveal that he owned a heifer and a small amount of corn and hay. Robert was reasonably prosperous; his estate was valued at over £30.[8] He was of sufficient status to serve in parish office.

The earliest mention of the Sandle family in Stourton is in 1553, when two of its members, Thomas and William,were serving as churchwardens[9] . Almost a century later, a John Sandle, was serving as parish clerk when he died in 1645.[10] In 1662,[11] 1670,[12] and again in 1683,[13]

1   WSHC 4314/1.
2   Holworthy, R., ed. *Dwelly's national records, vol.1. Hearth tax for Somerset 1664-5*. E.Dwelly, 1916, p.96.
3   WSHC P2/5/1355.
4   WSHC P2/5/796.
5   Ellis, op cit, p.8.
6   TNA PROB11/178.
7   WSHC P2/S/932.
8   Dwelly, E., ed. *Dwelly's national records vol.2. Directory of Somerset part 1*. E.Dwelly, 1929, p.136-7.
9   Calland, Gary. *St Peter's Stourton: a tour and history of the Church*. Henry Cadogan Hoare, 1910, p.57.
10 Ellis, op cit, p.67.
11 WSHC D/1/54/1/4.
12 Dwelly, E., ed. *Dwelly's national records vol.2. Directory of Somerset part 1*. E.Dwelly, 1929, p.137.
13 WSHC D1/54/10/5.

the churchwardenship was served by Robert Sandle,[1] who also served as sidesman in 1671.[2] In 1683, he presented a number of 'Papists', so was clearly not one himself. There were, however, recusant Sandles. Some Sandle baptisms and marriages seem to be missing from the parish register, possibly because they had been conducted by priests of the old religion.

Peter Sandle, the son of Robert, was probably a recusant. His wife Mary was cited to the Archdeaconry court in 1640, accused of being a Papist.[3] His son, another Peter, and his wife, Catherine, were cited to appear before the Archdeaconry Court in 1667,[4] and were again presented as Papists in 1674.[5] His papist connections are confirmed by the witnesses to his 1676 will, who included Mathew Stourton and Walter Barnes, two of the leading figures amongst Stourton recusants.[6]

Peter's descendants were still in the parish at the end of our period. His grandson James seems to have renounced his grandfather's faith by being confirmed in the Anglican church in 1711[7]; however, James's daughter Mary may have been the 'Papist' described as such in her burial entry in 1757.

The Shepherd Family

The Shepherds were another prolific Stourton family. In 1751 there were no less than five Shepherd households in the parish,[8] all of them probably related - and at least some of them Catholic recusants. The family could still be found in Stourton in 1831.[9]

In 1662, John, Abse, Eleanor, and Robert Shepherd were all presented as recusants.[10] Citations to appear before the Archdeaconry

---

1   Or possibly Robert senior and Robert junior.
2   WSHC D1/50/1.
3   WSHC D2/5/1/3. The nature of the accusation is not stated, but Papism is presumed given the number of other known Catholics cited to appear at the same time.
4   WSHC D2/5/1/8.
5   WSHC D1/54/6/5.
6   WSHC P2/5/796.
7   Hobbs, Steven, ed., *Gleanings from Wiltshire parish registers*. Wiltshire Record Society 63. 2010, p.226,
8   WSHC 383/259.
9   Hurley, Beryl, ed. *Miscellaneous censuses, 1695-1887, part II*. Wiltshire Family History Society, 1994, p.43.
10 WSHC D1/54/1/4.

Court were issued in 1667 to John, Robert (perhaps John's brother) and Isaac, Robert's son[1]; in 1668, the names of Catherine and Mary (Isaac's wife) were added to the list; in both 1668, and 1670, the first three names were repeatedly cited.[2] In 1674, and again in 1686, it was the turn of John and Isaac to be presented.[3] Fines were imposed on John Shepherd and his wife, and on Magdalen Shepherd, in 1678.[4] In 1683 Isaac and Mary his wife were also presented, together with Robert and his wife.[5] In 1703, Elizabeth Shepherd, widow, John Shepherd, with his wife, son and daughter, Robert Shepherd with his two sons and daughter, and William Shepherd and his wife, were all named as recusants.[6] It is probable these were all related, although their precise relationship cannot now be discovered. Whether they were related to the John Shepherd who served as churchwarden in 1681 is also not clear.[7]

As is natural, recusants associated with others of their own faith. John Shepherd witnessed the will of Charles Barnes in 1677/8.[8] Dorothy Barnes left Robert Shepherd her 'silver spoon & two silver salts and my best Holland sheet' when she died in 1726/7; he witnessed her deed of gift.[9] John Shepherd's marriage to Edith Rodway in the late seventeenth century was a marriage between members of the same faith. It may be that the same applied to the earlier marriage between John Shepherd and Joan Davies.

John and Joan had nine children between 1669 and 1693. Joan brought to her marriage her father Robert Davies's 1654 lease of five acres at Land Shire Hayes, which he had renewed in 1675.[10] It may have been the same John Shepherd, described as a linen weaver, who leased a cottage, orchard, garden and pasture at Bonham for 21 years in 1688.[11] In 1695, he leased a house. Edmund, his eldest son, renewed the lease

---

1 Robert's 1682/3 will was appraised by Isaac; his mother Mary acted as administrator; cf. WSHC P2/S/596.
2 WSHC D2/5/1/8.
3 WSHC D1/54/6/5; D1/54/11/5.
4 TNA E377/73.
5 WSHC D1/54/10/5.
6 WSHC D1/9/1/2.
7 WSHC D2/13/3.
8 TNA PROB11/357/185.
9 WSHC P1/B/939.
10 WSHC 383/723.
11 WSHC 383/381.

when his father died shortly afterwards.[1] In 1700, Edmund leased an additional five acres in the Lower Common.[2] He had already purchased the lease of a cottage and half an acre of land from John Edwards; in 1696/7, he took a new lease, naming his sisters Melior and Margaret as lives. On his death, it descended to Melior's husband, Robert Quill, who renewed the lease in 1741,[3] although a reversionary lease was granted to James Whitaker in 1742.[4]

There were several other John Shepherds in the parish, although most are poorly documented. We have already encountered John Shepherd, yeoman, who married Edith, the daughter of John Rodway, inheriting his father-in-law's cottage and an acre of land at Pool Close (originally leased in 1659); he renewed the lease in 1695, naming Edith, and his son Robert, as lives.[5] John served as homager in the manorial court on several occasions in the 1730s and 1740s. His death, and Robert's succession, was presented in the manor court in 1743.[6] Robert, like his father, served as homager, although he was fined six pence in 1745 for failure to appear.[7] Robert also witnessed a poor law bond in 1729.[8] By 1737, he held the Court House as devisee of John Bradden[9]; he sold it to James Helliker in 1746.[10]

The Target Family

Jeremiah Target, born in 1677, was baptised in Horsington,[11] as were his twin brothers William and Christopher (who both died within a day of their birth in 1683). Another Christopher was born subsequently, but his baptism cannot be traced. However, another William was baptised at Stourton in 1694, followed by Samuel in 1695. Jeremiah, Christopher, and Samuel all had children, although Jeremiah's did not survive infancy. Several members of the family were linen weavers.

---

1   WSHC 383/731.
2   WSHC 383/97, f.1; 383/99, p.15; 383/346; 383/348, p.3.
3   WSHC 383/97. f.3; 383/98, p.11; 383/348, p.3; 383/352.
4   WSHC 383/99, p.16.
5   WSHC 383/346; 383/733.
6   WSHC 383/353. His burial is not recorded in the parish register.
7   WSHC 383/353.
8   WSHC 1240/34.
9   WSHC 383/97, f.17.
10 WSHC 383/99, p.23.
11 Daniel, W.E., ed. *The parish register of Horsington in the County of Somerset 1558-1836.* 1907, passim, for the following baptisms.

Jeremiah followed the trade. So did Christopher, his son Thomas, and his grandson Thomas.[1] Christopher's father in law Robert Jaques was also a linen weaver.[2]

Jeremiah Target frequently appears in the historical record. He purchased a lease of three acres and a 'messuage' at Topp (in the manor of Bonham) in 1720.[3] In 1722, he was the assignee of two separate holdings in the manor of Stourton, including two cottages, the fulling mill, and five or six acres of land.[4] For one of these holdings he paid 1s 4d in rent; for the other the rent was 18s 4d – which he was still paying in 1744-5.[5] He regularly served as a homager in the manorial court between 1719 and 1750, although he was amerced in 1742 for failing to do so.[6] He also paid an 'acknowledgement' of 4d in 1745 for 'entring on Stourton Common.[7] In 1731 he served as a hundred juror.[8]

The inventory of Christopher, Jeremiah's brother, was valued at just over £92 when he died in 1710.[9] His son Thomas paid £160 for property in Gasper in 1711. He was also granted his mother's property at West Ball in 1714, which her father Robert had paid £224 for in 1655, on condition that she could continue to occupy it for her life. Thomas built a house on it, and settled the property on his wife, Martha (nee Perry), when they married in 1717. When he died in 1734, Martha had to renounce the administration of his estate to a creditor.[10] She did, however, continue to occupy the property, which she mortgaged to William White in 1746; two years later, Abraham Clifford of Knoyle, clerk, took over the mortgage.[11] Eventually, it was purchased by the Hoare family in 1785.[12]

1   WSHC P2/IJ/196; P2/T/545; 383/388.
2   WSHC P2/IJ/196.
3   WSHC 383/382.
4   WSHC 383/97, f.24-5.
5   WSHC 383/345.
6   WSHC 383/353.
7   WSHC 383/345.
8   Fowle, J.P.M., ed. *Wiltshire Quarter Sessions and Assizes, 1736*. Wiltshire Archaeological and Natural History Society Records Branch, 11. 1955, p.68.
9   WSHC P1/T/267.
10 WSHC P2/T/545.
11 WSHC 383/388.
12 For an abstract of the deeds, see WSHC 383/537.

Wadlow Family

The Wadlows or Wadleys were another family of minor gentry, who may perhaps have come from either Wincanton or Penselwood.[1] They cannot be traced in Stourton prior to the 1670s, but we know that, in 1671, Ann Wadlow, widow, with Richard Bailey her brother, surrendered a lease of ten acres of common land which had been enclosed.[2] Ann was the mother of Edmund Wadlow, who paid a fine of £50 to secure the reversion of her estate in 1683.[3] In 1688, Edmund was described as being of More Crichel, Dorset.[4] The only other life in the lease was his niece Sarah Wadlow (the daughter of his brother Thomas of Frome Selwood),[5] baptised at Stourton in 1685. Her two elder sisters had both been baptised at Stourton the previous year, although they were then aged seven and two respectively. Both were described as being of Frome Selwood.[6]

Edmund also had some connection with Winterbourne Stoke, north of Avebury. When he made his will in 1725,[7] he left his namesake Edmund, 'son of Edmund Wadlow of Winterbourne Stoke' (perhaps a nephew) his freehold property in Kilmington. Edmund, the devisee, had a brother John who was to inherit if he died. George Weston, also of Winterbourne Stoke, was Edmund's residuary legatee and executor. He was cited to appear in court in late 1725, when the apparitors identified him as 'possessor of the goods' of the testator, as he had yet to obtain grant of probate. The apparitors described him as being of Berwick St James.[8]

In 1681, Edmund had already purchased the reversion of 15 acres in Widenham after the death of his Uncle Richard,[9] and he continued to accumulate property. In 1688, he took a lease of Pound Close (4

1   Thomas Wadley of Wincanton was assessed on two hearths in 1664; cf. Holworthy, R., ed. *Hearth Tax for Somerset 1664-5*. Dwelly's national records 1. Fleet: E.Dwelly, 1916, p.88. One of the same name paid poll tax of £50 in Penselwood in 1641; cf. Howard, A.J., & Stoate, H.L., eds. *Somerset protestation returns and subsidy rolls*. Almondsbury: T.L.Stoate, 1975, p.245.
2   WSHC 383/109, f.75v.
3   WSHC 383/109, f.108r; 383/346.
4   WSHC 383/720.
5   WSHC 383/720.
6   WSHC 383/97, f.22.
7   PROB 11/606/58
8   WSHC D2/8/2.
9   WSHC 383/109, f.99v.

acres of land) from Lord Stourton.[1] In 1688, he leased eleven acres in Widenham, which he subsequently renewed in 1723.[2] This was probably the property described as eleven acres in the 1717 survey.[3] By 1693, he held four acres of land at Paradise, with his sister Sarah.[4] In 1706 he consolidated several leases by surrendering them and taking a new lease from Edward Lord Stourton; this included over 40 acres.[5] In 1713 he purchased the assignment of a lease of another tenement in Widenham from Mary Coffin.[6] He witnessed a deed of 1714 by which Alice Gullifer transferred her lease to her son Benjamin.[7] In 1717, he paid an entry fine of £190 to Sir John Meres, during the latter's brief lordship of the manor, for 22 acres.[8]

Edmund Wadlow served as tithingman in 1715, when he had to provide the crown with a soldier.[9] He regularly served as a member of the homage in Stourton's manorial court in the years before his death in 1725.[10] In 1723, the roof of his house was in poor repair; he was ordered by the court to replace rafters, and to have it thatched. His death was presented in 1725, when several heriots, amounting to £11 were said to be due to the Lord. In his will, he bequeathed £60 to the poor of the parish, which was to be used to pay fifteen poor persons four shillings every year.[11]

In 1723, Edmund had renewed his lease of Widenham, inserting the name of his nephew Edmund (his brother Thomas's son) as a life.[12] Edmund the younger probably did not move to Stourton until his uncle's death, and therefore not all of his family are recorded in the parish register. His wife, Mary, and his children, Richard and Ann, are recorded, but it seems likely that Thomas, Nicholas, and another Edmund were also his children. Edmund was buried in 1738. Thomas was the father of Hannah Lawes' bastard daughter, Mary; he

1 WSHC 383/720.
2 WSHC 383/97, f.27; 383/726.
3 WSHC 383/348, p.1.
4 WSHC 383/346.
5 WSHC 383/721.
6 WSHC 383/721; 383/97, f.20.
7 WSHC 1240/31.
8 WSHC 383/726; 383/97, f.22; 383/98, p.8; 383/99, p.26.
9 WSHC 413/12.
10 WSHC 383/353.
11 TNA PROB11/606/58; WSHC 383/706.
12 WSHC 383/726 (1723 lease).

was required to enter a bastardy bond in 1746.[1] He was described as a yeoman, so could probably afford to pay maintenance. It is possible that the Edmund, who was buried in 1738 was another son. So, probably, was Nicholas, who, as we shall see, continued the family name in Stourton.

Edmund served as churchwarden in 1733 and 1734.[2] It may have been during his terms of office that he erected the oversized gate which his successors in 1736 claimed hindered access.[3] He presumably inherited Widenham, as he served on the homage from 1731, although he died in 1741. He was singled out and fined one shilling in 1737 for his failure to attend. In 1731, he and other tenants agreed to fence in Tenants Common, which lay on the Hardway, to protect it against trespass from Kilmington. A similar problem was dealt with in 1734, when that part of the Common beside London Road was ordered to be fenced in. In 1736, he was ordered to 'plaish his hedge and dyke his ditch' at Widenham. Another order of the same date reveals that he had at least one under-tenant. William Bond was ordered to 'sufficiently repair his dwelling house lying at a place called Shave', which belonged to Wadlow. He was buried in 1741, and his death was presented in the manorial court in 1742.

The family name, as already noted, was carried on in Stourton by Nicholas Wadlow. He married Mary Lewis of Gasper in 1747 at Maperton. In 1751 he was invited to dine at Stourhead with two other members of his household.[4] No other Wadlow families seem to have been resident in the parish at that time.

The Whitaker Family

The Whitakers were not known in Stourton before James Whitaker married Ann Lamb at Chicklade 14th May 1730. They had six children between 1731 and 1741, although only three were baptised at Stourton. It may be conjectured that James Whitaker came to Stourton as a servant of the Hoare family. In 1727, he was paid £17 on account , plus another £25 15s. He also received £66 from 'the miller' on behalf of Mr Hoare.[5] Similar transactions are recorded in subsequent accounts.

1   WSHC 1240/28.
2   WSHC D2/11/14; D2/11/15,
3   WSHC D2/11/20.
4   WSHC 383/259.
5   WSHC 383/59.

By the 1740s Whitaker had become one of the leading tenants of the Stourhead estate. In 1742, he purchased two three-life leases of small properties at Stourhead, presumably close to the big house,,[1] and subsequently had a house built for himself on the waste. Thereafter, he regularly appeared amongst the homagers in the manorial court.[2] But most of the property he farmed was held on much shorter leases, in accordance with Henry Hoare's estate policy. From 1743 until the end of our period his rent was £120 per anum. It was sometimes in arrears.[3]

James Whitaker served as churchwarden in 1732,[4] and as overseer in 1736.[5] He nominated his wife's uncle John Lamb as churchwarden in 1744,[6] and was named as a trustee in the 1741 will of James Land, a Hoare family servant.[7] In 1737, he accepted Elizabeth Arnold as his pauper apprentice; she was to learn 'housewifery'.[8] His prominent position, however, did not shield him from having to give bond to the parish when his daughter Mary gave birth to a bastard son, Joseph, in 1753.[9]

The Windsor Family

Christopher Windsor was a Roman Catholic cordwainer, whose marriage to his wife Mary was not recorded in the parish register. It was probably conducted by a Roman Catholic priest. His children's baptisms may also have been conducted by that priest; several of them were interlined in the parish register, after other entries had been written up. The marriage of his son Joseph can also not be traced, perhaps for the same reason.[10] Christopher is mentioned in the 1670 will of William Lord Stourton as being one of the lessees 'of my newe inclosed common grounds lying neare Stourton Parke'.[11]

Christopher's estate was valued at just over £30 in 1692, including £20 in cash. He bequeathed his house, after the death of his

1 For details, see below p. 121..
2 WSHC 383/353.
3 WSHC 383/30.
4 WSHC D1/50/13; D2/13/6.
5 WSHC 1240/19.
6 WSHC 497/6.
7 WSHC P2/L/629.
8 WSHC 1240/19.
9 WSHC 1240/28.
10 He is mentioned in Christopher's will as having a son Francis; cf. WSHC P2/W/701.
11 TNA PROB11/339/297.

wife, to Joseph.[1] Joseph renewed the lease, paying rent of 1s 4d.[2] He subsequently moved to Hindon, although he was buried in Stourton in 1716. In 1725, his daughter Elizabeth was named as a life in the lease of a meadow to George Green, whom she subsequently married.[3]

1 WSHC P2/W/701.
2 WSHC 383/720. Indenture, 1693; 383/346; 383/352
3 WSHC 383/384. 1725 indenture.

4
Local Government in Stourton

S TOURTON, LIKE EVERY other parish in England, had its parish and manorial officers, its vestry and its manorial courts. Evidence for their activities is, however, limited. Our prime sources of information are the churchwardens' accounts[1] and the court book of the manor of Stourton,[2] both surviving only from the early eighteenth century. A number of documents relating to the poor law also survive, as do a number of visitation presentments. A few of the latter enable us to identify recusants; otherwise, they are not very informative.

Most of the parish belonged to the manor of Stourton, but there were also the manors of Bonham and Gasper. These smaller manors were in the tithing of Brook, which lay in Somerset, had its own separate officers, and was subject to the Somerset Justices. The whole of the parish, however, was in the Diocese of Salisbury – although one will from Gasper is known to have been proved in Wells.[3]

Power in early modern Stourton was in the hands of the lords of the manor – the Stourtons, and subsequently the Hoares. Many of their tenants served in parish and manorial office. Two institutions met regularly to consider the affairs of the parish: the vestry, and the manorial court.

The manorial lords attended neither of these bodies, but exercised their authority at a distance. Their status would normally have resulted in appointment as Justices of the Peace, which would have given them formal authority over most of the parish officers. Indeed, it has already been pointed out that Charles Lord Stourton was Lord Lieutenant of the county at the beginning of Queen Mary's reign. However, the Stourtons'

1 WSHC 497/6.
2 Primarily WSHC 383/353, although there are a few loose sheets elsewhere.
3 The will of John Baber of Gasper, husbandman, 1661; cf. 'Baber Family ', *Notes & Queries for Somerset & Dorset*, 5, 1897, p.179.

Roman Catholicism theoretically prohibited them from even being Justices of the Peace after 1558. Despite that, John, 9th Lord Stourton frequently sat on the bench in the 1580s.[1] The only subsequent exception to this rule occurred when the Catholic James II tried to re-model the bench in 1688. The then Lord Stourton was described as one of those 'fit to be made Deputy Lieutenants and Justices of the Peace'[2]; indeed, he sat on the bench in the Michaelmas sessions for 1685.[3] One of his stewards, George Knipe, sat with him.

Despite their usual exclusion from the bench, it is likely that the Stourton influence over the churchwardens may have prevented some presentments for recusancy from being made, despite the fact that churchwardens' prime responsibility lay to the bishop. After Henry Hoare purchased the manor, he almost certainly determined who was to serve – as can be seen in the appointment of Nathaniel Ireson, an outsider to the parish, but Hoare's personal architect.

Henry the Good never lived at Stourhead. Even when his successor, Henry the Magnificent, became a Justice of the Peace, he does not seem to have attended Quarter Sessions,[4] although he did take a settlement examination in 1746.[5] Participation in the work of Quarter Sessions, was not, however, essential to exercising influence over the appointment of parish officers and other matters of parish governance. Informal influence mattered just as much.

The lords did have formal power over the Stourton manorial court.[6] That power was normally exercised through manorial stewards,[7] who summoned and presided over meetings. The court required the presence of tenants as homagers, and appointed the hayward. All we

1   Johnson, H.C., ed. *Wiltshire County Records: Minutes of Proceedings in Sessions 1563 and 1574 to 1592*. Wiltshire Archaeological and Natural History Society Records Branch 4. 1949, *passim*.
2   Duckett, George. 'Proposed repeal of the Test and penal statutes by King James II in 1688', *Wiltshire Archaeological and Natural History Society magazine* 18, 1879, p.368 & 373.
3   WSHC A1/160/4.
4   The record of Justices' attendances in Quarter Sessions minute books may not be complete; the words 'and other their fellow Justices of the Peace' are regularly added to the lists of those in attendance; cf WSHC A1/150/19. The lists of *nomina ministrorum* in the sessions rolls have not been checked.
5   WSHC 1240/21.
6   We know little about the courts of the manors of Bonham and Gasper.
7   For stewards, see below, pp. 159-65.

know about the duties of the hayward is that he summoned the tenants to attend the manorial court.[1] The function of the court was to regulate the relationships between the copyholders themselves, and between them and the lord. Its role in registering changes in copyhold tenure will be discussed in chapter 6. The Lord also employed a bailiff, although all that we know of the office is that it was filled by William Moores under the 12th Lord Stourton, and that he acted at the direction of the steward when he sold off his deceased lord's animals.[2]

In August 1633, the court was convened as a 'court of survey', in order to consider the enclosure of 500 acres of waste land, hitherto used as a warren and as pasture. Most of the tenants agreed that enclosure would be advantageous to them, and Lord Stourton agreed that they should have two-thirds of the land to be enclosed, whilst he took one-third. 30 acres were reserved for poor cottagers. In order to secure valid title, Lord Stourton launched a collusive action, in order to obtain a Chancery decree confirming the enclosure agreement.[3]

The vestry was summoned by the churchwardens, and presided over by the rector. At the beginning of the seventeenth century, William King, tenant of the demesne, was expected to 'appear in the behalf of ... Edward Lord Stourton att the vestry.[4] When Henry Hoare became lord of the manor, it is likely that King continued in this role; he certainly witnessed Hoare's agreement with the rector to establish a school.[5]

Both manorial court, and parish vestry, met in the Court House, which was sometimes referred to as the Parish House, or the Church House,[6] although it seems to have been owned by the lord of the manor. Like most other houses in the parish, it was let on a three-life leasehold. However, the lease had an unusual condition: 'the Lord shall have sufficient room in the said cottage for his steward officers & servants to keep courts as often as occasion shall be and that the lessee will permit the churchwardens of Stourton and their successors against the feast of Penticost yearly for 6 weeks to have the use & occupacion of the said house to brew & bake in for the church ale there

1 WSHC 383/345.
2 TNA C22/708/55.
3 TNA C2/ChasI/S89/24.
4 WSHC 383/737.
5 WSHC 383/744.
6 This is the name used in the survey recording Charles Davies's 1607 lease; cf WSHC 4314/1.

till the time of Penticost is expired'.[1]

The relationship of the highway surveyor to the vestry and the manorial court is not clear – but it may be that it was not clear to contemporaries either. Many parishioners served as both manorial and parish officers, so it did not make much difference. We have no names of the surveyors, except in two possible instances. In 1726, Thomas Cook was paid a highway rate of 1s 7¼d by Henry Hoare, so presumably served as surveyor.[2] Twenty years later, Jeremiah Target may have served, as we will see. We do have a few orders by the homage relating to highways, which had to be enforced by the surveyor.[3] The maintenance of roads was seen as a manorial responsibility, and the court book contains various orders relating to them. The cost of repairs, however, was paid by the churchwardens, and is recorded in their accounts. In 1725, for example, Christopher Parsons was paid 15s 'for stones to men ye highways'.[4]

In 1703, a survey recorded that there was a 'waggon way through the woods'.[5] This may have been the 'way' that was regularly presented in the manorial court in the early eighteenth century. Tenants claimed to have a 'way ... through the Park, and through Davies's Ground, and Goat House' which enabled them to carry furzes from Great Coombe and Little Combe. A lease of 1746 reserved a right of way along a cart track to give access to Friezland Coppice.[6] In 1726, the homage complained that another way through the Park to the common had been 'stopped up' by the Lord, and ordered 'that the same road be laid open by Xmas next'. On the other hand, as has already been seen, in 1742, attempts to create a path from cottages on Stourton Lane across the land of Joseph Lampard were resisted. It is likely that the cottagers were seeking easier access to Stourton Common, and that Lampard complained to the homage about the 'treading down' of his fences. The homage merely presented the fact that the path led from the houses of Richard Edwards, John White, and John Goodland, without ordering any remedy. However, the cottagers were in trouble in the following year. John White and Edward Edwards (Richard's brother) were accused of making an encroachment

1   WSHC 383/99, p.23.
2   WSHC 383/58.
3   Presentments mentioned in the following paragraphs are from WSHC 383/353.
4   WSHC 497/6.
5   WSHC 383/253.
6   WSHC 383/353,

on the King's highway in Stourton Lane, and were ordered to throw it open again. Similarly, in 1746, Joseph Stone made 'an incroachment' on Stourton Common, 'by inclosing lately part of the highway below his house there'. When the next court was held in 1747, he had apparently done nothing about it, and was ordered to 'throw out the same', under penalty of ten shillings. In the following court, however, the homage agreed that 'he could have leave to keep' the enclosure, subject to the Lord's consent, and on payment of one shilling per year 'by way of acknowledgement'. Maybe the road at that point was wide enough to cope with encroachments.

Flooding also caused roads to be obstructed; in 1742, the homage ordered 'the water in the road going to Road Green ... to be thence conveyed away forthwith'. Two years later, the surveyor was ordered to 'amend' several roads in the parish: that between Road Green Gate and Baron's Gate; the road between Mr Barnes's gate and Knell Hill, and 'the road between James Cottrell's and Spencer's Mead stile'. Default meant the surveyor (who was not paid) would be fined ten shillings – a large sum in those days.[1]

Bridges were the responsibility of whoever had traditionally repaired them. In 1746, Jeremiah Target was ordered to repair the 'wooden bridge upon the head, or side, of Tucking Mill Pond'. Whether he did so as surveyor, or as the tenant responsible for the bridge, is not clear.

The duties of the churchwarden were many and varied. Originally, his role had been to ensure the fabric of the church was maintained – although the chancel remained the rector's responsibility.[2] In the sixteenth century, churchwardens' responsibilities were gradually extended, to include matters as diverse as the control of vermin, the morals of the parishioners, and the loyalties of Roman Catholics. The churchwarden was ex officio an overseer of the poor, and shared responsibility for the operation of the poor law with two other overseers.

It is probable that churchwardens had the assistance of two sidesmen, although surprisingly little is known of that office in Stourton. Two sidesmen, William Rose, and William Kenison, put their marks to the 1608 terrier.[3] John Jupe, sidesman, put his mark to the

1   WSHC 383/353.
2   The ecclesiastical activities of churchwardens are discussed in chapter 10.
3   WSHC D1/24/193/3.

1674 presentment.[1] The two sidesmen in September 1671 were John Humphreys and Robert Sandle.[2] That is all the evidence for sidesmen that we have, although it may be noted that Robert Sandle subsequently served as churchwarden in 1683,[3] and that various other members of the Jupe family also served.[4]

Churchwardens were appointed from the parish elite, although not from the family of the lord of the manor, who held too exalted a status to perform that function. Until the final decades of our period, they were generally leading tenants of the manor, who held office for a year or two before handing over to their successors. Richard Cuffe was one such; as we have seen, he was a substantial yeoman whose probate inventory was valued at £225 when he died in 1715/16.[5] He probably served on three occasions between 1685 and 1708.

Most churchwardens were natives of Stourton. However, a few were not. Nathaniel Ireson, as has already been seen, had no long-term connection to the parish. His status rested on the fact that he was employed to build Stourhead. He arrived in Stourton c.1720. Two years was an extraordinarily brief time for someone to spend in a parish before being appointed as its churchwarden, but Ireson took on that role in 1722.[6] The explanation probably lies in the fact that he was a master mason, and, as we will see, carried out a substantial re-ordering of the church during his term of office.

The church had probably been neglected under the Roman Catholic Stourtons. When he became lord of the manor, Henry Hoare gave the matter his attention, as a good Anglican should. It was almost certainly at his instigation that Ireson became churchwarden. There is a plaque in the church which reads 'This church was newly paved and seated and beautified 1722/3. Nathaniel Ireson, John Butcher, churchwardens'. Within three years, Ireson had bought Windmill Farm in Wincanton, and ceased to be resident in Stourton.[7] His time in Stourton was brief, but during it he made a considerable impact on the parish.

1   WSHC D1/54/6/5.
2   WSHC D1/50/1.
3   WSHC D1/54/10/5.
4   See above, pp. 61, 62.
5   WSHC P2/C/1004.
6   WSHC D2/13/4.
7   Colvin, H.M. *A biographical dictionary of British architects, 1600-1840*. Yale University Press, 1995, p.529.

In the late 1730s and 1740s, the pattern of office-holding changed; in that period, the office of churchwarden was almost monopolised by Joseph Lampard, John Bradden, and John Lamb. They were all leading tenants; Lampard, for example, paid more rent than anyone else in the parish. But as already noted, unlike most of his fellow wardens, he was not a native.

The maintenance of the church was (and is) the first duty of the churchwarden. In Stourton, the clearest example of that dictum was Ireson's work. Unfortunately, there is little evidence concerning routine maintenance until 1734. Thereafter, the churchwardens' accounts survive.[1] They show that church rates were regularly levied. In the 1730s and 1740s, one rate brought in £2. Usually at least two rates were imposed per annum. In 1737 and 1738, four rates had to be collected. No lists of ratepayers suvive. We do, however, know how the money from the church rate was spent. In 1741, for example, James Sparrow was paid 14s 4d for 'timber, nails & work about ye bells'. A 'plumers bill' for mending ye windows ye leads & soder', amounted to £1 10s. And 'to pans to hold ye white-washing' cost 8d. They were presumably used again in 1749, when additional expenses amounting to 8d were incurred 'when ye church was painted'. The churchyard also incurred expenditure; when it had to be fenced in 1749, 6s 3d was spent on 'posts and rails', and the labour involved in 'putting it up' cost 1s 4d.

In addition to maintenance work, the churchwardens had to pay Charles Evil 'for ringing gunpowder plot', as well as other expences. Record keeping also cost money: a 'skin of parchment for copying ye register' cost 1s 6d in 1745, and 'binding ye clarks book' (whatever that was) cost a further 4s. In 1750, Mr Wilkins was paid 2s 6d 'for writing out ye rates'. Unfortunately, his rate book does not survive.

Wine and bread for celebrating communion had to be paid for: 'wine for 12 sacraments' cost £1 17s 6d in the same year. Vermin eradication was another duty. The 1734 accounts are particularly full of payments for vermin: 'June 10 to Henry Hill for 1 doz & ½ of sparrows heads , 2d.

The costs of visitations also had to be met. Churchwardens, together with the rector, regularly attended the visitations of bishops and archdeacons, which might be held in Warminster, Hindon, or Salisbury.

In 1741, £1 0s 5½d was spent on court fes & expences at ye visitation at Salisbury'.

It was the duty of the churchwardens to make 'presentments' on the state of their parish – the fabric of the church, the conduct of the minister, the morals and religious inclinations of the inhabitants. Frequently, they reported 'omnia bene' – all well. But not always. In 1662, soon after the Restoration, the long-serving rector, Nathaniel Field, with his two churchwardens, presented a list of no less than 48 parishioners who were 'conceaved to be Popishly affected'.[1] In 1674, the list was only slightly briefer.[2] A few other presentments of papists were made, but mostly only mentioning a few names. Local people preferred to keep quiet about such matters; they needed to get on with their neighbours.

Churchwardens occasionally presented other matters. One of the earliest presentments of which we have record was made in 1584, when Robert Tape was presented as the reputed father of Jone Ryall's bastard, Mr Bonnam was accused of allowing a schoolmaster to teach without a licence, and the rector was accused of neglecting to preach sufficient sermons.[3] In 1674, a 'book of canons and homilies' was wanted.[4] The church was 'out of repair', and a 'hearst cloth' was needed in 1698.[5] 'Ye rectors barn and stable' were 'out of repair' in 1714.[6] In 1723 the 'frame of our sett of bells' was 'out of order', and William Maidment had not paid 18s due for his church rates.[7] The following year, the windows and leads of the church were 'out of repair'.[8] The 'parsonage house is repairing' was noted in 1726.[9] Mr Edmund Wadlow was in trouble in 1739 for 'putting up an oversiz'd gate in the foot way leading to our church wch hinders and obstructs many of the people of our parish in their way thither'.[10]

Occasionally, executors were presented for not obtaining grant of

1   WSHC D1/54/1/4. This is printed in Grout, Diana, & McAbendrath, Liz., eds. *Churchwardens' Presentments for 40 parishes between Warminster Salisbury and Downton. Volume 4.* Wiltshire Family History Society, 2014, p.8-9.
2   WSHC D1/54/6/5.
3   WSHC D1/43/5.
4   WSHC D1/54/6/5.
5   WSHC D1/54/16/5.
6   WSHC D1/54/24/5
7   WSHC D1/54/29/5.
8   WSHC D2/11/6.
9   WSHC D1/54/30/5. See below, p.182.
10 WHSC D2/11/20.

probate. 'Ye death of William Moor, William Moor his son possessor of his goods' was recorded in 1698.[1] In 1732, the apparitor was seeking the latter's son in order to ensure that he obtained probate for his father's estate. But he 'cou'd no learn out where his abode is'.[2] Citations, perhaps based on presentments, regularly summoned the 'possessors of the goods' of deceased persons to obtain grants of probate.[3] In 1725, for example, George Weston of Berwick St James was summoned as the executor of Edmund Wadlow.[4] In that case, however, the apparitor was too late; his will had already been proved in the Prerogative Court of Canterbury.[5]

Morality was a subject of frequent presentment. That could lead to action in the Salisbury Archdeaconry Court. The 1636-41 act books record several actions concerning fornication.[6] Margaret Combe admitted 'that she hath bin latterly delivered of a bastard childe begotten in fornicon', but pleaded that William Parsons had 'promised her marriage'. Soon after she had another bastard, and accused Alexander Davies of being the father. He too had 'promised her marriage'. Steven Bradden married Ann Combe 10th April 1639, but after their marriage they found themselves in the Archdeaconry Court accused of pre-marital fornication. But no baby arrived until 1642, when Steven was baptised on 16th June. One wonders if his baptism had been delayed. John Sandle was in a similar position after he married Edith Moores on 13th October 1634, although his son, Richard was baptised on 7th July 1634, before their marriage. Valentine Pitnie was sentenced to do penance for fornication before the rector of Stourton.

Almost a century later, in 1714, two couples, Charles Feltham and Ruth Mullens, and William Shepherd and Elizabeth Green, were presented 'for living incontinently'.[7] The practice of presentment was, however, dying out; increasingly, the churchwardens contented themselves with saying 'omnia bene' - all well.

The overseers of the poor (other than the churchwardens) were appointed by Justices of the Peace from names suggested by the vestry.

1 WSHC D1/54/16/5.
2 WSHC D1/47/3.
3 Many survive from the 1630s in WSHC D2/5/1/3-5 & 7.
4 WSHC D2/8/2.
5 TNA PROB 11/606/58
6 WSHC D2/4/1/16, f.29v, 95v, & 147r.
7 WSHC D1/54/24/5

Robert Jupe, a copyholder of the manor of Stourton, served in 1657[1];
he was succeeded in 1658 by Thomas Barnard.[2] John Lamb and John
Green were serving in 1670.[3] In 1682, Richard Bayley and John White,
as overseers, signed Thomas Stone's petition for a maimed soldier's
pension.[4] Francis Jupe, the tenant of the Barnes' family's farm at Rode,
and probably a relative of Robert Jupe, served c.1722.[5] Walter Barnes
also served on one occasion; in 1723 he owed £5 10s for the year he had
served.[6] In 1729, the overseers were William Jupe and John Williams.[7]
Thomas Hurdle and John Bradden were serving in February 1731/2.[8]
Unfortunately, we do not know the names of anyone else who served in
our period.

It was the duty of the overseers to relieve the parish poor.
Unfortunately, our evidence of their activities is very limited, although
it is clear that they were keen to limit their liabilities. They ensured that
paupers who were not 'settled' in Stourton were sent on their way; they
kept a watchful eye on those who came to dwell in Stourton, to make sure
they did not create liability for poor relief; they bound pauper children as
apprentices; they sought out the fathers of bastards to ensure that they
provided maintenance. But they also relieved the parish poor, and ran
a workhouse for those eligible for poor relief. When a foundling child
was left, presumably in the church door, the overseers would have been
responsible for her maintenance. It was probably the rector who gave
Mary Owen her name when she was baptised on 15th March 1741. The
overseers did not have the responsibility for long; she was buried on
23rd May.

Under the Elizabethan poor laws, the liability of parishes to pay
poor relief was determined by the settlement of claimants. In order to
determine where paupers were legally 'settled', a Justice of the Peace had
to conduct an examination. The travels of paupers revealed in surviving
settlement examinations for Stourton were discussed in chapter 2.

1   WSHC A1/110/T1657, 94;
2   WSHC A1/110/T1658, 137.
3   Dwelly, E., ed. *Directory of Somerset, part 1*. Dwelly's national records 2. Fleet:
    E.Dwelly, 1916, p.187.
4   WSHC AS/110/T1682, 81.
5   WSHC 383/740.
6   WSHC 383/740.
7   WSHC 1240/34.
8   WSHC 1240/35.

Those migrants who did not satisfy the settlement laws were only allowed to remain in Stourton under sufferance, unless they brought with them a settlement certificate by which the parish they came from acknowledged liability. Nine of these survive for our period amongst Stourton parish records.[1] William Feild in 1723/4 did not have such a certificate, but instead wrote a note promising to pay the overseers £5 if 'I do go to make myself any settlement' in the parish.[2] He was presumably allowed to remain. Stourton overseers themselves wrote settlement certificates for those who wanted to move to other parishes; William Brimson and his wife Elizabeth took one with them when they moved to Maiden Bradley in 1715.[3]

The travelling poor, however, might be relieved as they passed through Stourton; in 1746, the churchwardens' accounts record the payment of 6d 'to a soldier with a pass'.[4] Another curious entry records the payment of 6d to 'a person drown'd out by the sea'. These are the only such payments noted in the accounts, although it is probable that many similar payments were not recorded. The churchwardens' accounts of adjoining Mere record numerous payments to travellers, admittedly at a much earlier date.[5]

Some Stourton settlement examinations identify paupers who were removed to Stourton from other parishes. Thomas Dawkins, his wife Martha, and their two young children were removed from Pitton and Farley, five miles east of Salisbury, in 1733/4.[6] Similarly, John Evil, his wife and two daughters were removed from Kilmington in 1728.[7] And the constables escorted William Smart and his wife Joan back from Carisbrooke (Isle of Wight) in 1730. The Justices ordered that Ann Broadmead, Joan's daughter by her former husband, should accompany them. She was still a 'nurse child', so the Smarts must have been very recently married.

The Stourton overseers also sought to remove paupers or potential paupers who were not 'settled' in their parish. Several examples of their

---

1   WSHC 1240/21.
2   WSHC 1240/22.
3   WSHC 484/49/B.
4   WSHC 497/6.
5   Baker, T.H. 'The churchwardens' accounts of Mere', *Wiltshire Archaeological and Natural History Magazine* 35(110), 1908, p.226-7 (for 1592 payments).
6   WSHC 1240/26.
7   WSHC 1240/26.

actions can be mentioned. In 1658, Thomas Barnard, the overseer, petitioned Quarter Sessions to remove John Land, who had married a parishioner, but had been in residence at Kilmington for three months.[1] The Coffin family - James, Jane, and two infants – were removed to Henstridge (Somerset) in 1733.[2] Henry Cooper, his wife, and four children, were removed to Kilmington in 1738.[3] The Kilmington overseers challenged the removal at Quarter Sessions, but were unsuccessful, and had to pay costs of 40s. All four of the Cooper children had been baptised in Stourton, but Henry himself was described as 'of Kilmington' when he married at Stourton in 1728/9.

The Stourton overseers were not always successful in removing paupers from other parishes. When they tried to remove Robert Alford, Joan his wife, and Elizabeth their ten-year old daughter, they were rebuffed by Quarter Sessions. The overseers of Mere successfully appealed against the removal order, leaving the Stourton overseers to pay costs of 10s.[4] The Stourton overseers were more successful in 1730, when Kilmington appealed against an order to remove Henry Cooper, his wife, and their four children, to Kilmington. This order was signed by Henry Hoare, the lord of the manor, together with Richard Willoughby, another local Justice of the Peace. Quarter Sessions rebuffed the Kilmington overseers, who were ordered to pay costs amounting to 40s to their Stourton counterparts.[5]

There is only evidence of one other appeal by the Stourton overseers against removal orders from other parishes. In 1678, they appealed against the removal of Edward Panier from Fonthill Gifford, but again were rebuffed by Quarter Sessions, and had to pay costs.[6]

Some paupers suffered severely at the hands of officialdom, especially those deemed to be 'vagrants'. William Lewis, aged eight, was one of these. He was brought before the Dorset Quarter Sessions, and 'suffered punishment by law as he ought'. In other words, he was whipped. The Quarter Sessions were probably sitting in Shaftesbury, as the Shaftesbury constable was ordered to escort the boy to his parish of

---

1   WSHC A1/110/T1658, 137.
2   WSHC 1240/26.
3   WSHC A1/130; A1/150/19.
4   WSHC 438/42.
5   WSHC A1/160/7. Michaelmas session, 1730.
6   WSHC A1/160/4. Hilary Sessions, 30 Charles II.

birth, Stourton.[1] Similarly, in 1750 Mary Morland was found 'wandering and begging' in Downton, and adjudged to be 'a rogue and vagabond', although there is no record of a whipping for her. She claimed that 'being in great want she was obliged to ask charity'. She also claimed to have been born in Stourton, and was returned there, although there is no record of her baptism in the parish register, and her surname is otherwise unknown in the parish.[2] In 1736, 17s 4d was paid by the churchwardens, presumably to the constable, 'for carrying vagrants', that is, removing them from the parish.[3] It is likely that the constable in question was John Bradden. He was paid 12s 8d a little later for the same reason. However similar entries do not recur in the churchwardens' accounts.

Bastards were particularly unwelcome to the overseers. Their maintenance could be a continuing and substantial cost to the parish, at least until they were old enough to be apprenticed. When Thomasine Chandler died in 1615, she was owed 30s by the overseers for looking after 'Roberte a base poore boy',[4] whose care had presumably fallen on the parish. If fathers could be identified, they were required to enter a bond to pay for their bastards' maintenance. They could best be identified by examining their mothers – and although Justices of the Peace carried out formal bastardy examinations, midwives were encouraged to discover information whilst mothers were in labour! Margery Bayley charged John Perry of Tisbury with being the father of her 'bastard man child' 'at the tyme of her deliverie' in 1657.[5] Perry was apprehended by the Alvediston tithingman, but ran away. That led to a warrant against the tithingman for neglect of his duty, but eventually the parish came to an agreement with Luke Dyer, who must have been a relative of Perry, to pay maintenance.[6] There is no record of the baptism of the baby, although he was to remain in Stourton, presumably with his mother.

When Joan Baker identified Charles Gover as the father of her unborn child in 1738, he and his father Peter were bound in £40 to meet

1 WSHC 1240/26.
2 WSHC 1240/26.
3 WSHC 497/6.
4 WSHC P2/C/279.
5 WSHC A1/110/61657, 94.
6 The Stourton churchwarden who signed the overseer's petition was named Nicholas Dyer, so there may have been some connection.

'any costs, damages, charges and expenses' which the parish might sustain as a result of the pregnancy.[1] This was the standard condition for a Stourton bastardy bond in this period.

Phyllis Cooper moved from Gasper to Tucking Mill just before her bastardy examination was conducted in 1728, perhaps because she had lost her place on account of her pregnancy. The father was Humphry Scammel of Garve Hill, in the parish of Marston Bigot. His father, another Humphry, lived in Gasper. Humphry the younger had quite possibly encountered Phyllis whilst visiting his father. Father and son, together with Roger Bird and John Earbery, both also of Marston Bigot, were required to enter bond.[2]

The father of Jane Miles's son, who does not appear to have been baptised in Stourton, was a cordwainer from Bayford, in the parish of Stoke Trister. Philip Read was required to stand bound with Thomas Barnard, yeoman, who may be presumed to have been a relative.[3]

We have already met Thomas Wadlow, who fathered a bastard in 1746 . He was a yeoman; his father had been a member of the homage. But he was treated no differently from other fathers of bastards. He too had to enter a bond.[4] The mother was a young widow, Hannah Laws (nee Jupe), who had married John Laws in 1738. Her husband died in 1742, leaving her with two young children; she was probably already claiming relief when Wadlow made her pregnant. Or perhaps she was in service in the Wadlow house when her master took advantage of her? And what was the role of Thomas's widowed mother, Mary, who stood bond with him?

The Justices were not always able to examine the mothers of bastards before the delivery of their babies. On 8th March 1744/5, Betty, the bastard child of Elizabeth Deacons, was baptised. A bastardy order was not made until 17th June, when William Noak of Kilmington, labourer, and Jeafry Noake of Shaftesbury, yeoman (presumably William's father) entered a bond with conditions similar to those entered by Gover and Scammel.[5]

Bastards who did become a charge on the poor rates, together with the legitimate children of other paupers, would have been apprenticed as early as possible – probably at age 7 or 8. We have ten apprenticeship

1   WSHC 1240/28.
2   WSHC 1240/28.
3   WSHC 1240/28.
4   WSHC 1240/28.
5   WSHC 1240/28.

indentures, which will be discussed in chapter 8. It might be noted here, however, that only one (or possibly two) of the masters found by the overseers were Stourton parishioners. The laws of settlement dictated that overseers were only liable to pay poor relief to those who were 'settled' in their parish. And one of the criterias for determining 'settlement' was apprenticeship to a master 'settled' in the parish. By sending pauper apprentices out of the parish, overseers were avoiding any future liability to poor relief.

The case of David Boyt illustrates the way in which the overseers operated. The probability is that the family came to Stourton in 1707, when they leased a tenement in Bonham, and presumably gained a settlement, although the lease was surrendered shortly afterwards.[1] In the mid-1740s the family were tenants of Charlton's Close. The family do not appear in the parish register until 1749, and other Stourton records rarely mention them, However, David Boyt junior, although he was a married man with a daughter, acknowledged himself to be the father of Martha Owen's bastard daughter in October 1728, and was bound in £40 to ensure he maintained the child.[2] Indeed, his father conditionally assigned his messuage at Norton Mead to the parish officers as a guarantee that he would do so.[3] It would appear that Boyt failed to find the maintenance, as the property was seized by the parish officers soon after.[4] Boyt had also made the mistake of establishing a settlement in Batcombe (Somerset). In the following March, the Justices ordered his removal to that parish.[5] He was not, however, to be kept away. By 1738, he had returned to dwell with his father in Stourton, 'without the consent of the said parish he not being a parishioner'. Consequently, he 'occasioned' the churchwardens and overseers to be 'uneasy' that he might gain a settlement, become a parishioner, and hence become a potential liability. They therefore insisted that his father entered a bond to pay £40 if Boyt should become a parishioner 'without the special licence and consent' of themselves.[6]

Curiously, at the same time as his son was being investigated for the paternity of Martha Owen's child, David Boyt senior was negotiating

1 WSHC 383/541.
2 WSHC 1240/28.
3 WSHC 1240/33.
4 WSHC 1240/33.
5 WSHC 1240/26.
6 WSHC 1240/23.

the assignment of his lease of Norton Mead to the overseers – although he continued to reside there himself until his death in 1779. Even more curiously, another David Boyt was serving as overseer in 1783.[1]

Boyt's property, together with a tenement formerly in the tenure of Mary Slatford,[2] provided the land for the erection of a workhouse, and for the planting of a willowbed, which was leased to William and Andrew Hoskins of Gillingham for ten years from 1730.[3] They were to 'sett in a good and sufficient quantity of willow stocks in that part of the ground now sett out & unplanted', and to 'leave the whole ground well filled with such willow stocks' at the end of their tenancy. The lease yielded the vestry an income of £3-05-00 per annum. The willowbed was extended in 1737, when Hoare purchased the property next door from George Green.[4]

The workhouse was established in order to take advantage of the provisions of the Poor Law Act of 1722, which permitted parishes to erect workhouses where paupers could be set to work in return for relief. It may have been the first such workhouse in Wiltshire, and was almost certainly erected at the instigation of the Hoare family. Henry 'the Magnificent' was responsible for securing the surrender of Mary Slatford's lease in 1727. His father's 1725 will left a substantial sum of money for erecting and supporting workhouses and charity schools; perhaps the Stourton workhouse benefited from this.[5] It probably also benefited from advice from the S.P.C.K., which was taking a coordinating role in the erection of workhouses nation-wide.[6]

Presumably, workhouse inmates were expected to make baskets from the produce of the willow beds. The workhouse, with its orchards, garden and barn, was said to be worth £4 per annum in c.1756.[7] It is mapped in a deed of 1739 showing the willow bed beside a pond Henry Hoare had created[8] .

We know little about the inmates of the workhouse in our period.

1   Hobbs, Steven, ed. *Wiltshire glebe terriers 1588-1827*. Wiltshire Record Society 56. 2003, p.408.
2   WSHC 383/97, f.37; 383/98, p.3.
3   WSHC 1240/35.
4   WSHC 383/384.
5   Oxford Dictionary of National Biography **www.oxforddnb.com**
6   Cambridge University Library SPCK Abstract Letter Book D2/18, p.8909 & 8947.
7   WSHC 383/740.
8   WSHC 383/719.

Six inmates attended the Christmas dinner at Stourhead in 1751.[1] In the 1750s several of their burials were recorded in the parish register. Ironically, one of them was David Boyt. Despite his father's bond, he was buried in 1756 'from ye workhouse'. Another was Mary Cooper – probably a relation of Henry Cooper – who was also buried in 1756. Interestingly, she and another relative, Hannah Cooper, had been amongst the nineteen 'masterless' persons, without visible means of subsistence, who had been ordered to find a master by a Somerset Justice of the Peace in 1720.[2]

One of the earliest inmates, in 1729, was James Hurden, the son of John and Katherine Hurden, and nephew of Peter Torteshall of Chideock. When his uncle 'out of his natural love and affection' wanted to remove him, he had to enter a bond for £60 with the overseers before they would let him out. Interestingly, the person bound with Torteshall was no less than Charles Stourton of Bonham.[3] The Hurdens evidently had Roman Catholic connections: Chideock was the home of the Catholic Lady Arundel in the late sixteenth century,[4] and the Torteshall family was well known for its Catholicism.[5]

The workhouse was funded under the will of Henry Hoare, the lord of the manor, who died in 1725. His memorial inscription records that Hoare ' gave by his last will two thousand pounds, for erecting and encouraging charity schools and workhouses'.[6]

One reason why the overseers would not allow James Hurden to leave the workhouse without a bond from his uncle was that they wanted to control the activities of the poor. That control was normally exercised through the master and servant relationship. When the poor who had 'nothing to live on by theire labour and worke' refused to enter service, they aroused suspicion, and could be compelled to find a master. In 1624, the Mere Hundred jury presented George Spender of Stourton 'for that he do lyve as an idle person'.[7] In 1720, the churchwardens and

---

1   WSHC 383/259.
2   WSHC 1240/3.
3   WSHC 1240/34.
4   *Calendar of State Papers Domestic ... 1591-1594.* HMSO, 1867, p.488.
5   Williams, J. Anthony *Catholic recusancy in Wiltshire, 1660-1791.* Catholic Record Society, 1968, especially p.199, note 107.
6   Calland, Garry. St Peters, *Stourton: a tour and history of the church.* Henry Cadogan Hoare, 2010, p.77.
7   WSHC A1/110/T1624/127.

overseers of Gasper complained that there were no less than nineteen men and women in the tithing who were not in service. The constable (or tithingman) was ordered by one of the Somerset Justices to 'warne' them all to find a master; otherwise he was to 'cause them to be and appeare before me'.[1]

We know very little about the constables of Stourton in our period. We do know that Thomas Davies served as tithingman c.1580, and Edith Blanford succeeded him.[2] Alexander Adams, described by the jury of Mere Hundred as Stourton's tithingman, was presented for failing in his duty in 1640; he had not reproved some 'sturdie beggars and rouges' for 'tipling and taking tobacco' in the church porch.[3] In 1651, Stourton's constables were required to raise a rate for the relief of plague in neighbouring Maiden Bradley, although by 1654 some of the money demanded was still outstanding.[4] Mathew Combes served as tithingman in 1658, when he, together with Edward Gibbs, the churchwarden, presented 38 recusants to Quarter Sessions.[5] Robert Jupe succeeded Combes in 1659, although Gibbs continued to hold office; Jupe and Gibbs presented 39 recusants.[6] In 1742, the tithingman of Stourton was discharged by Quarter Sessions.[7] The churchwardens' accounts record the payment of rates for the Marshallsea and for the county gaol. Such rates were normally collected and paid by the parish constable (also known as the tithingman), although in Stourton the task seems to have been done by the churchwardens. Or perhaps it was the custom for the same individual to hold both offices. In 1734 and 1735, payment was made by Joseph Lampard, who was then serving as churchwarden. In 1746, it was noted that Mr John White, the then churchwarden, 'must gather one rate for the tithing account' – presumably also for these rates. John Bradden was serving as churchwarden in 1734, when, as already noted, he was paid 12s 8d by Joseph Lampard (his fellow churchwarden) 'for carrying vagrants'. The removal of vagrants was the duty of the constable.

---

1   WSHC 1240/3.
2   TNA LR11/34/463.
3   WSHC A1/110/t1640,76; printed in Cunnington, B.Howard, ed. *Records of the County of Wilts, being extracts from the Quarter Sessions Great Rolls of the Seventeenth Century*. Devizes: B.Simpson & Co., 1932, p.134.
4   WSHC A1/110/T1654, 102.
5   WSHC A1/110/T1658, 116.
6   WSHC A1/110/T1659, f.125.
7   WSHC A1/165/6.

Other entries in the accounts relating to the duties of the constable include mention in 1734 of 'a plate and nails for ye stocks & setting on' cost 2s 4d.[1] In 1746, 'the tithingman's bill' for 'county stock money' came to £2 4s 10d.

Constables were responsible for the recruitment of the militia. The Mere constables perhaps recruited Thomas Bennett of Stourton to serve on their behalf in 1594; he was paid 8d. In 1715/16, Stourton was required to send one soldier to serve.[2] The only person found 'liable to send souldiers' in the parish was Edmund Wadlow, and the only person found 'fitt to go soldier' was Joseph Stone. Wadlow presumably paid for Stone's deployment. Two decades later, he served as the constable of Mere Hundred.[3]

Constables were also required to press soldiers when the country was at war. There is no direct evidence of Stourton men being pressed; however, both sons of John Williams from neighbouring Mere were sent to serve in the Isle of Rhe. One was killed; the other severely injured. In 1628, their father petitioned Quarter Sessions to allow him to build a cottage in Mere, as the son who had been killed had been the last life in his lease. He could not afford to pay a fine to renew the lease, but was able to rent a small plot of land on which a cottage could be built, provided that the bench would allow him to do so.[4] One wonders if Jeremy Williams, who served in the Royalist army during the Civil War, and who petitioned for a pension in 1662, was a relative.[5]

We also have very little evidence concerning taxation during our period. Church rates have already been discussed. These were not the only duties imposed in the parish; a variety of other rates and taxes were levied. In 1691, the Stourton collectors for the assessment were John Walter and Richard Smart; they collected just over £28.[6] Taxation was an ever present issue in Stourton. In 1723, Francis Jupe, the tenant of Rode, had to pay £2 3s 10½d for poor rates, £1 11s 6d for church rates, 9s 3¾d for highway rates and 3s 4½d for tything rates.[7] In the same year, Henry

1 WSHC 497/6.
2 WSHC 413/12.
3 Fowle, J.P.M., ed. *Wiltshire Quarter Sessions and Assizes, 1736*. Wiltshire Archaeological and Natural History Society Records Branch, 11. 1955, p.69.
4 WSHC A1/110/T1628, 139.
5 WSHC A1/110/T1661, 100.
6 WSHC 413/32.
7 WSHC 383/740.

Hoare paid land tax £3 6s 11¼d, poor rates £2 14s, church rates 13s 9d, highway rates 13s 10½d, and a tything rate of 1s 8¼d.[1] In 1735, Quarter Sessions confirmed Stourton's poor rate assessment.[2] The parish was expected to contribute to county rates; in 1747, the churchwardens had to pay 'the tithingman's bill county stock money'.[3] We know that land tax was levied in the parish in 1720, as Henry Hoare had to allow his tenants 28s 6d.[4] Sadly, no assessments survive for our period.

The activities of most parish officers were supervised by Justices of the Peace, either acting alone, or sitting in Quarter Sessions. Some of the responsibilities of the lone justice have already been discussed, especially in relationship to the poor law. They also had criminal responsibilities, and regularly examined both offenders and witnesses. It is difficult to identify specifically Stourton matters amongst Quarter Sessions documents, since there are too many unindexed documents to search. Alexander Green had to enter a bond for £20 to appear before the bench in 1626 to answer for some misdemeanour.[5] In 1628, John Bradden had to do the same.[6] In 1648, John Freak laid an information against his servant, Edith Courtney, whom he suspected of stealing a gold ring and other items.[7] We know that in 1741 Robert Smart of Stourton was found not guilty of stealing four quarters of mutton.[8] We know too that Richard Newman, yeoman, was indicted in 1730, but his offence is not stated.[9] A few examinations and informations from Gasper can be found amongst Somerset records. Sir Henry Berkeley's examination of a suspected thief from Gasper in 1625[10] will be discussed below.[11] In 1693, William Ashe examined William Duffett, who was suspected of poaching, as he had been found with a net. He had had a violent altercation with the tithingman.[12] A few years later, in 1707, Mr John King gave a Justice an information against James Sparrow and

1   WSHC 383/58.
2   WSHC A1/150/19.
3   WSHC 497/6.
4   WSHC 383/58.
5   WSHC A1/110/M1626/44.
6   WSHC A1/110/E1628/19.
7   WSHC A1/110/T1648, 114.
8   WSHC A1/150/19.
9   WSHC A1/65/6-7.
10 Somerset Heritage Centre Q/SR/53/68.
11 See below, p. 154.
12 Somerset Heritage Centre Q/SR/193a/1-2.

Thomas Alford, who had assaulted him on the road between Silton and Gasper, and 'wth a cudgel' had 'struck out one of his eyes'.[1]

If Justices wished to, they could send such examinations and informations to Quarter Sessions. There were also petty sessions. Little evidence for these survive, although we know that they sat at Hindon in 1650.[2] Prosecution of criminal offences had to be carried out by victims, who were sometimes unwilling to do so, due to the cost, the difficulties of obtaining witnesses, and the reluctance to accuse neighbours who would continue to be neighbours after their court appearances. Hence William Green of Stourton had to enter into a bond to prosecute Thomas Hanson in 1592, and seems not to have appeared, although we know no more than that.[3] A number of local names are recorded in the minutes of Quarter Sessions proceedings for 1578: Thomas Garret, John Gullyford, William Britten and John Jupe were all indicted for trespass, found not guilty, but nevertheless had to pay fines of 20d each – perhaps for hunting in Selwood.[4] In the 1610s, the right to hunt in Selwood was at the centre of a controversy between Lord Stourton and Sir Maurice Berkeley. Berkeley, a deputy lieutenant for Somerset, and several times a Member of Parliament, was a strong puritan. Although there is no mention of religion in the relevant Star Chamber papers, it may be suspected that the religious proclivities of the two disputants had something to do with their dispute. The dispute itself was carried on by proxy between their respective servants. Several serious affrays took place on the borders of Stourton Park and Selwood Forest. Richard Bayley, one of Lord Stourton's keepers, twice suffered serious injuries that threatened his life, once by the thrust of a pike. The dispute between the two sides was not dealt with at Quarter Sessions; instead, both sides initiated complaints in Star Chamber.[5]

Local government was severely strained during the Civil War, especially when fighting took place in the parish. By June 1645, Stourton

---

1   Somerset Heritage Centre Q/SR/244/5.

2   WSHC A1/110/T1650, 82.

3   Johnson, H.C., ed. *Wiltshire County records: minutes of proceedings in Sessions, 1563 and 1574 to 1592*. Wiltshire Archaeological Society Records Branch 4. 1949, p.146

4   Johnson, op cit, p.42. The text does not actually state their parish, but these were all names well known in Stourton, and they were associated with others from Kilmington.

5   TNA STAC8/256/26; STAC8/73/13.

was at the centre of the club movement. The clubmen of Frome Selwood, Gillingham and Mere sought to halt the fighting. They were genuinely neutral, rather than being tinged with Royalism or Parliamentarianism.[1] That did not apply to all Stourtonians. In 1655, eight men from Stourton, including two shoemakers, four husbandmen, a miller, and Lord Stourton himself, were suspected of Royalism.[2]

Procedure at Quarter Sessions began by means of presentment before the Grand Jury. Jurors were selected from freeholders' books compiled by high constables. For Wiltshire, these are available for 1708, 1712, and every year or two from 1730.[3] However, we do know the names of a few earlier jurors from Stourton. In 1626 Henry Baron was a juror[4]; in 1657, Robert Gapper served[5]; in 1659 Thomas Banister served[6]; in 1669, Adam Cuffe served.[7] In the 1730s, the freeholders' books regularly name between three and five Stourton freeholders. They are therefore far from complete listings of those who might be considered eligible to serve, and do not include any members of the Roman Catholic community – such as the Coffins or the Barnes. The same names frequently re-appear – especially Jeremiah Target, Thomas Hurdle, Edmund Wadlow, and George Green. In the 1740s the pattern changed, probably due to the fact that Henry Hoare, the Magnificent, took up residence at Stourhead after his mother's death in 1741. His name first appears on the jurors' list for 1743, in association with Jeremiah Target. Thereafter, Hoare's name appears by itself. It is likely that Hoare recognised that the status of the Grand Jury had risen in the previous decades, and that whereas in previous years it had been manned by yeomen and minor gentry, now jurors were increasingly drawn from the county gentry and aristocracy. He therefore felt that his name should appear (although he was himself a Justice of the Peace), and that the names of his tenants should cease to do so. Nevertheless, the earliest surviving jurors' list for Somerset, dated 1763, and covering the tything of Brook (that is, Gasper), show that Henry Hoare was quite happy for Thomas Target (probably Jeremiah's

1   Sharp, Buchanan. *In contempt of all authority: rural artisans and riot in the West of England, 1586-1660.* University of California Press, 1980, p.238.
2   British Lbrary Add. Mss 34012.
3   WSHC A1/265.
4   WSHC A1/110/T1626/101.
5   WSHC A1/110/T1657, 57.
6   WSHC A1/110/T1659, 188.
7   WSSHC A1/10/T1669, 62.

great nephew) to serve in the neighbouring county.[1] In practice, there is no record that Henry Hoare was ever actually called upon to serve on the Grand Jury. The only other evidence of Stourton presence on a jury is that John Smith of Stourton was accused of serving as a juror at the Royalist 'illegal Assizes' during the civil war, and fined £20 by the County Committee in consequence.[2] But his name has not been found in any other document of the period.

Jurors also had to be selected to sit on the hundred juries which made presentments at Quarter Sessions.[3] Stourton fell in the Hundred of Mere, which normally made presentments once a year at Trinity sessions.[4] Lists of jurors names can be found amongst the Quarter Sessions rolls. There were usually three or four Stourton names on these lists. Most were probably yeomen; William Barnard, yeoman, served in 1629, and again in 1632[5]; Walter Tabor, yeoman in 1631.[6] In 1731, Thomas Hurdle, Edmund Wadlow, George Green, and Jeremiah Target served[7]; their names have already been mentioned in connection with the lists for the Grand Jury. They were all prominent figures in the parish; three were yeomen, and one described himself as a gentleman. It is likely that the role of Hundred jurymen was becoming more attractive to leading parishioners. A century earlier, in 1615 no less than three husbandmen from Stourton served, together with one yeoman.[8] Mathew Combes, husbandman, served in 1637.[9] Edward Sutor, a linen weaver, served in 1640.[10]

It was the duty of the hundred jurors, and the hundred constables, to make presentments at Quarter Sessions. Their seventeenth-century presentments are full of the names of recusants. These will be discussed in chapter 10. But they also made presentments on matters such as the

1 Somerset Heritage Centre Q/RJl 28/9a.
2 Wylen, J. 'The Falstone day book', *Wiltshire Archaeological and Natural History Society magazine* 26, 1892, p.383.
3 WSHC A1/110. The Mere Hundred jury normally made presentments at Trinity sessions, held at Warminster, at least in the 1630s.
4 Fowle, J.P.M., ed. *Wiltshire Quarter Sessions and Assizes, 1736.* Wiltshire Archaeological and Natural History Society Records Branch, 11. 1955, p.99.
5 WSHC A1/110/T1629/158; /T1632/147.
6 WSHC A1/110/T1631/80.
7 Fowle, op cit, p.68.
8 WSHC A1 /110/T1615/93.
9 WSHC A1/110/T1637/207.
10 WSHC A1/110/T1640.

punishment of vagrants, the state of the alehouses, and the state of the highways. On two occasions they presented individuals for causing damage to Stourton roads. In 1639, William Leversett of Kilmington dug up the road on Whitesheet Hill to carry away 'mame', that is, malm, which was a type of limestone used as foundation stones for walling.[1] He was accused of causing 'great prejudice' to Stourton inhabitants', and 'the spoyle of the highway there'.[2] In 1640, it was the turn of William Jefferies, a maltster, who had 'spoilled the highway at a place called Longland'.[3] In 1633, they presented that Thomas Read had been punished for swearing 'by setting in the stockes'. He had also been presented as a recusant.[4] George Green was another swearer who was punished in the stocks, in 1655.[5] A few Stourton names are mentioned amongst the Hundred Constables, for example, William Barnard in 1666, and Richard Bayliffe in 1672.[6]

It is also necessary to mention the Hundred Courts. Unfortunately, there is very little evidence surviving relating to the activities of the Mere Hundred court, although it is clear from the jurors' presentments at Quarter Sessions that it was a liberty of the Duchy of Cornwall, and that a court was held every three weeks.[7] A court was also regularly held for the Somerset Hundred of Norton Ferris, which included the tithing of Brook covering the western portion of the parish. An estreat book from the Hundred Court has survived, listing fines imposed by the court between 1625 and 1630.[8] A few Stourton parishioners are named, but little can be said concerning the court's activities.

1   Wright, Joseph. *The English dialect dictionary, vol.4.* Oxford University Press, 1905, p.22.
2   WSHC A1/110/T1639/123.
3   WSHC A1/110/T1640/76.
4   WSHC A1/110/T1633/140.
5   WSHC A1/110/61655, 95. It is not clear whether he was of Stourton's blacksmith's family, or whether he was of Mere.
6   WSHC A1/110, passim.
7   WSHC A1/110/T1622/117; A1/110/T1623/131.
8   Somerset Heritage Centre DD\S\WI/32.

5
Wealth and Poverty in Stourton

STOURTON KNEW EXTREMES of wealth and poverty in our period. The Stourton family were seriously wealthy. John Aubrey estimated that they were worth at least £20,000 in the seventeenth century.[1] In 1638-9, Lord Stourton himself claimed that he had an income of about £1500 per annum.[2] The family's property included, of course, not just the manor of Stourton, but also a variety of other estates in various parts of the country. By 1651, however, after the ravages of civil war, the estate was said to be worth no more than £800 per annum.[3] In seventeenth century circumstances, even that was seriously wealthy. The £6000 dowry provided for the 11th Lord's daughter Mary in 1648 has already been noted. But the estate became seriously encumbered with debt. When it was sold to the mortgagor, Sir Thomas Meres, in 1714, the price was £19,400. But, as already noted, a mere £775 was left to Lord Stourton after the mortgage was taken into account.[4] Henry Hoare, who purchased the estate in 1717, was much wealthier; he was a London banker. As has already been seen, the Hoares spent over £20,000 on building Stourhead, and much more on their landscaping and gardening activities.

By contrast, there was much poverty in the parish. Its extent can be demonstrated from the hearth tax returns for the tithing of Brook (usually referred to as Gasper).[5] In 1664, there were 33 taxpayers,

1 Mowbray, Lord. *The history of the noble house of Stourton.* Elliot Stock, 1899, p.1.
2 *Calendar of State Papers Domestic Charles I, vol. 13, 1638-9.* HMSO, 1871, p.472.
3 Green, Mary Anne Everett, ed. *Calendar of the proceedings of the Committee for Compounding with Delinquents &c., 1643-1660 ... cases 1643-1646.* HMSO, 1890, p.1294.
4 Mowbray, op cit, p.514.
5 Sadly, returns for the Wiltshire portion of the parish do not survive.

mostly paying on just one or two hearths. Exemption certificates are not available for this levy, although three householders were too poor to pay.[1] In 1670, exemption certificates do survive[2] – although the actual assessment is missing. No less than 25 householders were exempt on the grounds of poverty. Assuming that the number who paid in 1670 was the same as the number in 1664, over 40% were too poor to pay the tax.

Normally, it is possible to assess relative wealth and poverty from tax returns. Unfortunately, there are none for the parish that are comprehensive. The hearth tax documents referred to above only cover a small part of the parish. The only tax document that is useful for this purpose is for the 1642 grant of £400,000.[3] This lists the amounts paid, but does not indicate the basis of assessment. Mr. Field, the rector, headed the list of taxpayers, paying £1 17s. As we will see, his probate inventory suggests that he was perhaps the wealthiest individual in the parish, apart from the lord of the manor. The latter, Lord Stourton, heads a separate list of recusant taxpayers; he paid £6 8s – four times as much as the rector.

There were 25 ordinary taxpayers in 1642, plus 25 recusants (including several wives). Four of the former paid 10s 4d each; seven paid between 3s and 10s, twelve paid between 1s and 3s, and one paid 6d. These figures support the conclusion that there were several individuals in the parish whose wealth sharply differentiated them from most of the inhabitants. There were also a substantial number who could afford to pay a few shillings. But the great majority were either too poor to be liable, or were able to avoid payment.

Recusants were much less likely to escape payment. Lord Stourton himself was the only recusant liable to pay the 1642 grant. However, recusants who were not liable nevertheless had to pay a poll tax of 2s 8d. The 24 who did so were supposedly poorer than those who paid the grant. It is noticeable that whilst no less than five members of the Barnes family were assessed as recusants to the poll tax, three others paid the subsidy without being classed as recusant. The assessments of the latter were, admittedly high: Walter paid 10s 4d, William 7s 3d, and Robert 10s 4d. But Robert himself was described as 'sessor'. One

1   Holworthy, R., ed. *Hearth tax for Somerset 1664-5.* Dwellys' national records 1. Fleet: E.Dwelly, 1916, p.96-8.
2   Dwelly, E., ed. *Directory of Somerset part 1.* Fleet: E.Dwelly, 1929, p.136-7.
3   TNA E179/259/25. pt.1.

wonders how far he was responsible for limiting his family's liabilities.

If, as has been suggested, Stourton had more than 100 households in our period, then fewer than half of them paid the grant. It is likely that some who should have paid escaped assessment. Nevertheless, it is clear that, as in the case of the hearth tax, more than half were too poor to pay.

Another possibility for assessing wealth is provided by probate inventories. These only record moveable goods and leasehold property; they do not record copyhold or freehold land, and cannot therefore be used to establish total wealth. They are also unreliable guides to individuals' wealth. Richard Rogers was described as a gentleman in his 1602 inventory,[1] and some of the goods his appraisers listed support the designation; for example, he had a hauberk (a coat of mail) worth ten shillings, and books valued at four shillings. Yet the total valuation placed on his goods was a mere £12 4s 5d. The inventory was ostensibly dated May 1602, but it was not produced in court until May 1604. One wonders if his son, as administrator, removed items before the inventory was drawn up, or if the old man was living with his son. He had a 'little table borde', and even 'table napkins' – yet no seating whatever was recorded.

Despite this criticism, inventories do provide an indication of relative wealth. For the period between 1558 and 1724, 78 inventories survive (although two are damaged and without totals). There are none for later periods. Prior to 1650, none relate to wealthy individuals. Indeed, three of the five surviving inventories for the period 1575 to 1599 were valued at under £10, and only one was over £50 (but only just). In the first half of the seventeenth century, only five of the twenty-three inventories were valued at over £50.

That changed in the second half of the century. It is likely that the enclosure of 1633 boosted the wealth of some manorial tenants. Between 1650 and 1674, four of the eleven inventories were valued at over £100. Two of them related to rectors. Nathaniel Field's 1666 inventory, as already noted, was valued at £762 10s 2d.[2] His successor, John Derby owned goods valued at £181 10s when he died in 1671.[3] Thomas Stourton, the brother of the 11th Lord, who died in 1670, was worth £620, mainly

1 WSHC P2/R/77.
2 WSHC P1/F/134.
3 TNA PROB4/21045.

in cash and desperate debts, that is, debts for which he had no bonds.[1]
The fourth, Francis Jupe, a mere yeoman, was worth less; his inventory
was valued at £190.[2]

Men of lower status were generally worth less. Robert Davies, who
died in 1667, was perhaps one of the wealthier husbandmen. His status
has to be inferred from the small number of sheep and cattle recorded in
his inventory, and from the fact that he leased seven acres; he had goods
valued at £56 7s.[3] Mathew Combes, whose status as a husbandman is
explicitly stated in his inventory, had possessions of lesser value; he
died in 1671, with goods worth £28 11s 4d.[4] Throughout the following
decades, that was fairly typical. Seventeen of the thirty-one inventories
recorded between 1675 and 1699 recorded valuations of between £20
and £40. In that period, there were only two high value inventories: a
yeoman, Thomas Barnard, possessed goods said to be worth £600 4s
when he died in 1681.[5] When William Jupe, the son of Francis Jupe,
whose inventory we have already noticed, died in 1683, he was worth
less than his father had been, but his inventory was still valued at a not
inconsiderable £113 13s 4d.[6]

In the twenty-five years from 1st January 1700, four of the seven
inventories were valued at over £100. John Hill, who described himself
as a yeoman, but whose inventory suggests he was a mercer, was the
wealthiest, with £381 10s 11d.[7] His son married the rector's daughter.

Many Stourton people benefited from an expanding economy
in the century following the Restoration in 1660. The proportion of
inventories with valuations under £20 gradually decreased as time
passed. In the second decade of the seventeenth century, four of the
six inventories were in this category. For the last half of the century,
the proportion decreased from 66% to 19%. Only one of the seven
inventories for the period 1700-1724 had a similar low value.

Prosperity, however, did not entirely account for the fact that
the proportion of inventories showing low levels of wealth was
decreasing. Another reason was that those who should have undertaken

1   TNA PROB4/6892.
2   WSHC P2/IJ/181.
3   WSHC P2/D/265.
4   WSHC P2/C/630.
5   WSHC P2/B/990.
6   WSHC P2/IJ/181.
7   WSHC P2/H/1092.

administration of deceased estates increasingly felt that goods worth less than £20 were not worth taking through the process of probate. If the value of the goods was small, the cost of probate could exceed their value. And for many, there was a narrow gap between self-sufficiency and poverty. John Humphreys, a yeoman, was paying rent of £30 per annum for a property at Blackslough in the 1720s, probably on a yearly tenancy. When he died, his widow kept the tenancy till the year was up, then relinquished it. In 1734/5, his son John was forced to undergo a settlement examination, and was ordered to be removed from Wincanton to Gasper, with his wife and two children.[1]

We have already seen that there were many poor in Stourton. Many had cottages – hovels – on the commons, as will be seen in chapter 9. When the waste was enclosed in 1633, thirty acres were reserved for them. Ten indentures for pauper boys apprenticed by the poor law overseers survive amongst the parish records; it is likely that more have been lost. Henry Hoare's new workhouse was needed to cater for the parish's many paupers.

The wealth and poverty of Stourton, as in the case of most rural parishes in our period, was based on land. Those who had land, whether they were freeholders, leaseholders, or copyholders, had some degree of wealth, and of protection against the vagaries of the economy. Those who did not could easily be reduced to poverty and pauperism.

The structure of land-holding was a major determinant of the prosperity of the community, and of the social and economic relationships of its inhabitants. It forms the topic of our next chapter.

---

[1]   Somerset Heritage Centre Q/SR/303/26; Q/SR/303/59.

6
Land Owners, Tenants, and Discontent

ESTATE RECORDS FOR the parish of Stourton are sparse before the late seventeenth century, although there are a few earlier deeds and leases. It is probable that the estate archives were destroyed when Parliamentary troops ravaged Stourton Castle in 1644.[1] It is also possible that they were lost when Walter Barnes of Shaftesbury, the then steward, died in 1657; he had kept all of Lord Stourton's 'writings' in his personal possession, and his executors had to be sued in order to secure their return.[2] Another possibility is that George Knipe never returned the court rolls and other papers in his possession when he was dismissed as steward c.1692.[3]

A survey of 1633 for the manor of Stourton, presumably made when the waste was enclosed by Chancery decree, has recently been discovered.[4] A few seventeenth-century deeds and leases survive; some are recorded in Lord Stourton's entry book.[5] A variety of rentals and surveys are available. Surveys were taken in 1693,[6] c.1694,[7] 1717,[8] and 1719.[9] the latter two after the respective purchases of Sir Thomas Meres and Henry Hoare. Further surveys were made in 1722/3, 1744, and 1745.[10] Henry Hoare

1   Firth, C.H., ed. *The Memoirs of Edmund Ludlow, Lieutenant General of the Horse in the Army of the Commonwealth of England, 1625-1672*. Clarendon Press, 1898. Vol.1, p.97.
2   TNA C6/303/26.
3   TNA C6/303/26.
4   WSHC 4314/1.
5   WSHC 383/109.
6   WSHC 383/346.
7   WSHC 383/352
8   WSHC 383/348.
9   WSHC 383/256.
10 WSHC 383/97-99.

bought 'books to enter court rolls' for 12s 6d in 1719.[1] One of these was probably used to compile the 'book of entries', which preserves minutes of the manorial court from 1719 until 1749.[2] There are also many deeds and leases.

These records enable us to reconstruct the late seventeenth and early eighteenth century tenurial pattern for the manor of Stourton. A small number of deeds and leases are also available for the small manors of Bonham and Gasper. For Bonham, there is also the entry for Thomas Stourton in the 1717 register of Papists estates, which effectively provides us with a survey of the manor.[3]

A fairly detailed description of Stourton manor was written in 1704. It estimated the value of the house and 950 acres of demesne at £11,000. There were 49 leasehold and copyhold tenements worth £4000. They produced £200 per annum by 'renewing leases and copies', although it was thought they would be worth £550 if taken in hand. Rents received totalled £396 per annum. The advowson was reckoned to be worth £600, as the incumbent was old. There were 'comons and royalties of vast extent', especially fishing rights on the River Stour from its source to the sea, which brought in rents and 'acknowledgements' from all the villages en route worth £100. That totalled £16,096. In addition there were 'two very good new stone built farme houses' worth £1200, and timber valued at £4000 which could be sold.[4]

The timber was probably sold. Sir Thomas Meres paid £19,400 when he bought the estate in 1714.[5] His purchase included not just the manor of Stourton, but also a water mill, the farm at Coldcot, fishing rights in the River Stour, and the advowson, as well as the manor of Stourton Caundle and other Dorset property. His son sold the estate to the banker, Henry Hoare, in 1717. The Stourton portion was estimated to be worth over £1100 per annum when Henry Hoare 'the Magnificent'

1 WSHC 383/58.
2 WSHC 383/353. The record was kept in a book rather than a roll. Rough drafts of some minutes are also in 383/345; this also includes presentments for 1707.
3 Somerset Heritage Centre Q/RRp1/14. Stourton's property in Wiltshire is recorded in a separate Wiltshire register; cf. WSHC A1/310/4.
4 WSHC 383/255.
5 Mowbray, Baron. *The History of the Noble House of Stourton, of Stourton, in the County of Wilts.* Elliott Stock, 1899, vol.1, p.530-31.

succeeded his father in 1725. About half of that was accounted for by demesne lands which Henry's mother held in jointure, the other half by leases upon lives.

Until the late sixteenth century, it is likely that land in the manor of Stourton was generally held by copy of court roll. Grants of copyhold property were made in open court, and entry fines could be charged. Heriots 'according to the custom of the manor' were payable. The custom was set out in 1819: 'at the death of each and every customary tenant seised the Lord may reserve and recover a heriot of best beast or goods, or a commuted sum in lieu thereof'.[1] This appears to have been the custom throughout our period. The fees normally charged were set out in 1693, when the foreman of the homage and other homagers were asked by the new steward to state them. They replied that 13s 4d was due for every copy, 1s for every admittance to a tenancy, £1 5s for every lease, and 6s 8d for 'copy licence' (presumably a copy of the court roll).[2] Some copyholders held for their own lives only; others for three lives. Tenants' heirs were automatically admitted to copyholds when the manorial court was held.

Manorial custom gave the widow of the first-named life an automatic right to occupy her husband's tenement after his death.[3] In 1731, the homage presented that the 'antient custom' of the manor was that 'the purchaser of any copyhold tenement ... his widow only shall enjoy her widowhood and not ye widow of any other person whose life shall be in the copy'.[4] The custom had, apparently, been proved in the Court of Chancery,[5] although no trace of the relevant case has so far been found amongst Chancery records. Amongst the property held by Mary Coffin, the Papist, when she registered her estate with Quarter Sessions in 1717, was a coppice, garden, and thirty acres of meadow, held for her widowhood in accordance with manorial custom. She paid rent of £1 4s 8d, plus a cock, but she claimed it was worth £23 per annum to her.[6] A complication of the custom was that if the widow re-married she automatically forfeited

---

1   WSHC 3117/13.
2   WSHC 383/346.
3   WSHC 383/97; 383/256, f.4. The widows of succeeding lives, however, had no right to succeed their husbands; cf WSHC 383/113.
4   WSHC 383/353.
5   WSHC 383/113; 383/257.
6   WSHC A1/310/1.

her copyhold estate. Mary Slatford suffered this fate in 1726.[1]

The role of the manorial court in the government of the parish, and in agreeing to the 1633 enclosure, has already been discussed. It also had an important role in estate administration. Stewards were responsible for holding the manorial court, negotiating tenancies, collecting rents, and generally administering the estate. Their role is discussed in chapter 10. The lords themselves had no need to be directly involved in estate administration, although sometimes they were, as when 'my Lord himself' granted sixty acres of common at Bonham to his nephew, Thomas Stourton, in 1671.[2]

The manorial court ceased to meet during the Civil War. In 1650, however, the Interregnum authorities permitted Walter Barnes to hold courts. He was also allowed to become the yearly tenant of two-thirds of Lord Stourton's lands in Wiltshire, Dorset, and Somerset.[3] Thereafter, the court was held annually, although court books do not survive for the seventeenth century. In the early eighteenth century, there were usually eight or ten members of the homage present.[4] Meetings continued until the nineteenth-century[5]; in 1819, for example, the Court Baron was summoned to conduct a perambulation of the boundary. The numbers in attendance, however, had drastically declined; only two members of the homage were present in 1829.

All tenants of the manor owed 'suit and service', and were liable to be amerced if they failed to attend; one shilling was regularly demanded from absentees. The court proceeded by means of presentment by the homage, apparently consisting of the tenants, although a presentment of 1744 ordered that 'no cottagers shall serve on the homage at this court'.[6] A hayward was regularly elected; Francis Swetnam held the office from 1723 until 1731, Charles Evil from 1739 till 1747, and George Green until the end of our period.[7] One of the hayward's duties was to 'warn' the homagers to attend court; the steward regularly sent him a notice to do

1   WSHC 383/353.
2   WSHC 383/109, f.75r.
3   Mowbray, op cit, vol.1, p.494; Mayo, Charles Herbert, ed. *The Minute Books of the Dorset Standing Committee, 23rd September 1646 to 8th May 1650.* Exeter: William Pollard & Co., 1902, p.364-5.
4   WSHC 383/353.
5   WSHC 3117/13.
6   WSHC 383/353.
7   WSHC 383/353.

so.[1] Curiously, in 1723 the notice was sent to Nathaniel Ireson (who had recently served as churchwarden), although it was also addressed to the Hayward.[2]

Certain customs of the manor were regularly presented[3]: timber for gates, stiles, and repairs was to be taken from tenants' own lands; 'curbs for wells, watling rodds, and spike gadds' were to be taken from Broom Wood; sheep were not to be kept on the common, in Great Coombe, or in Little Coombe between Lady Day and St Andrews tide. Tenants were not to keep sheep on the common and pen them on another lord's land, under penalty of 6s 8d, and the rector – or his under-tenants - was not to keep sheep on the highways. In 1742, that order was extended: 'We present that no person ought to keep sheep in the highways belonging to this manor at any time of the year'. 'Ridgeling horses, mangey horses', and 'ridgling bulls' were not to be kept on the common at any time, under penalty of 3s 4d. Increasing pressure on the commons, led to the presentment of 1742 objecting to 'all persons surchargeing the Common with any cattle', and insisting that 'no person shall keep more sheep or cattle on the Commons in the summer than they can winter respectively on their severall tenements'.[4] In 1745, the homage was driven to list the tenants who had rights of common on Stourton Common, and threatened the large fine of 6s 8d on anyone else 'turning in on the same common any sheep or cattle'. In the following two years, several individuals fell foul of this presentment, and were fined; Joseph Stone was fined twice.

The deaths of tenants were regularly presented. In 1719, for example, the homage presented that 'William Perman, a copyhold tenant of this manor, is dead since the last court, and that the estate is fallen into the Lord's hands'. In 1726, it was presented 'that Robert Green a leasehold tenant of this manor is dead since ye last court and that Geo Green his son is the lord's next tenant'. The deaths of Alexander Green in 1731, of Thomas Green in 1732, and of his son Thomas in 1745, were similarly reported. Such entries in the court rolls frequently note the name of the next tenant; when Robert Slatford, gent., died in 1723, his widow Mary was admitted to his copyhold, and the record notes that

1   See WSHC 383/345 for a notice to Charles Evell do so in 1743.
2   WSHC 383/345.
3   For most of the following presentments, see WSHC 383/353. Customs were presented by the homage in 1819; see WSHC 3117/13.
4   WSHC 383/353.

a heriot was due. If the heir was a minor, then the court decided who was to serve as guardian. In c.1642, for example, the court decided 'by special direction from the Lord of the manor' that Robert Barnes should undertake the guardianship of his nephew Thomas Barnes.[1]

Manorial custom was not, however, static. The Stourtons began the process of converting copyhold to three-life leaseholds in the seventeenth century. The process was dis-continued when the Hoares purchased the manor; they decided to consolidate the manor into large farms held on short leases. Although copyholders continued to hold property, most only held dwelling houses and cottages; by the end of our period, there was very little agricultural land held by copyhold, and three-life leases were gradually being phased out.

In 1694, there were 27 copyholders, and 24 three-life leaseholders.[2] By 1745, only six copyholders remained; all of their copies dated back to the Stourton era in the late seventeenth century. Leaseholders paid an entry fine, and took a lease lasting for three named lives, or ninety-nine years. Sometimes heriots were payable. Leases were not granted in the manorial court, although leaseholders continued to owe suit and service. That could apply even to short-term leases; in 1743, when he was proposing to take a new lease of Stourton Farm, Joseph Lampard noted that 'he hopes to be excused in the future' from customary obligations such as having to plough his lord's lands.[3]

Conversion to leasehold depended on copyhold land falling into the hands of the lord, and was therefore a gradual process. When Robert Jupe died in December 1675,[4] his copyhold estate fell into the Lord's hands. His widow had to pay an entry fine of £45 to secure a lease of the property in order to continue occupying it.[5] Edward Wadlow's lease of thirty-nine acres in 1707 included two tenements which had formerly been copyhold.[6] Similarly, in 1722/3, William Cuffe held copyhold land at Widenham granted in 1695 at a rent of 6s 8d, with a heriot 'according to custom'. He surrendered it in 1724, and the property was granted to William Burrell by lease in 1724, at the same rent, but with a heriot of £1

---

1   WSHC 383/109, f.6v.
2   WSHC 383/352, f.3.
3   WSHC 383/751.
4   Ellis, John Henry, ed. *The registers of Stourton, County Wilts., from 1570 to 1800.* Harleian Society register series 12. 1887, p.71.
5   WSHC 383/109, f.91r.
6   WSHC 383/721.

10s.[1] Leasehold heriots were very variable; they could, as in this case, be more than four times the rent. In other cases, they were set at nil. Both rents and heriots were sometimes payable, partly or wholly, in hens or cocks.

Until Henry Hoare purchased the estate in 1717, both copyholders and three-life-leaseholders could surrender their tenancies in order to obtain a fresh grant naming additional lives, thus obtaining greater security of tenure, and meeting the needs of growing families. In 1677, William Jupe, yeoman, surrendered a lease of ten acres of land at Upper Broom Hayes granted in 1653 to Francis Jupe, and obtained a fresh grant for the lives of himself, Hannah his wife, and Gertrude his daughter.[2] Similarly, Robert Tabor surrendered his lease of a cottage, and inserted the names of his two sons in a new lease, taken out in 1693.[3]

Sometimes, existing tenants simply assigned their interest to another. Robert Green, for example, secured a lease of seven acres in 1673 by procuring a surrender from the existing tenant.[4] George Green purchased the residue of the term of a lease of Upper Broom Hayes from Robert Green in 1714.[5] John Edwards purchased an assignment of the Gover family's lease of Windsors tenement in 1745. Five years later, he surrendered the lease in order to obtain a re-grant.[6] Robert Tabor assigned his cottage to John Coake of Iwerne Courtney in 1717, although the latter sold it back to another member of the Tabor family in 1723.[7] In 1727, the same lease was assigned to Henry Miles of Stourton.[8]

It was possible to purchase the reversion of a lease or a copyhold tenancy. The survey of 1722 records that Charles Barnes had been admitted to eleven acres previously held by Elizabeth Combes deceased, by a reversionary copy of court roll dated 1688.[9] When Robert Barnes died in 1672, he bequeathed premises to Mary his daughter; when she married Richard Coffin, Coffin purchased the reversion for his own and his son Robert's life.[10] Mary was the last surviving life in this lease

1   WSHC 383/97, f.39; 383/353.
2   WSHC 383/721.
3   WSHC 383/726.
4   WSHC 383/721.
5   WSHC 383/721.
6   WSHC 383/754.
7   WSHC 383/726.
8   WSHC 383/726.
9   WSHC 383/97, f.35.
10 WSHC 383/723. Recited in lease to William Reynolds, 1707.

when she entered her estate on the register of Papists' estates in 1717.[1] In 1742, James Whitaker, yeoman, paid £15 to secure a reversionary lease of a dwelling house and pasture which was then in the possession of John and Robert Smart. He would enter the property only on their deaths.[2]

Leases (but not copyholds) could be bequeathed. Christopher Target's 1708 will provided for his family by leaving his 'loving wife' Joan 'all my estate for life'. That included the 'house I do now live in', which was to descend to his son John on Joan's death, for the residue of the term.[3] Walter Sparrow's lease of Bonham Plain was bequeathed to his son James in 1713, 'until ye terme of yeares be completed'.[4] In 1723 Henry Hoare purchased the residue of a 1696 lease which had been bequeathed by Christopher Alford to his son Samuel, and which Samuel himself had sold to Henry Clarke of Mere in 1707.[5] In 1731, Henry Hoare purchased leases formerly held by William Reynolds, which he had bequeathed to his wife Mary. She was paid £300.[6]

The Stourtons, and subsequently the Hoares, had a number of important tenants. Some of these were large farmers who held by short leases; they will be discussed below. There were also two important leaseholders who held for three lives. In the early seventeenth century, Robert Barnes, who had purchased the freehold of Rode in 1601, obtained leases of Topp Tenement, Shave Farm, and Greene's Ground.[7] Shave remained in the family, descending to Robert's grand-daughter Mary Coffin, who, as has been seen, entered it in the register of Papists' estates in 1717.

That register also reveals that Thomas Stourton, brother of Lord Stourton, and heir to the peerage, also held seventeen acres in the manor of Stourton by copy in his wife's name.[8] The total value of his Wiltshire estate was said to be £9.[9] He was also, of course, the lord of the manor of Bonham (in Somerset), which will be discussed below. After the sale

1   WSHC A1/310/1.
2   WSHC 383/736.
3   WSHC P1/T/267.
4   WSHC P2/8/1163.
5   WSHC 383/726. For the original lease, see 383/734.
6   WSHC 383/739.
7   WSHC 383/719; TNA C8/325/121.
8   WSHC A1/310/4. Thomas Stourton made entries in both the Wiltshire and the Somerset registers, as his property in Stourton lay in both counties.
9   WSHC A1/311/9.

of the main Stourton estate, he was responsible for ensuring that the family retained property in Stourton, and for ensuring the future of the Catholic congregation.

Copies of court rolls and leases were important documents to tenants; they could not afford to lose them. No fewer than twelve cottagers were unable to show the steward any 'grant or demise' in 1717. The problem was not confined to cottagers; more substantial tenants also had difficulties. Mr Charles Barnes claimed a copyhold property of 29 acres, but 'refused or could not produce the copy'.[1]

The formal documentation of tenancies does not routinely mention sub-tenants, who may consequently be hidden from view.[2] Mary Coffin's entry in the 1717 register of Papists' estates records that both her leasehold and copyhold property at Shave had been sub-let to Richard Garret. Not only that, but Garret himself had further sub-let it to John Mitchell.[3] In the same year, James Stourton, who tenanted sixteen acres of his family's former manor, was an absentee, thought to be living in Jersey, and presumably had sub-tenants.[4] He died in 1721,[5] and his heir, Lady Elizabeth Stourton, probably inherited them; in 1745, she had three sub-tenants: Christopher Parsons, Thomas Hurdle, and John Target.[6] When Edmund Wadlow, yeoman, of More Crichel (Dorset) took a reversionary lease of four acres of pasture at Pound Close, he intended to sub-let it.[7] His tenant in 1736 was William Bond.[8] In 1717, Thomas Davies of Stour Provost was the tenant of two acres on the manor of Bonham, which he sub-let to Mary Moores.[9] When William Roberts surrendered his copyhold in 1731, his sub-tenant was Francis Jupe.[10]

Sub-tenants sometimes merely sought to pasture a horse or a bullock on the common. In 1707, William Moores and John Bradden were both presented for 'letting their common', and in 1743 the homage

---

1   WSHC 383/348, p.2.
2   The 1745 survey 383/99 mentions sub-tenants occasionally, but whether it does so consistently is not clear.
3   TNA FEC1/1294; WSHC A1/310/1.
4   WSHC 383/348, p.1.
5   WSHC 383/345.
6   WSHC 383/99, f.1.
7   WSHC 383/720.
8   WSHC 383/353.
9   Somerset Heritage Centre Q/RRp/1/18.
10 WSHC 383/345.

banned sub-letting to non-Stourton parishioners.[1]

Sub-tenants were not, however, necessarily the poorest. Charles Barnes, a prominent figure in the parish, was the sub-tenant of Richard Coffin for a tenement with an acre of arable in 1717.[2] Farmer William King, perhaps the most substantial tenant in the manor of Stourton, rented, by verbal agreement, thirteen acres of copyhold held by Thomas Stourton, which was recorded in the 1723 Papists' register.[3]

Presentments in the manor court occasionally identify sub-tenants when ordering tenants to repair their properties.[4] Thus in 1723, William Barnard was named as an under-tenant of John Edwards when they were both ordered to 'sufficiently repair and amend the dwelling house' and barn on their property, 'the timber and roof of the said house being very ruinous', and the roof of the barn being 'much in decay'. George Green was allowed to sub-let one of his holdings to Roger Helliker – probably a relation of his son-in-law, James Helliker - who in 1730 was ordered to 'repair his dwelling house by thatching ye same & repairing the north wall of the said house being much in decay'. A similar order was made against another under-tenant, Henry Cooper, in 1737.

Tenants were expected to keep their property in repair, and were allowed to cut timber that was growing on their land for that purpose, by assignment of the steward. The homage kept a close watch on what was happening.[5] When Richard Cuffe in 1707 felled twelve trees to 'repaire and build a barne', without assignment, it ordered 'that the reparations be viewed & the number & value of the trees inquired into'. At the same court it was presented that Richard Coffin had felled trees, and ordered 'let the number & vallew of these trees be enquired into'.

The court also kept a close eye on the need to maintain buildings and fences, and frequently ordered tenants to undertake repairs. In 1740, George Green was accused of allowing 'his barn lying within this manor to fall into decay and likely to fall down'; the homage ordered him to rebuild it. The order is marked 'done' in the court book.[6] Similarly, in 1722 Mrs Mary Coffin was required to repair her barn, and John Jenkins,

---

1   WSHC 383/345.
2   WSHC 383/348, p.4.
3   WSHC A1/310/4.
4   WSHC 383/353.
5   The following presentments for 1707 are in WSHC 383/345.
6   WSHC 383/353.

under-tenant to Mr. Robert Slatford, to repair his dwelling house.[1] The
death of Edward Dyer in 1707 was the occasion for his widow to be
ordered to re-build a small outhouse which had fallen down; the bailiff
was ordered to 'view the premises to see what is necessary to be rebuilt'.
Similarly, in the same court, Mr Charles Barnes was presented for
allowing 'one outhouse to fall which must be rebuilt'; he was threatened
with forfeiture if the property had not been rebuilt within twelve months.
Threats to impose penalties were not without substance. In 1735, John
Edwards was fined 40s for his failure to erect a gate and fence as ordered
at the previous court, and was threatened with a further fine of £4 if he
failed to do so by March 1736.[2]

Boundaries were also important. In 1736, Edmund Wadlow was
ordered to 'plaish his hedge and dyke his ditch' where his land abutted
against Henry White's ground. He was given just a month to do the
work, under penalty of 40s for failure.[3] Had his animals been straying
into Henry White's fields? A similar order was made against Francis
Jupe in the following year, although the penalty for failure was set at
just 10s. The difference was probably that Jupe's boundary lay on the
highway, so animals would stray there, rather than damage another
tenant's property. The importance of adequate fencing was emphasised
by Farmer Heal in the 1750s, when he launched vigorous complaints
against Joseph Lampard's farming methods. At the bottom of Whitesheet
Hill, he complained, 'there is no fence now to prevent the sheep of Mere
flock to come into the corn'.[4]

The average size of a copyhold or three-life leasehold tenancy was
small.[5] In 1724, William Cuffe and his sister surrendered their copyhold
holding of a cottage, garden, and one acre close, together with a four
acre close in Widenham. This was a fairly typical holding, although
there were larger ones: in 1730, Thomas Martin surrendered a 130 acre
copyhold estate which had been in the occupation of Anne George for
her widowhood. Conversely, some tenants merely leased a cottage, with
perhaps a garden. In 1693, two labourers, Edmund Ryall and George
Edwards, were both negotiating to take leases of property consisting of a

1   WSHC 383/345.
2   WSHC 383/353.
3   WSHC 383/353.
4   WSHC 383/721.
5   See WSHC 383/353 for this paragraph.

cottage and garden, which would be rented for 1s 4d each.[1] In the same year, Joseph Windsor paid an entry fine of 5s, with a rent of 1s 4d, for a cottage which had previously been in his mother's tenure.[2] Two decades later, in 1717, there were twelve cottagers, most of whom paid 1s 4d rent.[3]

Cottages were not necessarily just for labourers. The Court House, which was leased by Robert Green upon the surrender of William Jupe in 1683,[4] was described as a cottage; it must have been a fairly substantial building to permit the manorial court to hold its meetings there.

Some occupiers held neither copyhold nor leasehold property. There were eleven such cottagers in 1719.[5] In 1738, no less than six individuals were presented for having 'lately erected cottages or dwelling houses ... upon ... Stourton Common without leave or licence from the Lord of this manor'; they 'ought to pull down the same or take leases from the Lord'.[6] By the time of the 1745 survey,[7] numbers had been reduced to six cottagers without leases on Stourton Common; they each paid an 'acknowledgement' of one shilling to the Lord of the manor.

Estate policy changed under the Hoare family. In the eight years before his death in 1725, Henry the Good refused to renew any three-life leases, or to allow his tenants to add 'lives' to them, except in special circumstances. He sought greater flexibility in his management of the estate, and wanted to create larger farms on shorter leases. Those leases which were made normally specified that the tenant was not to sub-let without the lord's permission.[8] Consequently, when Henry died, his successor was able to note that 'this estate is now chiefly standing out upon one & two lives'.[9] The policy only applied to land; houses and cottages continued to be leased or copyholds granted.

Hoare's policy was not entirely new. The Stourtons had also let some large properties on short leases. In 1678, William Moores leased a farm in 1678 – probably the home farm, or perhaps part of Shave, but that is not stated. He took it for nine years only, at the substantial rent of

1   WSCH 383/346.
2   WSHC 383/720.
3   WSHC 383/348, p.2.
4   WSHC 383/109, f.106r; 383/346, minit 6a.
5   WSHC 383/348, p.2.
6   WSHC 383/353.
7   WSHC 383/99.
8   See for example, Henry Hoare's lease of Rode to William Edwards, 1736; cf.WSHC 383/719, and his lease to James Whitaker, 1742; cf. 383/736.
9   WSHC 212b/6265.

£234 per annum. There is no mention of an entry fine.[1]

William King was another substantial tenant holding a short-term lease. In 1717, he held the 'farm house and demesne lands' of Stourton, under a twelve year lease made to him in 1709.[2] In the same year, he also took a lease of part of Shave. Although most of its terms are unfortunately unreadable, his lease did require him to sow French grass and clover, to spread dung yearly, and to make other improvements.[3] The 1722 map shows that William King farmed a substantial proportion of the eastern half of the parish.[4]

Coldcot was one of the larger farms, although technically it was not a part of the manor of Stourton. It had been purchased by Edward, 10th Lord Stourton in 1601 for £260.[5] In 1627, William Barnard leased 86 acres there; he also had the right of pasture on the commons of Stourton, Norton, and Pen.[6] By 1717, Coldcot had been rented for many years by Farmer John Mitchell.[7]

By 1749, Hoare's policy had seen results.[8] The numbers of copyholders and three-life leaseholders had been drastically reduced. Property valued at £96 was in hand. 'Manor rents', presumably received from a number of cottagers and husbandmen, totalled a mere £16 16s 2d, and there were five other small tenants, most of whom paid under £5. There were, however, three tenants who each paid rents of over £100 per annum: Thomas Hurdle paid £104, James Whitaker £120, and Joseph Lampard no less than £396. Their rents were not always paid on time; at Michaelmas 1749, all three of the major tenants were in arrears – two of them by more than a year. Joseph Lampard owed £227, James Whitaker £154, and Thomas Hurdle £170.

Lampard was the tenant of Stourton Farm, the property formerly tenanted by Farmer King. He leased it in 1744 for a term of twelve years, paying £357 rent per annum.[9] If he ploughed up any meadow or down, he was to pay an additional £10 per acre. His lease was not identical

1   WSHC 383/109, f.93.
2   Probably for some 20 years; King stated in 1710 that he had lived in the parish for eleven years, cf. 383/364.
3   WSHC 383/720.
4   WSHC 383/316.
5   WSHC 383/718.
6   WSHC 4314/1.
7   WSHC 383/348, p.2.
8   For these figures, and the rest of this paragraph, see WSHC 383/30.
9   WSHC 383/721.

to King's; it included various properties at Gascoynes, Widenham, and Search, which had recently fallen into hand. In 1744, his land totalled 569 acres. By 1749, he was paying an extra £39 for a lease of additional land at Widenham.[1] He was also the tenant of Coldcot, which in 1743 he wished to relinquish, preferring a lease at Widenham.[2] In 1745, Thomas Hurdle was paying rent for both Coldcot and Shave.[3]

Lampard, like other tenants, sometimes paid rent in kind. In 1746, £4 15s was 'paid by oats'. Other farmers paid rather larger sums; in the same year, James Whitaker's 'carriage of timber meant that £22 10s 4d was credited to him as rent, and Christopher Parsons paid £3 1s 3d by 'a bill of oates & vetches'. The following year, the sale of sheep to his landlord reduced the cash needed to pay Hurdle's rent by £51.[4]

These major tenants had little security of tenure, despite the size of their holdings. Their wives and families had to be provided for. The Hoares recognised their need for greater security by granting them three-life-leases of smaller properties. Thomas Hurdle took a three-life lease of ten acres at Widenham in 1724, paying an entry fine of £45, and naming his son John and his daughter Basil as the lives.[5] Similarly, in 1742, James Whitaker was granted two leases, both 'in Stourhead'. One was the reversionary lease of a dwelling house and 3 acres of pasture; the other gave him two meadows totalling five acres. The total rent was a mere 13s 1d per annum.[6]

Whitaker's payments on these properties were probably included in the 'manor rents' mentioned above. However, in 1746 he decided not to wait for the lease of the dwelling house to fall in, and arranged to have a house built on the waste in Stourton Lane, next to his farm. The lease does not mention a consideration, and the rent was a mere 2s 6d per annum.[7] The previous tenant in fact died the following year, so Whitaker was able to take possession of the property.[8]

Following their purchase of the manor of Stourton, the Hoares were eager to buy up property in the locality, both in Stourton, and in

1 WSHC 383/30.
2 WSHC 383/751.
3 WSHC 383/29.
4 WSHC 383/30.
5 WSHC 383/745.
6 WSHC 383/709; 383/736.
7 WSHC 383/736.
8 WSHC 383/353.

places such as South Brewham and West Knoyle. The process in Stourton began in 1723, when Walter Barnes sold Henry Hoare of London, goldsmith, various properties in Bonham for £230. A few months later, Barnes transferred the mortgage on Rode which he had from his mother to Hoare.[1] George Green took a lease of a small meadow called Harweth (in the manor of Bonham) in 1725, for an entry fine of £12 paid to Lord Stourton. Twelve years later, Henry Hoare realised that he needed the land for his landscaping; it adjoined 'a certain piece of ground covered with water called the Lake'. He had to pay for it; after twelve years the lease would normally have been worth less, but Green was able to drive a hard bargain, and was able to assign it to Hoare for the same amount that he had paid for it. In 1742, Hoare surrendered the lease to Lord Stourton and took a new one.[2] Similarly, Walter Barnes of Shaftesbury was able to sell Hoare land that belonged to Rode, close to the parish workhouse, which had been partly converted into a pond; following a hearing in Chancery, the price of £55 was decided in 1739 by the arbitration of Thomas Freke of Wyke (Dorset). Hoare agreed to create watering places for cattle at the edge of the pond, and to allow Barnes to pasture his cattle there until he was able to enclose it.[3] Similarly, in 1738, the executors of Edmund Wadlow wanted to dispose of his lease of land in Stourton Street. Hoare was prepared to pay £162 to purchase the lease; it is likely that he incorporated the property in his gardens. Landscaping could also be mentioned in leases. Joseph Lampard was required by his 1744 lease to allow Henry Hoare to plant an avenue of trees from Stourhead to Whitesheet Hill.[4] Building also required land; when Hoare built a brick kiln at Road Green, he compensated his tenant by paying £6 for an assignment of the land required.[5]

Walter Barnes was not the only land-owner who borrowed money from the Hoare family. In 1740, Joseph Charlton of South Brewham owed Henry Hoare £159 16s. He paid his debt by selling Hoare a meadow called Lower Mead in Gasper.[6]

Property might also be leased from other landowners; in 1755, Hoare reached an agreement with Rev Montague Burton to continue

1   WSHC 383/719.
2   WSHC 383/384.
3   WSHC 383/719. See also TNA C11/2072/19.
4   WSHC 383/721; 383/751.
5   WSHC 383/98, p.10; 383/750.
6   WSHC 1617/1/5.

his occupation of several pieces of glebe land known as the Plantation and the Cribbes.[1]

Bonham

The documentation for the two smaller manors in the parish is limited, although, as already noted, the details of Bonham entered by Thomas Stourton in the 1717 register of Papists estates effectively provides us with a full survey.[2] The manor was leased to the Stourton family for several centuries[3] before, in 1592, Walter Bonham leased its 'capital messuage' and 18 acres of demesne to Thomas South, and, subsequently, to Peter Pytney in 1605 at a rent of 2s and a fine of £3 5s.[4] A chief rent of £4 per annum was paid to the lord of the manor of Norton Ferris. In 1645, Thomas Stourton, the then lord of the manor, was paying this to Edward Combe.[5]

We do not know when the Stourtons re-acquired the lease, although it was in the possession of Thomas Stourton (the brother of the 11th Lord) in 1645. In that year, he was convicted of recusancy, and the revenue from two-thirds of his land became liable to seizure (although legally he retained actual ownership). The details of seizure have not been traced; however, we do know that in 1655, he complained that 'for want of keeping courts in the said manor, the houses and woods had fallen considerably into decay'.[6]

In September 1657, the revenues were leased out to Walter Barnes of Shaftesbury, who, as has been seen, was already the lessee of the manor of Stourton. He was clearly acting on behalf of the Stourton family. A few months later, Thomas Stourton was granted a twenty-one year lease of the property himself, paying £40 per annum.[7] The authorities frequently found that the most efficient way of dealing with recusant seizures was to lease the property back to the recusant himself.

1   WSHC 383/755.
2   For the earlier history of Bonham see Bonham, Carol. 'Notes on the manors of Discove and Bonham on the Wiltshire-Somerset border from the 12th century', *Hatcher Review* 2(15), p.228-32.
3   Mowbray, op cit, vol.2, p.589.
4   WSHC 383/380.
5   TNA E367/2238.
6   Williams, J.Anthony. *Catholic recusancy in Wiltshire 1660-1791*. Catholic Record Society, 1968, p.211.
7   Mowbray, op cit, vol.1, p.455; TNA E367/879, & E367/2238.

By 1655, Edward Combe[1] of Netherhampton had acquired some interest in the manor; in that year he leased an acre of arable in Bonham (parcel of Norton Ferris manor), together with various other property, to Susan Tyte of Gasper, widow.[2] The manor was subsequently purchased by the Stourton family; in 1670, it was used as part of a family settlement.[3] After the sale of the manor of Stourton, Bonham was the only property in the parish still owned by the Stourton family. Thomas Stourton (subsequently the 14th Lord), was the manorial lord, although he probably did not reside; Bonham House was in the tenure of his brother Charles. The manor remained in the hands of the Stourton family until 1785, when it was purchased by Henry Hoare – although even then the Stourtons reserved the chapel for use of the Catholic congregation.[4]

No court rolls survive for Bonham. However, a few copies granted to copyholders survive. In 1698, Alexander Green was granted an acre of arable by copyhold. In 1725, William Bracher was admitted to two acres of pasture at Topp; Thomas Davies, Samuel Lamb, and Stephen Penny were the homagers. Two years later, Bracher took a lease of a dwelling house, stable, and garden, 'some years since inclosed erected and built by him' in Topp Lane.[5]

The introduction of leasehold tenancies was occurring in Bonham at the same time as in the manor of Stourton. Hon Thomas Stourton let a cottage, orchard, garden, and a small pasture there to John Shepherd in 1688, but the lease was only for twenty-one years.[6] In 1704, five years before the lease expired, his son renewed it for another twenty-one years.[7] Another cottage at Bonham was let in 1716 to Mary Evans of Shaftesbury, this time for three lives, for an entry fine of four pounds and a rent of

1   In 1641 he is mentioned in the Norton Ferris poll tax return; he was assessed to pay the enormous sum of £100; cf. Howard, A.J., & Stoate, H.L., eds. *Somerset protestation returns and subsidy rolls*. Almondsbury: T.L.Stoate, 1975, p.245.
2   WSHC 383/538.
3   WSHC 383/380.
4   Hoare, Richard Colt. *The Modern History of South Wiltshire*. John Bowyer Nichols & John Gough Nichols, 1822, p.89; the conveyance is printed in Mowbray, op cit, vol.1, p.589-91.
5   WSHC 383/382.
6   WSHC 383/381.
7   WSHC 383/381.

sixpence.[1] Similarly, John Edwards, yeoman, took a lease of a dwelling house in Bonham with four acres of land in 1720.[2] Five leases from the 1720s and 1730s are listed in a manorial survey compiled probably in the 1780s; the largest was of sixteen acres, and two were merely of cottages.[3]

In 1717, the manor included seventeen small leasehold properties, including the capital messuage at Bonham let to his brother Charles Stourton, and nine copyhold tenements, some of which were in hand.[4] There were five cottages built on the waste, whose occupiers had neither leases nor copies of court rolls. The manor also included property in the open field of Norton Ferris.[5] Unfortunately, the register does not give acreages; however, it is unlikely that any tenant occupied more than a few smallish fields. The only possible exception to this rule was the ground known as 'three score acres' leased to Charles Stourton in 1717, which bounded property in Topp Lane let to William Bracher in 1727.[6]

Gasper

The manor of Gasper was larger than Bonham, but by the late sixteenth century its ownership was divided. In 1599, a quarter of the manor was included in the marriage settlement of Henry Ashford of Ashford, Devon.[7] At some time in the sixteenth century, another quarter of the manor had been held by Thomas Stoughton and William Walrond. By 1639, this had descended to Thomas Presley, who sold it to Roger Stile of Gasper, yeoman. It was held 'of the chief lord of the manor of Norton Ferris'.[8] Two decades later, in 1657, Stile purchased Five Acres from John Presley, yeoman (probably Thomas's son).[9] Five Acres seems to have descended to Alexander Dyer, serge weaver, who leased it to Robert Jaques, linen weaver, in 1679.[10] Jaques had already acquired a quarter of the manor in 1655. Some of this property descended from Jaques to his daughter Joan Target, and, in 1714, became a part of the dowry of her daughter in law, Grace Parfitt, who married Jeremiah

1   WSHC 383/381.
2   WSHC 383/721.
3   WSHC 383/132.
4   Somerset Heritage Centre Q/RRp/1/14,Register of Papists' Estates.
5   WSHC 383/382. Copy of court roll dated 1698.
6   WSHC 383/382.
7   Somerset Heritage Centre DD\SF/2/1/6.
8   WSHC 383/536.
9   WSHC 383/536.
10 WSHC 383/388.

Target.[1] At the same time, West Ball and Hall Close, presumably part of the manor, were leased to Thomas Target, another of Joan's sons. Subsequently, some of the property came into the possession of Martha Target, widow, and her son Thomas, linen weaver, who mortgaged 'that newly erected messuage, tenement or dwelling house' called West Ball, with various other property including Oat Close, in 1747 and 1748 for £200.[2] Five years earlier, in 1742, Samuel Target, yeoman, had similarly mortgaged land adjoining Five Acres.[3] Thomas Target's quarter of the manor of Gasper totalled 26 acres, 'very convenient for stocking cattle on Gasper Common'. It was said to be worth £750 c.1785.[4]

The rest of the manor of Gasper was in diverse hands. Thomas Gapper[5] quitclaimed various meadows in Gasper to William Evil, yeoman, in 1648. In 1701, Maurice Williams's lease of twelve acres of land in Gasper stated that it had once been owned by William Dodington, as part of his manor of Gasper.[6] In 1694, Alexander Dyer of Bower Hinton, Martock, gave his son, also named Alexander, a 1000 year lease of a dwelling house in Gasper.[7] In 1693, Robert Combe mortgaged his portion of the manor for £400.[8] When he died, his brother Edmund of Lincolns Inn inherited his estate, and the mortgage became the subject of dispute in Chancery.[9] In 1702 his heir, Edmond Combe of Lincolns Inn, sold his interest to John Keene, serjeant at law.[10] This was probably the property sold to Sir Isaac Rebow of Colchester in 1719,[11] which he leased for ten years to Thomas Williams in 1729, without an entry fine, but at a rent of £42 per annum.[12]

1   WSHC 383/535.
2   WSHC 383/388. For abstract of Thomas Targett's title, see 383/537.
3   WSHC 383/535.
4   WSHC 383/537.
5   He was from Cucklington, or perhaps Stoke Trister. In 1641, he was assessed to pay £20 for the poll tax of that year; cf. Howard, A.J., & Stoate, H.L., eds. *Somerset protestation returns and subsidy rolls*. Almondsbury: T.L.Stoate, 1975, p.244.
6   WSHC 1617/1/4.
7   WSHC 383/536.
8   WSHC 383/539.
9   TNA C6/389/79.
10 WSHC 383/539.
11 Ellis, John Henry, ed. *The Registers of Stourton, County Wilts., from 1570 to 1800*. Harleian Society publications 12. 1887, p.viii.
12 Somerset Heritage Centre DD/BR/gf2.

The manor of Gasper also included the farm at Rode, which was in the tenure of Edward Lord Stourton in 1601, when it was purchased by Robert Barnes.[1] Rode stayed in the ownership of the Barnes family into the eighteenth century. In 1704, Walter Barnes mortgaged it to his mother Dorothy.[2] In 1717, he leased four acres of pasture called Oat Close to John Bradden of Gasper.[3] In the same year, he also leased Bonham Grounds to his sister, Mary Barnes.[4] Most of Rode was actually being farmed by Francis Jupe, who was granted a new lease for thirteen years in 1723, at a rent of £40 per annum.[5] Shortly after, Henry Hoare purchased a life interest in Rode for £230.[6] By 1729, his successor had also acquired Bonham Grounds and the property tenanted by John Bradden, although only for the life of Walter Barnes.[7] In 1735, the latter was able to lease and release his (presumably) reversionary interest in Rode to his son Walter, together with the Three Swans at Shaftesbury.[8] Even so, Henry Hoare was able to lease Rode to William Edwards in 1736, although the tenant was prohibited from sub-letting.[9] By 1740, Rode had reverted to Walter Barnes the younger, who took out a mortgage of £300 on it.[10] Eventually, however, it came into the hands of the Hoare family. Its boundaries were perambulated, and its customs presented, at the manorial court held in 1819.[11] The customs in Gasper were much the same as those in Stourton.

Matters of Contention

The people of Stourton were not always content with their lot. Disafforestation and enclosure were major issues in our period, as was the housing of the poor. The reactions of cottagers to the threatened losses of their livelihoods as a result of enclosure have already been discussed. Selwood and Brewham Forests were the nearest areas to Stourton subjected to disafforestation in the early seventeenth century;

1   WSHC 383/719. It is described as being a part of the manor in Somerset Heritage Centre Q/RRp/15.
2   WSHC 383/719.
3   WSHC 383/388.
4   WSHC 383/719.
5   WSHC 383/740.
6   WSHC 383/719.
7   WSHC 383/719.
8   WSHC 383/719.
9   WSHC 383/719 & 383/726.
10 WSHC 383/719.
11 WSHC 3117/13.

indeed, they bordered on the parish, and the tenants of Bonham claimed property rights in Selwood. When Selwood was disafforested, that part of the common of Norton Ferris which lay within the manor of Bonham (and was within the bounds of Selwood) was enclosed by agreement made in 1631 between William Combe (presumably lord of the manor of Norton Ferris), Edward Lord Stourton, and Robert Barnes. It is not clear which parish this property lay in. However, Lord Stourton was allotted sixty acres of the waste alongside Rode Brook, next to Topp Wood. An enclosure of ten acres was assigned to Robert Barnes, for his freehold at Rode (he was also the lessee of Topp Tenement[1]). The cost of fencing and hedging was to be shared between the parties, and Combe was to be paid the value of the trees on the land allotted to Stourton and Barnes; these would presumably have been previously reserved for Combe as lord of Norton Ferris manor. The remaining third of the common, was to remain open for the manorial tenants of Bonham.[2]

A few years later, in 1633, Lord Stourton decided to enclose 500 acres of waste ground within his own manor of Stourton. This enclosure has already been discussed, but nibbling at the edges of the remaining commons continued. These nibblings were frequently controversial. The cottages in which the poor lived were frequently erected on commons or waste land without permission. These cottages would not have been substantial constructions, but merely wooden frames occupying minimal space, and erected at minimal cost, perhaps even overnight. Such cottages were banned by statute in 1588/9, unless they stood in at least four acres of land – the minimum thought necessary to support a family. Otherwise, they were thought likely to attract the undesirable poor, who were unwilling to accept statutory wages, refused permanent employment, poached and pilfered as opportunity offered, and would probably claim poor relief.

Such people suffered when the manorial homage sought to restrict access to the commons; they were in danger of losing their ability to support themselves. In 1730, ten manorial tenants agreed to enclose 'Tenants Common' which lay on the Hardway, in order to prevent the men of Kilmington from trespassing, and 'for the improvement of our severall estates'.[3] Four years later, complaint was again made in the

1   TNA C8/325/131.
2   WSHC 383/719.
3   WSHC 383/353.

manorial court that 'the cattle belonging to the inhabitants of Bruham,[1] Kilmington, and others, do often trespass', and it was resolved to make 'a sufficient hedge & ditch' against the London Road. In 1745, both Jeremiah Target and Walter Sparrow paid 4d 'for entring on Stourton Common',[2] although whether this related to enclosure is not clear. Sparrow, or perhaps his father, had 'a way into the common from his house', for which he paid 4d in 1694.[3]

The process was continued in 1748, when all the tenants of the manor agreed to determine their respective rights of common, and to 'go the bounds of ye said manor' with the steward on 26th December. Unfortunately, the subsequent orders of the homage are missing. We cannot now discover the reactions of eighteenth-century Stourton cottagers to restrictions on common grazing, presentments against their cottages, and enclosure.

1   i.e. Brewham.
2   WSHC 383/345.
3   WSHC 383/352.

7
Agriculture in Stourton

S TOURTON WAS HEAVILY dependent on the land, as is demonstrated by the importance attached to the recording of ownership and tenancies. There were some very substantial farmers. Robert Barnes probably fitted that category; in 1672, he bequeathed 'all my corn hey cowes horses sheepe and other beasts and cattle' to his kinsmen George Knipe (Lord Stourton's steward), and to John Warham. Barnes was evidently farming the property he leased at Shave, but no inventory survives to describe his farming practices.[1] Nor do inventories survive for other substantial farmers, such as William King or John Mitchell. Lord Stourton himself died in 1685; there is no inventory for him either, but the depositions of witnesses in the Chancery case his heir brought against George Knipe in 1693 reveals some details of his stock. William Moores, his bailiff, bought twelve oxen and steers, together with 'plow tackling' and some hay, for £41. His deceased Lord also had ten cows, some pigs, horses worth £10, oats worth £24, and substantial quantities of hay and peas. Another witness, Thomas Morgan, noted that he had two waggons.[2] He evidently ran a substantial farm in Stourton terms, although it was small in comparison to his total wealth.

There were a multitude of small farmers, including many who had other occupations and merely kept a pig or a cow. Anthony Newman, for example, was a turner, but he mentioned his cattle, hay, and fodder in his 1632 will.[3] John Trembie described himself as a turner in his will, but was described as a husbandman in his 1678 inventory.[4] It recorded three cows and a bullock worth £8, and two acres of corn worth £3. There is no direct evidence of livestock in the inventory of Joan Davies, widow,

1   TNA PROB11/341/162
2   TNA C22/708/55.
3   TNA PROB11/178. The will was proved in 1638.
4   WSHC P2/T/292.

which was appraised in 1632, but she nevertheless had hay worth 4s, and hard corn worth £5.[1] Most of our evidence regarding crops and livestock is derived from the inventories of smaller yeomen and husbandmen, and of tradesmen who leased a field where they could keep a cow.

Cattle were kept for three purposes: for milk, for beef, and to provide motive power. They were regarded as part of the family, and given names: John Kerbey had a 'cowe called bosse'[2]; Thomasine Chandler gave a 'cowe called Nam' to her daughters.[3] Stourton was a dairying parish. Milk was used for making butter and cheese. Probate records contain many references to them, and to the implements used in their preparation, such as cheese vats and cheese presses. Sometimes, cheese was kept in such quantity that it must have been for sale. John Kerbey in 1603 had 'twenty cheeses and two dozen of butter' worth 10s.[4] The 1602 inventory of John Tovey shows that he had butter and cheese worth no less than £6.[5] 'About seven hundred of cheese one old cheese two chees racks', were to be found in Thomas Barnard's 'Chamber over the Kitchin' in 1681/2.[6] It is also clear that butter and cheese was used for domestic consumption. Income from cattle could also be obtained by hiring them; Julian Leversuch's 1583 inventory records that he received £1 2s from John Myller 'for the hyre of the said cowe'.[7]

Oxen and bullocks were kept for the plough and the harrow, and then killed off for beef. Calves might also be kept for their meat. William Britten referred in his 1562/3 will to 'my two myddlemost oxen as they gooe in the plowe'.[8] John Kerbey had four 'byeff fatts' in 1693, presumably for storing beef.[9]

Sheep were kept primarily for their wool; both sheep and wool are frequently mentioned in inventories. Some yeomen had large flocks. When Robert Barnes took a lease of land at Shave in 1603, he was allowed common of pasture for 'seaven score sheepe'on Stourton Common, as well as for his cattle.[10] Five years later, John Porter had a hundred sheep

1   WSHC P2/D/168.
2   WSHC P2/K/72.
3   WSHC P2/C279.
4   WSHC P2/K/72.
5   WSHC P2/T/58.
6   WSHC P2/B/990.
7   WSJC P2/1/33.
8   WSHC P2/4Reg/132B.
9   WSHC P2/K/72.
10 WSHC 4314/1; C2/ChasI/S89/24.

worth £24.[1] In 1691, Thomas Barnard had 90 sheep and lambs worth £18; he also had '5 ways of flew wooll' worth £7, which presumably came from his spring shearing.[2]

Smaller flocks were possessed by John Ellis in 1620 (31 sheep, plus 10 lambs, worth £5),[3] Robert Davies in 1667 (21 sheep worth £3 10s),[4] and Richard Cuffe in 1688/9 (30 sheep worth £3).[5] The value of a sheep was not high, so it was within range of poorer men. Thomas Bacon, whose inventory was valued at £8 10s 4d in 1604, had three sheep worth 10s.[6] Julian Leversuch's sheep, like his cow, were hired out.[7]

Wool was, of course, also found amongst the possessions of those engaged in the textile trades. Peter Pitnie, for example, who had no livestock, did have wool valued at 6s when he died in 1612.[8] It was presumably waiting to be spun.

Mutton was probably rarely eaten. In 1719, Henry Hoare had to pay 3s 9d for 'mutton sent to Stourton when Lord Digby was there'.[9] For most people, pigs were the main source of meat. They are mentioned in twenty inventories, and were mostly valued at no more than a couple of pounds. Even the poorest decedents could afford to keep them. In 1589, for example, Steven Bradden had six pigs valued at 3s 4d; the total of his 1590 inventory was £3 3s 8d.[10] Almost a century later, in 1680, a relative, John Bradden had two pigs valued at ten shillings; his inventory was valued at £39 12s 4d.[11] Pigs were kept for domestic consumption. Flitches of bacon are frequently mentioned in the inventories. At least one farmer paid his rent in pigs. Henry Hoare's accounts record that 'piggs sold at Knoyle' reduced Thomas Hurdle's rent by £3 18s 9d in 1747.[12]

Poultry offered eggs, which must have been a staple food for poorer inhabitants. They are missing from many inventories, probably

1   WSHC P2/P/163.
2   WSHC P2/B/990.
3   WSHC P1/E/29.
4   WSHC P2/D/265.
5   TNA PROB4/25439.
6   WSHC P2/B/252.
7   WSHC P2/1/33.
8   WSHC P2/P/191.
9   WSHC 383/58.
10 WSHC P2/B/115.
11 WSHC P2/B/959.
12 WSHC 383/30.

because appraisers did not consider that their value was sufficient to make it worthwhile listing them. However, Rinold Jupe had 'two cocks & sixe hens' worth 3s 4d in 1601,[1] Robert Davies had 'seven poulles' worth 2s 5d in 1622,[2] and Margaret Porter had 'pultry' valued at 1s 2d in 1608/9.[3]

Meat was not the only product from dead livestock. There were several tanners and shoemakers (or cordwainers) in the parish, who tanned hides and made them into shoes. Fat from animals was used for making tallow for candles: John Gildon was apprenticed to a London tallow chandler in 1693.[4]

Horses were kept to provide motive power, and were sometimes harnessed to the plough. In one entry in William Tovey's 1602 inventory, there is reference to 'oxen & 2 horse beasts one olde carte with all the furniture', as if both oxen and horses together could be used to pull the cart. Horses were also kept for riding; in 1669 Thomas Stourton had two geldings worth £20 at Bonham, but no interest in agriculture whatsoever.[5] His brother, William Lord Stourton, when he died in 1685, had two coach horses for his carriage, together with a Welsh nag, together worth £20; they were sold to Mr Freke of Shrowton (Dorset).[6]

Several inhabitants were apiarists. John Porter in 1608 had 'six stocks of bease' worth 13s 4d.[7] In the following spring, his widow had only three 'stocks' left, worth 10s.[8] Thomasine Chandler, widow, had 'a stocke of bees' worth 5s in 1615[9] . In 1677, Andrew Lamb's 'stocke of beese' was worth 4s.[10] The honey must have been a welcome addition to a diet which was otherwise sugarless.

There was also a warren for 'coneys', that is, rabbits. In the 1610s, Lord Stourton had sufficient coneys to keep his household well supplied, and also to sell them to neighbouring gentlemen – provided he could keep out the 'riotous persons' from neighbouring parishes who

1   WSHC P2/IJ/37.
2   WSHC P2/D/133.
3   WSHC P2/P/164.
4   London Apprenticeship Abstracts 1442-1850 **www.findmypast.co.uk**
5   TNA PROB4/6892.
6   TNA C22/708/55.
7   WSHC P2/P/163.
8   WSHC P2/P/164.
9   WSHC P2/C/279.
10 WSHC P1/L/185.

were challenging his right to a warren, and poaching large numbers.[1] A little over a century later, in 1721, Henry Hoare ordered the warren to be stocked with 250 coneys. When Joseph Reed became gamekeeper in 1724, he was instructed 'to mend or make any netts which herafter there may be occasion for to take fish connies or any other game'.[2] His instructions also mention the pigeons and ducks to be found on the estate, all of which would have been found on the table at Stourhead. An additional building had to be constructed at 'ye warren house' in 1729.[3]

Dogs are not mentioned in the inventories. However, we know that they were kept. In the early sixteenth century, Robert Barnes, kept them for hunting deer and coneys. A dog was shot in a dispute over hunting rights in 1613.[4] A little over a century later, in 1727, Mrs Hoare paid a man to keep puppies, and £9 was spent 'for stone to lay the dog kennil'.[5]

A variety of different crops were grown. Wheat, oats, rye, barley, and peas were all common. Wheat produced flour for bread-making; barley was used for malting and brewing, and to feed horses and pigs, who also ate peas, beans, and oats. Acreages were generally small; in 1579, for example, John Genyns had an acre of wheat, ten acres of rye, and twelve acres of oats, as well as corn in the barn worth ten shillings. He also had an acre of peas and beans. However, oats could be important. Joshua Cox's accounts as steward of Henry Hoare record that Farmer King was paid £62 1s 2d for 'his bill of oats, straw etc' in 1727.[6] Similarly, Joseph Lampard was paid £48 8s in 1740 for 'two bills of straw, oats, running of horses in the Park, plow timber etc'.[7]

Many farmers made hay for feeding their animals during the winter. When Susan Goddard bequeathed her cattle to the Banister children in 1657, she also gave them 'all my hay at my liveinge in Gasper for the winteringe of the foresaid cattell'.[8] Hay was sometimes stored in barns, but hay ricks were common. Francis Jupe's hay rick was worth £8

1   TNA STAC8/256/26.
2   WSHC 383/114.
3   WSHC 383/59.
4   TNA STAC8/73/13.
5   WSHC 383/59.
6   WSHC 383/59.
7   WSHC 383/61.
8   TNA PROB 11/271/250.

in 1662.[1] In 1692, William Green, who was described as a blacksmith in his inventory, nevertheless had '3 ricks of hay & some in a house'.[2] Not only hay was stored in ricks: in 1602, William Tovey had 'one wheate ricke' worth £2 13s 4d.[3] Ricks required thatching, to keep out the rain, so sixteenth- and seventeenth-century Stourton thatchers would have had plenty of work after the harvest.

Straw was also important, although not frequently found in inventories. In 1622, Robert Davies had hay and straw together worth £2 6s.[4] It was needed for thatching, but was also used as bedding for the cattle in winter. It was not so long since it had also been used to fill straw pallets for men to sleep on.[5]

Some farmers ground their own corn (although others were obliged to grind at the lord's mill). Rinold Jupe had a 'grindle stone' worth 1s in 1600.[6] John Bacon's grinding stone was worth 6d in 1638.[7] In 1676, Peter Sandle's grinding stone was worth 7s, but may have been used for working with wood rather than for grinding corn: he was a turner.

It is likely that gardens supplied many vegetables, although their minimal value mean that they are rarely mentioned in inventories. Peter Pitnie, however, had 'a garden of cabbeges' worth 6s 8d in 1602.[8] John Presley left his son the garden next to his kitchen in his 1670 will.[9] William Poor similarly bequeathed gardens to two of his children in 1682.[10] Gardens and orchards are frequently mentioned in leases, but little is said of what was grown. Apples were probably a regular crop, and cyder was certainly made. In 1721, William Maidment had 'one apple mill & sider presse' valued at £2.[11] Its value suggests a commercial operation, but Nathaniel Field's apple roaster was probably for domestic use only.[12]

1 WSHC P2/IJ/143.
2 WSHC P2/G/535
3 WSHC P2/T/58.
4 WSHC P2/D/133.
5 Harrison, William. *The description of England,* ed. Georges Edelen. Cornell University Press, 1968, p.201.
6 WSHC P2/IJ/37.
7 WSHC P2/B/673.
8 WSHC P2/P/191.
9 WSHC P2/P/476.
10 WSHC P2/P/560.
11 WSHC P2/M/925.
12 WSHC P1/F/134.

The importance of woodland in the parish was emphasised in chapter 1, and in chapter 4 we examined the way in which the manorial court supervised the felling of trees for repairs to tenants' properties. The importance of timber in the parish is not immediately obvious from probate records, until one considers the extensive information provided by inventories concerning furniture and other goods made from wood. The production of such goods required the planting and harvesting of trees. Wood for fuel was also important. We have already seen that many cottagers were dependent on the fuel they could collect on the commons. Unlike them, Henry Hoare did not have to collect fuel himself. Instead, he paid £1 'for wood for firing' in 1723.[1] The importance of coppicing was sufficient to make it worth while for the rector to sue a parishioner for tithes on faggots taken from a coppice in 1671.[2]

Fish were also farmed. Medieval lords had created a series of fishponds in Six Wells Bottom, and the Hoare's development of the lake is likely to have resulted in the availability of more fish. In 1648, Giles Jupe's lease of Pond Close expressly forbade him to take fish in the pond.[3] Emanuel Swetnam's 1651 lease of a mill in Stourton permitted his lord to allow water to run out of his pond for the purpose of fishing.[4] An account of the number of fish put into the ponds at Stourton in 1721 and 1722 reveals that they were well stocked with perch, tench, and trout.[5]

Fish were also available further downstream. The lords of the manor claimed the right to fish in the River Stour from its source in Stourton to its mouth at Christchurch, a right which the lords of the manor of Christchurch formally acknowledged by sending two roach salmon to Stourton every year.[6] In 1722, Henry Hoare formally exercised his right to fish at Sturminster Newton; he instructed all the millers in the vicinity to open their flood gates to make fishing easier.[7]

Mixed farming was the norm, perhaps with an emphasis on pastoral farming. Poorer husbandmen tended to concentrate on animal husbandry; wealthier yeomen tended to have more of their capital

1   WSHC 383/58.
2   TNA E134/23Chas2/Mich7.
3   WSHC 383/348, p.4.
4   WSHC 383/724.
5   WSHC 383/114.
6   WSHC 383/113.
7   WSHC 383/97.

invested in arable crops. Husbandmen needed their cows and their pigs to provide food from day to day, but yeomen with bigger acreages could better afford to wait for a return from their fields of wheat, oats, and rye. The rest of this chapter will be devoted to showing how this worked out in individual cases.

When Stourton Farm was leased to Joseph Lampard in 1744, the lease included detailed instructions on husbandry.[1] Lampard was 'to plow and sow the arable part thereof in a due course of husbandry', and not to 'impoverish the same'. His corn was to be ground in the lord's mill. He was expected to 'keep sufficient sheep'. At the end of his tenancy, he was required to sow 218 acres with corn, and was given the right to use two barns 'for the laying in and threshing out the same' until twelve months after the expiration of his term. His landlord was to 'cut and cleanse the fern growing ... in the Park' – ten acres each year for the first two years, but twenty acres per year thereafter. It was the intention of both landlord and tenant 'to fold and fodder his sheep and cattle there ... and to make the ... Park part of the premises into a clean and good sheep sleight'. He was also to maintain the farm house, stables, and other outhouses. The tenant was to pay for 'straw and reed for thatching the dwelling'. Hoare was to pay for a new barn to be constructed at Search, adjoining the one already there. And if he decided to demolish the 'great stone barn', he would rebuild another elsewhere, 'with three good threshing floors'. The same applied to any stables or other outhouses he wished to demolish.

Lampard's husbandry was the subject of complaint from Farmer Heale.[2] It is not clear what Heale's status was, but he was particularly concerned at the lack of ditches against fences, and enumerated several gateways which lacked gates or posts. Heale thought that his field of sown grass in Little Broom Wood would be damaged by sheep unless a small hedge was planted to defend it. He also complained that Heale had 'shredded' trees so that there was 'hardly one left on the farm'.

Other landowners also sometimes made provision for husbandry in their leases. When Walter Barnes let Rode to Francis Jupe in 1723, he required his tenant to 'carry forth and lay in good husbandrie like manner all the dung and soil thereof upon the same lands and not elsewhere'. He also expected an additional fifty shillings per annum for every acre Jupe ploughed up.[3]

1   WSHC 383/721; 383/751.
2   WSHC 383/721.
3   WSHC 383/740.

In the six inventories surviving from the late sixteenth century, only two directly mention arable crops. In 1558, Thomas Jennens[1] had five steers worth £1 each, two kine, two heifers and two yearlings (with an illegible value), and a mare and colt worth 13s 4d. He also had 'corn in the barn & fyld' worth £4, and 'a wayne with all plowghe gere therto pertaynyge' valued at £2. The total value of his inventory was £21.

John Genyns,[2] who died in 1579, had goods valued at just over £50. His investment in agriculture was a little more varied. He had corn in the barn worth ten shillings, an acre of wheat and ten acres of rye, together worth £7 6s 8d, twelve acres of oats valued at £4, and an acre of peas and beans worth 6s 8d. He also had 'a weane ropes & yowckes fullo and a peire of oythes', ie a wain, yokes, spoked wheels, and a harrow. His motive power was provided by yokes of oxen and steers. He also had six bullocks, five 'kine', and a bull; together, his cattle were valued at £13 13s 4d. In addition he had sheep and lambs worth £10, six pigs worth £1, and a cock and six hens worth 2s. The sheep provided him with wool valued at 10s, which he may have intended to spin and/or weave himself.

Other inventories reveal less investment in agriculture. In 1591, Edmund Davies, with an inventory valued at £20 6s 8d, had a single cow worth £2, and no crops. But his inventory was taken in November. It also listed £12 in cash, and a winnowing sheet – suggesting that his crop for that year had just been sold.

In the first half of the seventeenth century, there were 24 inventories, 21 of which mention livestock and/or crops. The value of John Porter's 1608 inventory[3] was £87 2s 10d; he was the wealthiest decedent of the period. His cattle – six 'kine' and two heifers – were valued at £16. He had a hundred sheep valued at £24, which had evidently been recently sheared, as he had wool valued at £3. There were pigs worth £2, and horses - an old mare & two colts, plus an 'old croppold mare', together valued at four guineas. His poultry were worth a mere 1s 4d. His crops included three acres of wheat worth £3, three acres of rye worth £2, an acre and a half of rye worth £1, and hay valued at £4. He was also an apiarist; his 'six stocks of bease' were valued at 13s 4d. His implements included 'seaven cheas fats' worth 2s, and a 'chees preas' worth 7s; evidently he made cheese. He also had an 'old iron bound

1   WSHC P2/G/5.
2   WSHC P2/G/32.
3   WSHC P2/P/163.

carte and eithes [harrows] with harnes for two horses', worth £1, 'a side saddle two pack saddles a tange one girse' worth 4s, (the tange and girse were used to fasten loads on the pack saddles), and 'two payre of prang two rakes six seams two hoockes & hachett' worth 3s. These would have enabled him to harvest his crops, and to carry his cheeses to market.

Porter's death was followed in the following spring by that of his widow, Margaret. She was his residuary legatee, but he had also made bequests totalling just over £24. Her inventory[1] was valued at £40 6s 6d. By the time she died, she had sold off or disposed of much of her husband's stock. The value of her cattle was £8 – half that of her husband. Instead of a hundred sheep, she had 'twelve cupple of ewes and 9 lambes' valued at £3 2s; she had also disposed of much of her husband's wool, although what was left was worth £1. She had disposed of two of his mares, and was left with just one mare and a colt worth £2. There were no pigs, but there were 'foure flytches of bacon', probably 'hanging from the roof', worth £1 6s 8d: the pigs had been killed and were ready for the table. She only had three 'stoockes of bees', compared to her husband's six, but her appraisers valued them more highly than their predecessors had done. Margaret probably had the same poultry as her husband had owned; they were worth just 2d less than his. Her crops included 'eight acres of wheat and one upon the ground'; presumably her husband's crops had been harvested and sold (although she still had 'two busshels of wotte' (oats) worth 3s 4d, perhaps waiting to be sowed), and her wheat had been sown in late autumn or winter. By the spring, much of her husband's hay had been fed to her cattle, but what was left was valued at £1 10s. She still had the 'iron bound cart and eythes with harnis for two horses', the 'side saddell one packe sadle a tange & a girsse', and the ' two payre of pronges two rakes six seaves two hookes and a hatchett'. She also still had the 'seaven cheese vats, and the 'cheese presse'. Her inventory also identifies a 'winoinge sheet' worth 2s 6d', and used for winnowing the corn. It had probably been missed by her husband's appraisers.

John Ellis was a contemporary of the Porters, whose 1620 inventory was valued at just over £81.[2] His arable was rather more extensive than is revealed in other inventories; it totalled seventeen acres of rye and oats, with a total value of £21 6s 8d. He also had four oxen, valued at £14, to

1   WSHC P2/P/164.
2   WSHC P1/E/29.

provide the motive power for his plough, together with 'one weyne & the plow harnes' worth £3 6s 8d. Like the Porters, he also had 'kine'and other cattle, together with a horse and pigs. His 'iii henns & a roust cock' were worth 1s 8d.

Most of the inventories for the early seventeenth century record the wealth of poorer husbandmen. They generally had a similar mix of interests. Thomas Bacon, whose 1604 inventory[1] was valued at a mere £8 10s 4d, had cattle valued at £4, two pigs worth 8s, 3 sheep worth 10s, corn valued at 10s, and 16s worth of hay. Similarly, William Kenison's 1611 inventory, valued at just over £26, recorded cattle worth £13 18s 8d, a mare and a colt worth £3, three pigs valued at £1, and a ram worth 6s. His two acres of wheat were valued at £1 10s. He also had 'two quarts of mustard seed'. The widow, Elizabeth Jupe, had no arable at all when she died in 1617; her inventory (valued at just under £25) included 'one mare and coult (£3), foure kyne (£6), and 23 sheep (£5 15s). By contrast, William Bayley had wheat and barley in the field valued at £5; the total of his inventory was £7.[2]

In the half century following 1650, there were 42 inventories; 35 of them included valuations of agricultural produce. The rector, Nathaniel Field, was the wealthiest decedent, with an inventory valued at just over £726. When he died in 1665/6, he was evidently farming the glebe himself, rather than leasing it. It was one of the larger farms in the parish, covering just over 90 acres.[3] A third of it was planted with oats and rye, together worth £28 10s. The 'implements for the plough' which his oxen pulled were worth £8, and provided the means by which he cultivated the soil. Field also had wheat, rye, and oats worth £60 in his barn, although this may have been tithe produce, rather than from his own land. His cattle were worth £49. They included three yoke of oxen, as well as cows, heifers, yearlings, and a bull. He also had six pigs worth £4, and sheep valued at £18 10s. A late sixteenth-century terrier records that the rector was entitled to feed 200 sheep on the common.[4]

It is worth comparing Field's inventory with that of John Derby, his successor, which was taken just five years later, in 1671.[5] Derby was

1   WSHC P2/B/252.
2   WSHC P2/B/570.
3   WSHC D1/24/193/1-5.
4   Hobbs, Steven, ed, *Wiltshire glebe terriers 1588-1827*. Wiltshire Record Society 56. 2003, p.406.
5   TNA PROB4/21045.

probably poorer than his predecessor, but he still had more than most; his inventory was valued at £181 10s.[1] He had 'corne in the barne and one the ground' valued at £50, but unfortunately his appraisers did not give any more detail. The inventory was taken in winter, so he would probably have disposed of some of his tithe corn, and the fields would have been sown. The appraisers did not specify whether any of his 26 head of cattle, worth £52, were oxen (although some of them probably were). He also had three mares (£10), 'about sixty sheepe and lambes (£20), and foure swine in the bartone (£1-10s). The total value of his livestock and arable was £133 10s, which compares to his predecessors £160.

Thomas Barnard, who died in 1681 was another wealthy yeoman. His inventory was valued at just over £600.[2] Almost three-quarters was cash in hand. He possessed comparatively little arable, just two acres of wheat and two acres of barley, together worth £18, although he also had hay worth £4 6s 8d. His cattle were valued at £26 10s; they included a yoke of oxen, a bull, six cows, nine heifers, and three calves. The presence of a 'cheeston' and milk vessells worth £4 12s in the inventory suggests cheese making. He also had 90 sheep worth £18.

The Jupes were another prominent family in the parish. The inventories of Francis Jupe (1666) and his son William (1683) both survive, enabling us to compare their farming practices. Francis's inventory,[3] taken in October, totalled just over £387. His tackling for husbandry, valued at £10, presumably included ploughs, harrows, and other implements used to grow his crops. He had completed harvesting his 1666 crop when he died, as he had 'tow rickes of wheat and masling in his barton, (£15), together with pease unthreshed valued at £5. In his barn at Widenham, he also had 'barley unthreshed (£9), and oates unthreshed (£15). His death caught him in the middle of sowing for the following year; he had 24 acres of corne sowed & to sowe (£32). He also had a rick of hay worth £8, which would provide winter fodder for his cattle (£43 10s). They included five yoke of oxen,

1 This figure may, however, be misleading. The inventory refers to 'some bonds as appears by the will', but does not value them. The will itself does not directly mention bonds, but the inventory may be referring to the £200 he left to his grand-daughter, Mary Ians. That would more than double the value of the inventory.

2 WSHC P2/B/990.

3 WSHC P2/IJ/143

for ploughing, plus four cows and seven heifers. He also had three mares, a nag, and two colts (£14), together with 90 sheep (£27), and pigs (£5).

When William Jupe, Francis's son, died in 1683, his inventory was valued at £113 13s 4d,[1] much less than his fathers'. He had inherited the lease of Little Broom Hayes from his father, but it is likely that his brother Francis was given his father's lease of Upper Broom Hayes.[2] That explains, at least in part, why William was not as wealthy as his father. His livestock consisted of '6 head of rother cattle (£12), 3 horses and one sucking colte (£10), and one pig (13s 4d). They were more important to him than his arable crops, which consisted of corne uppon the ground worth £12.

In this period, livestock continued to be more important than arable for the smaller husbandmen. In 1682, William Poor, husbandman, had cattle worth £5, and horses worth £3, but apart from his hay, valued at £2, he had no arable crops. His inventory was valued at £39 13s 6d.[3] When his widow Mary died a year later, she similarly only had '2 keene and one mare , valued at £4 10s, with hay worth £1 10s. William Perman's 1690 inventory was valued at £36 15s 4d, although he described himself as a yeoman.[4] He merely had a cow, a mare, and a colt, valued at £5, but again no arable.

Only 8 post 1700 inventories survive. Six of them mention agriculture, but only two reveal any investment in arable, other than hay. The poorest decedent of this period was Robert Trouk, whose 1701 inventory was valued at just over £19 . He had no interest in arable at all, but did have an 'old mare' (13s 4d), and 3 'small cows (£6 9s).

Richard Smart's appraisers valued his 1701 inventory at just over £70.[5] They listed 'wheate in the barne & in a reeke' (£10), severall 'parcells of oates pease & fatches' (£8), and two 'hay reekes' (£8). His livestock was worth slightly more: 'a hogg in the sty'(£2), four horses (£7 10s), four cows (£13 10s), and eleven sheep (£3). He also had a few poultry, but these were lumped together with wood to be valued. His implements included 'a cart two horse harnesse a dung pott a paire of harrowes a paire of drafts an old waine bedd & appurtennces' (£3).

1   WSHC P2/IJ/181.
2   See above, pp.60-1.
3   WSHC P2/P560.
4   WSHC P2/P/626.
5   WSHC P1/S/666.

Three inventories of this period were valued at over £100. Only Richard Cuffe's showed a substantial investment in agriculture.[1] His interest in arable cultivation is demonstrated by the fact that he had four oxen, with 'a payre of ayes and sull', that is, harrows and a plough. The inventory was taken in January 1715/16, so his harvest of the previous year was stored in 'too ricks of corne' worth £12, although some of it may have already been sold. The £90 he had 'in readey money in hous and upon band and morgres' may represent, at least in part, the value of crops sold. But at the time of his death his major interest was in livestock; apart from his oxen, he also had 'twenty best' ('beasts', that is, cattle), valued at £40, and a hundred sheep worth £30. In addition, he kept three horses, presumably for riding, and kept three pigs for bacon.

By contrast, neither Richard Green nor John Hill were primarily farmers. Green's inventory was valued at £108 13s, but he merely had six sheep, a hay rick, a 'gilden', and a colt. In his will he is described as a linen weaver.[2]

Similarly, John Hill of Gasper, yeoman,[3] kept a cow and a calf (£2 10s), ten sheep (£2 10s), and two mares and two colts (£18). He also had two hayrickes in the meadow (£6). But his inventory was valued at £381. Much of it was devoted to his 'shop goods'; he was primarily a mercer.

For Green and Hill, involvement in agriculture was secondary to their primary occupations. Many other Stourton inhabitants similarly had a few pigs, sheep, or cows, but earned their livelihoods in non-agricultural pursuits. Their activities are the subject of the next chapter.

1   WSHC P2/C/1004.
2   WSHC P1/G/33.
3   WSHC P2/H/1092.

8
Status and Occupations in Stourton

THE TERMS 'GENTLEMAN', 'yeoman', and 'husbandman' denoted the status of many Stourton inhabitants in our period. In a status conscious society, they had real meaning. Only the lords of the manor had the status of county gentry; the heads of the Stourton family were peers of the realm, whilst the Hoare family who succeeded them were immensely wealthy. There were a number of minor gentry families in Stourton; in chapter 3 we have already met the Barnes, the Coffins, and the Wadlows, amongst others. Such men were generally owners of freehold estates. We have also met the Greens and the Hills, some of whom claimed gentle status. Both these families also had members who were blacksmiths – a worthy trade, but perhaps not one associated with gentle status.

Below the gentry were the yeomen, who were generally substantial yeomen holding three life leaseholds. John Bradden, yeoman, provides a good example. In 1710, he paid a £14 entry fine to the Hon Thomas Stourton for seven acres of land in Bonham; he paid another £30 for a lease of land at Bonham in 1725,[1] which he used as a dowry when he married Mary Cable.[2] Two years later, he found another £126 to take a reversionary lease of more property in Bonham.[3] On the same day, his nephew's widow, Ann Bradden, paid £30 to take a lease of land in Gasper. One wonders whether the uncle helped to find the money.[4]

Some yeomen were sufficiently prosperous to operate as substantial money lenders. William Moores, for example, was owed £200 on bond by Edward, 13th Lord Stourton, when the former died in 1698.[5] He had

---

1   WSHC 383/540.
2   WSHC 383/541.
3   WSHC 383/541.
4   WSHC 383/541.
5   WSHC P2/M/770.

served as bailiff to the 12th Lord, and had been responsible for selling some of his livestock after his death.[1]

Husbandmen could also be lease or copyholders, but generally held smaller pieces of land. For example, Robert Davies, husbandman, took a lease of five acres at Land Shire Hayes, sometime part of Shave Farm, in 1654.[2] In 1706, Edward Edwards, husbandman, leased the cottage at Pockadilla, paying an entry fine of a mere five shillings, and a rent of 1s 4d. In the following year, he leased another cottage, this time paying no entry fine, but, again, rent of 1s 4d.[3] On the death of his father in 1744, Mathew Davies, husbandman, renewed his lease of a messuage and 3 acre meadow lying near the Tucking Mill. He also took a 'narrow strip of ground' 'out of the Park', which had been in the occupation of Joseph Lampard, the farmer of the demesne.[4]

Labourers were at the bottom of the pile, but the more prosperous amongst them could still be leaseholders. In 1693, John Edwards, labourer, paid an entry fine of 5s for a lease of a cottage in the Town. It had a garden, and the rent was 1s per annum.[5] In the same year, Edmund Ryall and George Edwards were both labourers leasing cottages with gardens, but with no other land, at rents of 1s 4d each.[6] In 1705, Ryall renewed his lease, but this time he was described as a husbandman.[7]

These status terms sometimes indicated that the person in question was engaged in agriculture, but sometimes not. Wills frequently record a status term, but the accompanying inventory states the occupation of the decedent. People were not always consistent in the use of status and occupational terms. It was also true that many people combined an interest in agriculture with some other occupation. Those involved in cloth-making and other trades frequently invested occasionally in a pig, a cow or a few poultry. So did the clergy and other professionals. Occupational labels in this period can be very misleading, since the boundaries between occupations were much more fluid than they are today. Many described themselves as yeomen or husbandmen, implying that they were farmers – but the evidence of their inventories

---

1 TNA C22/708/55
2 WSHC 383/721.
3 WSHC 383/721.
4 WSHC 383/353.
5 WSHC 383/731.
6 WSHC 383/346 & 383/726.
7 WSHC 383/738.

sometimes suggest that they followed other trades. John Rodway, for example, described himself as a husbandman – but there is no evidence of husbandry in his inventory (apart from his 'chattle lease' valued at £10). There is, instead, a trendle, which suggests that he was a spinster.[1] Other tradesmen catered for the needs of the agricultural community, for example, blacksmiths, wheelwrights, carpenters, and masons.

The Hoare family's activities at Stourhead meant that there were plenty of opportunities for labourers and tradesmen. In the early eighteenth-century, the demolition of the castle, the building of Stourhead, the digging of the lake, and the landscaping of the gardens, must all have had considerable and continuing effects on the economy of Stourton. In 1736, Francis Faugoin, who had recently been appointed as the Hoare family's gardener (probably at Quarley), purchased a copy of John Evelyn's translation of Jean de Quintinye's *Compleat Gard'ner*, and wrote his name in it.[2] In 1747, he came to Stourhead,[3] and spent most of the next half century supervising the development of Stourhead gardens. Almost thirty years later, he was still serving as steward, and was presumably in charge of the fifty men who were 'constantly employed in keeping the pleasure grounds, rides, etc., in order'.[4] His memorial inscription in the churchyard states that, when he died aged 72 in 1788, he had been 'stewart' of the Hoare family for forty-eight years.

Some of those given work by the Hoares were casual workers, from outside of the parish; for example, the 'man sent to Stourton about glazing of tyles' in 1722, who was paid 5s.[5] Others spent much of their career at Stourhead. One of them was William Helliker, who was employed as a gardener by Henry Hoare in the early 1740s.[6] This book's focus, of course, is on the community, not on Stourhead itself, so there will be only limited mention of the tradesmen who built and fitted out the Hoare family's new mansion, and of the servants who staffed the

1   WSHC P2/R/418.
2   **http://catalogue.swanngalleries.com/** (search 'Quintinye')
3   Dodd, Dudley, ed. *The Letters of Henry Hoare, 1760-1781*. Wiltshire Record Society, 71. 2018, p.261-3.
4   Climenson, Emily, ed. *Passages from the diary of Mrs Philip Lybbe Powys of Hardwick House, Oxon., A.D.1756 to 1808*. Longmans Green & Co., 1899, p.169.
5   WSHC 383/58.
6   Dodd, op cit, p.261. His marriage licence bond (Sarum Marriage Licence Bonds **www.findmypast.co.uk**) states that he was a gardener in 1745, but he had left the Hoare's employ by 1747.

house. But it is important to appreciate that the presence of the family increased the opportunities available not just for tradesmen, but also for professionals such as stewards and medics.

Our discussion of specific occupations must begin with those trades on which agriculture depended, or which depended on agriculture. Of these, the miller was perhaps highest in status, since he had to be of sufficient standing to lease a mill. There were at least two mills in the parish. In 1619, both were 'lately reedified', and were leased to William Moon for a £10 entry fine. The property included a dwelling house, a malt mill, a grist mill (for processing malt for brewing), and an acre of meadow. Moon's lease was for twenty years, but by 1633 he had assigned it to Walter Board.[1] It was probably this property that changed hands again in 1651. By then, it had been in the tenure of John Eveleigh, but was leased to Emanuel Swetnam of Mere, miller. Our source adds that Swetnam had common of pasture for two 'kine', and for a horse. It seems likely that Swetnam was related to John Swetnam, who had a mill in Gasper in the late 1620s.[2] Swetnam's lease was for seven years, at a rent of £20. He was also required to grind wheat, malt, and other corn for the Stourton family without taking toll.[3] Swetnam presumably surrendered his lease in 1658,[4] as in that year John Eveleigh again leased it, together with a rood of land in Paradise, and rights in the Park. Like Swetnam, he was obliged to 'grind the Lords corne toll free'.[5] By 1663, however, Swetnam was leasing two mills: Stourton Mill, which presumably carried the obligation to grind the Lord's corn, and Swetnam's Mill.[6] Our source states that the latter had been erected some forty years earlier, so Swetnam's two mills were probably those leased by Moon in 1619 (although it probably gained its name after Swetnam took possession).

In 1699, the mill was again let, this time to Philip Pitman, for a term of ten years.[7] In 1717, a mill was 'in hand', although subsequently let

1 WSHC 4314/1.
2 Somerset Heritage Centre DD\S\WI/32.
3 WSHC 383/724; 383/109, f.177v.
4 But in 1663 Swetnam was sued for tithe due for the previous 6½ years from two mills; cf TNA E 126/8/136.
5 WSHC 383/109, f.41v.
6 TNA E 126/8/136.
7 WSHC 383/724.

to Miller Keynes for £10.[1] The mill was again let in 1735, when Thomas Turner leased two pairs of milling stones at Cascade Mills. The lease was for twenty-one years, at a rent of £22.[2] In 1744, a new mill with a house was due to be erected on land in Gasper close to the head of the pond; the property was leased to William Curtis, although whether this was to be a corn mill or a cloth mill is not clear.[3] It was evidently on the site of an old mill, as William Moores paid his final half-yearly rent of 10s on Lady Day 1745.[4] Curtis paid £2 per annum.[5] The millers profited from the fact that some leases required tenants to grind their corn at their lord's mill.[6]

In 1822, two mills were mentioned by Colt Hoare. There was still a large mill operating at Gasper, but another had been destroyed in the process of landscaping.[7] That was probably the grist mill, which was demolished in 1811.[8]

The flour produced by Stourton's corn mills was used by bakers to make bread. It is likely that most people had their own ovens where they could bake their own bread. However, the houses of the poor were not always so equipped. There was therefore a need for a baker in the parish, although, a few years after our period, Henry Hoare tried to provide hand mills so that the poor could grind their own corn.[9] It is also possible that the manorial lords employed a baker. William Rose was working as a baker in the early seventeenth century; in 1606 he was named as overseer in the will of Elizabeth Jupe (although he did not have to act as such until 1617).[10] In 1622, he acted as surety for the

---

1 WSHC 383/348, p.2.
2 WSHC 383/748.
3 WSHC 383/97, f.53; 383/98, f.9; 383/99, f.33.
4 WSHC 383/29.
5 WSHC 383/345.
6 See for example Joseph Lampard's lease of Stourton Farm, 13th July 1744; cf. WSHC 383/721.
7 Hoare, Richard Colt. *The Modern History of South Wiltshire*. John Bowyer Nichols & John Gough Nichols, 1822, p.53.
8 McKewan, Colin. *Stourhead Lake Project 2005: Survey and Excavation of the Lakes at Stourhead House*. Nautical Archaeological Society, 2006. Online at **https://nauticalarchaeologysociety.org/sites/default/files/u9/NAS%20 Stourhead%20Master%20composite%20Report-01_sml.pdf**
9 Woodbridge, Tim. *The Choice*. Dotesio Publishing, 2017, p.202.
10 WSHC P2/IJ/68.

administration bond of Peter Pitnie.[1] He also signed the 1608 parish terrier as sidesman.[2] He was evidently respected in the parish, although the Rose family is rarely mentioned in other Stourton sources.

It has already been suggested that Richard Hunt of Gasper was a baker in the post-Restoration period; the hearth tax return records his 'private hearth'.[3] In the early eighteenth century, the need for a baker was met by Richard Edwards, who occupied a cottage and an acre of common in 1705.[4] His name (or that of his son?) recurs in 1744, when he was occupying a cottage formerly leased to Richard Coffin. In 1751, when John Target was invited to Christmas dinner at Stourhead, he was described as a baker.[5] No other Stourton bakers have been identified.

The butchering trade also depended on agriculture. John White, butcher, was the master of several apprentices (discussed below) during the first half of the eighteenth century. He was a prominent parishioner, serving as churchwarden from 1745 to 1747,[6] and regularly serving on the manorial homage between 1720 and 1748,[7] although he only leased a cottage and a couple of fields.[8] Robert Smart was the only other known Stourton butcher; his trade probably had something to do with his appearance at Quarter Sessions on a charge of stealing four quarters of mutton in 1741.[9]

Tanning was another trade which depended on agriculture. Tanners turned animal hides into leather. There were several tanners in Stourton. Thomas Gapper, who sold property in Gasper in 1648, was a tanner.[10] He was probably related to Robert Gapper of North Cheriton (Somerset), tanner, who leased a Stourton dwelling house and two closes in 1663.[11] Robert Slatford of Brewham (Somerset), who surrendered his lease of 6 acres in Widenham in 1688 to obtain a re-grant, was also a

1   WSHC P2/P/191.
2   WHSC D/1/24/193/3
3   TNA E179/256/16, pt.18.
4   WSHC 383/99, f. 24.
5   WSHC 383/259.
6   WSHC D1/54/38/5; D2/11/26; D1/54/40/5.
7   WSHC 383/353.
8   WSHC 383/97, f.26; 383/98, f.12.
9   WSHC A1/165/5. f.117; A1/150/19.
10 WSHC 383/536.
11 WSHC 383/721.

tanner.[1] So were John Stroud, who died in 1685,[2] Robert Feltham, who administered Mary Poor's estate in 1683,[3] and Robert Sandle, who leased a house at Bonham in 1669,[4] and whose inventory was written in 1686.[5] Sandle's estate was valued at just over £28.

Sandle's appraisers described him as a tanner, but he described himself in his will as a 'cordwinder', that is, a cordwainer. The trades of tanners and cordwainers (shoemakers) were closely related. Several other shoemakers are mentioned in Stourton. Robert Wilmot, shoemaker, was cited to appear at Quarter Sessions as a recusant in 1658.[6] Robert Browne, 'cordwinder', served as the administrator of Robert Jaques in 1688.[7] In 1693, Joseph Windsor took a lease of a cottage then in possession of his mother. He was a cordwainer.[8] John Coake, another cordwainer, purchased the assignment of a Stourton cottage in 1717, but probably never lived in the parish; when he sold it in 1723, he was described as of Tollard Royal.[9] Two cordwainers brought settlement certificates from other parishes in order to settle in Stourton. Henry Perfect came from Mere in 1727; Joseph Millard came from Bruton in 1737.[10]

Carpenters and masons also played important roles in Stourton's economy. The earliest reference we have to a mason is from 1611, when George Hilgrove, rough mason, petitioned Quarter Sessions for relief after his house was burnt down.[11] Francis Hilgrove, mason, was probably a relation; he is mentioned in his daughter Julian's 1628 marriage licence bond.[12] In 1735, Walter Barnes granted Richard Arnold, a mason, the lease of a house, orchard, and garden at Topp in Rode.[13] As has been seen, the manorial court books record many orders to tenants to have their houses and barns repaired. Their leases usually granted them sufficient timber to carry out repairs. The timber would have

1   WSHC 383/721.
2   WSHC P2/S/939.
3   WSHC P2/S/939.
4   WSHC 383/109, f.70v.
5   WSHC P2/S/932.
6   WSHC A1/110/T1658, 113.
7   WSHC P2/IJ/196.
8   WSHC 383/346; 383/720.
9   WSHC 383/726.
10 WSHC 1240/20.
11 WSHC A1/110/T1611, 111.
12 Sarum Marriage Licence Bonds **www.findmypast.co.uk**
13 WSHC 383/98, p.35.

been worked by carpenters. Tenants needed to call on the services of the parish's carpenters, masons, and other building tradesmen. In 1738, for example, Thomas Hurdle was ordered by the court to repair his barn.[1] The 1739 presentments record that the work was 'not done', and he was fined twenty shillings for his neglect. But in 1740, we learn that John Green, a carpenter, was paid twelve guineas 'for repairing Thos Hurdle's barn'.[2]

Work was also available elsewhere. Two masons, Andrew Smith and Mathew King, two plasterers, Francis Cartwright and Timothy Coney, and two carpenters, Thomas Spinks and Richard Young, appraised the cost of repairing the Rectory in 1726.[3] Whether they actually did the work is not stated.

Building tradesmen were far from being at the top of the social pyramid, but could be reasonably self-sufficient. George Hilgrove, whose losses by fire in 1611 have already been mentioned, had been relatively well off before the fire. The property burnt included 'his dwelling house & barne, an oxstocke, with part of his houshould stuffe' He was not able to bear the loss, which had reduced him to a 'poore estate', and in need of assistance.[4]

When Walter Sparrow, carpenter, died in 1713, he had leasehold property in Brewham, as well as at Bonham.[5] Richard Arnold, mason, was sufficiently well-off in 1745 to hold a lease of Tops Tenement, with a dwelling house, orchard, garden, and half an acre of land, for which he had recently paid a fine of £7 10s to Walter Barnes.[6] He subsequently leased a further ¾ acre at the Moor, adjoining Rode.[7] The only probate inventory we have for a carpenter – that of John Humphreys in 1694 – was valued at just over £72. His working tooles were valued at £1 1s 2d.[8] Nathaniel Ireson out-did all of these tradesmen; as we have seen, he was responsible not just for the building of Stourhead, but also for a wide range of other buildings in the region.[9]

1   WSHC 383/353.
2   WSHC 383/61, f.5.
3   WSHC D/1/61/1/37.
4   WSHC A1/110/T1611, 111.
5   WSHC P2/S/1163.
6   WSHC 383/98, f.35 & 37.
7   WSHC 383/99, f.35; 383/749.
8   WSHC P1/H/570.
9   See above, p.58.

Masons worked in stone or brick. In 1743, Henry Hoare established a brick kiln at Road Green, in order to meet the demand for brick at Stourhead.[1] Hoare had 'banked in and inclosed' about an acre, and secured 'liberty of digging for earth and clay' from his tenant.[2] The kiln presumably provided employment for several labourers.

Tradesmen able to build or repair roofs were also needed, as will be seen in the next chapter. Most pre-Stourhead houses were thatched, and in the early eighteenth century the Hoares continued to pay for thatching work. The Stourhead accounts show that, in 1726, John Edwards was paid £1 12s 4d in 1726 for 'thatching work'.[3] In 1729, three years later, 'Wise the thatcher', was paid £3 14s.[4] Other thatchers are mentioned elsewhere. In 1729, George Howell viewed the Rectory, and estimated that it would cost £2 11s to re-thatch.[5] In 1741, John Richards, thatcher, leased a cottage.[6]

Building tradesmen could obviously turn their hands to a variety of tasks. In 1727, John Edwards the thatcher was paid £3 18s for his 'glazier's bill of work done' on Hoare property in Brewham.[7] Mr Moger 'the plumber', similarly had a range of skills; his bill for 'plumbing and glazing about Stourton House', amounting to £4, was paid in 1740.[8]

Probate inventories are also full of wooden goods made by turners, or, sometimes carpenters. Anthony Newman was a turner, and bequeathed his tools to his step-son when he died in 1638.[9] Thomas Read, who was regularly cited as a recusant, was described as a turner when he was cited to appear at Quarter Sessions in 1658.[10] Peter Sandle described himself as a turner when he died in 1676.[11] John Tremby, turner, died in 1678.[12]

Houses on the Hoare's estate began to lose their thatch in the eighteenth and nineteenth centuries. It was replaced by tiles, and

1   WSHC 383/99, p.37.
2   WSHC 383/750.
3   WSHC 383/58.
4   WSHC 383/60.
5   WSHC D1/61/1/37.
6   WSHC 383/97, f.5.
7   WSHC 383/50.
8   WSHC 383/61.
9   TNA PROB11/178
10 WSHC A1/110/T1658, 113.
11 WSHC P2/5/796.
12 WSHC P2/T/292.

thatchers were gradually replaced by helliers. In 1727, Peter Gover was
paid £5 12s 6d 'for tiling the house'; a year later he had 28s for 'mending
tyling about ye house'.[1] In 1749, when he and his mother assigned
their lease of Windsor's Tenement to John Edwards,[2] Gover was still
describing himself as a hellier.

Blacksmiths were also important, for both the lord of the manor,
and for his tenants. Descriptions of the metal goods blacksmiths made
and repaired occupy much space in probate inventories. Arable farmers
needed to have ploughs, harrows, and other implements. Their horses
had to be shod. Blacksmiths may have been involved in making and
repairing the armour required at musters, and worn by local soldiers
during the Civil War. Bills for 'smith's work' in the church are frequently
mentioned in Stourton churchwardens' accounts for the 1730s and
1740s.[3]

We have already traced the activities of two blacksmith families. At
least five members of the Green family followed the trade between 1626
and 1750. Alexander Green, blacksmith, obtained an alehouse licence
in 1615, as we will see. He had to appear for some misdemeanour at
Quarter Sessions in 1626.[4] The inventory of a relative, Robert Green,
was valued at over £88 in 1688; his new anvills & bellows and some
hammers were worth £1 2s.[5] He was able to lend Lord Stourton £40.
In 1691, his son William was described as a yeoman in his will, and
a blacksmith in his inventory, although the value of his inventory was
lower at just under £40.[6] In 1732, Thomas Green, William's brother, was
sufficiently prosperous to have his will proved in the Prerogative Court
of Canterbury. There is no inventory, but the will records freehold estates
at Cole, and leasehold estates in Stourton and Shepton Montague.[7]

Towards the end of our period, the Hill family also became
involved in the trade; John Hill, the son in law of the rector, was
responsible for the 'smith's work' in the church mentioned above. He
is first mentioned as a blacksmith in 1723, when he stood surety for

1   WSHC 383/59.
2   WSHC 383/754.
3   WSHC 497/6.
4   WSHC A1/110/M1626/44.
5   WSHC P2/G/518.
6   WSHC P2/G/535.
7   TNA PROB11/659/92.

John Hartgill in the latter's marriage licence bond.[1] In 1743, he leased a dwelling house with a smith's shop, other outhouses, a garden, and a plot 'formerly wast ground'[2]; the buildings had been 'lately erected'.[3] In the same year, Thomas Green similarly leased a dwelling house, a blacksmiths shop, and seven acres of land.[4] There was evidently scope for two blacksmiths to be active in Stourton. We do not know of any wheelwrights in Stourton, although Thomas Evil was apprenticed to a wheelwright in the early 1740s. He failed to complete his term.[5]

The textile industry was important in Stourton. Many people spun wool; a number of 'turns', that is, spinning wheels, are recorded in inventories. Spinning was a task in which many participated; on summer evenings spinsters could be seen sitting at their turns outside most houses, having perhaps spent the day in the fields. Dual occupations were suited to a pastoral economy, which did not require as much labour as arable farming. There were, of course, also many artisans in the parish who relied entirely on the money they could earn from such tasks, and did not have access to land on which they could run a pig or two. Stourton was in one of the most important textile areas in sixteenth and seventeenth century England; it stood on the edge of Selwood Forest, where many cottagers engaged in weaving, at the same time supplementing their income from the unenclosed woods and pastures of the royal forest (at least, until they were enclosed).

There were many weavers in the parish. For example, Leonard Shuter of Gasper, linen weaver, was accused before Sir Henry Berkeley, JP, of stealing parcels of yarn found in his house in 1625.[6] John Sandle was identified as a weaver in his son's 1633 baptismal entry. John Bradden's 1643/4 inventory[7] records that he had wool worth 2s when he died; he was probably a weaver. In 1688, John Shepherd, linen weaver, leased a cottage from Hon. Thomas Stourton, for a fine of £3, and a rent of 2s per annum.[8] In 1693, John Jupe, weaver, tenanted a cottage and

1   Sarum Marriage Licence Bonds **www.findmypast.co.uk**
2   WSHC 383/752.
3   WSHC 393/98, p.8; 383/99, p.27; 383/752.
4   WSHC 383/99, p.14.
5   WSHC 1240/21.
6   Somerset Heritage Centre Q/SR/53/68.
7   WSHC P1/5/354.
8   WSHC 383/381.

five acres of common.[1] Richard Green had yarn worth £60 at his death in 1704.[2] Joseph Stone owned half of a copyhold cottage in Bourton, which he sold to another linen weaver in 1715/16.[3] Alexander Dyer, serge weaver of Gasper, had a close called Five Acres in Gasper, which he leased to Robert Jaques, linen weaver, in 1679.[4] In 1687/8, when Jaques died, he had two looms, together with flax and yarn, together valued at almost £8.[5] His son in law, Christopher Target, also a linen weaver, stood surety for the administration of Jaques' estate. Christopher's son Thomas was also a linen weaver when he died in 1734.[6] Another linen weaver, Richard Feltham of Gasper, was of sufficient status to mortgage his property for £38 in 1738; the mortgagee was William Bracher, a tailor.[7] Marriage licence bonds identify many linen weavers and other cloth workers; the earliest was John Shuter in 1628.[8] Similarly, in 1750, John Orchard, linen weaver, joined with John Lamb, yeoman, to take a bond from John Bell of Silton, also a linen weaver, to pay £26.[9]

The trade could be relatively prosperous. Jaques estate was valued at a substantial £97 11s.4d.[10] When Richard Green, 'linen weaver', died in 1704, his estate was valued at £108 13s.[11] The Stourton paupers apprenticed to the trade of 'broad weaving' at Mells in the 1730s were being given a useful skill.[12]

Fulling was another important process in the textile trade. There were some who combined the trades of weaver and fuller. Giles Jupe described himself as a 'linen weaver' in 1708,[13] but he also owned a fulling mill; his 1695 lease also included a tenement, orchard & garden, ponds, with 12 acres of meadow and pasture.[14] The 1717 survey shows

1   WSHC 383/346 & 352.
2   WSHC P1/G/333.
3   Dorset History Centre D-1216/1/8.
4   WSHC 383/388.
5   WSHC P2/IJ/196.
6   WSHC P2/T/545.
7   WSHC 1617/1/4.
8   Sarum Marriage Licence Bonds **www.findmypast.co.uk**
9   WSHC 1617/1/4.
10 WSHC P1/G/333.
11 WSHC P1/G/333.
12 See below, p.172.
13 WSHC 383/382.
14 WSHC 383/348.

that he was still there.[1] In 1720, the 1708 lease was surrendered, and a new one was granted to Jeremiah Target, also a linen weaver.[2] Target was also assigned the 1695 lease, which was still in force in 1745, although at that date the mill had been 'down time out of mind'.[3] It had, however, probably provided much employment

The sale of the cloth produced in the textile process depended on drapers and mercers. Attention has already been drawn to the activities of John Hill, whose inventory reveals interesting evidence of the mercers trade.[4] Robert Molton of Kilmington, linen draper, was negotiating for the reversion of a tenement of 21 acres in Stourton in 1693.[5] We have already mentioned the death of Nicholas King, the son of a former rector, at Seville in 1649. He was a wealthy merchant, who bequeathed 500 pieces of eight to the poor of Stourton. It is quite likely that he was trading in Stourton cloth.

Some cloth, however, stayed in Stourton, to be made into clothes by local tailors. Thomas Butler, presented for recusancy in 1659, was a tailor.[6] Two other tailoring families can be identified. The brothers Adam and Francis Cuffe were both tailors when they administered their father's estate in 1668/9.[7] Another brother, Richard, described himself as a tailor when he leased the house next door to Walter Barnes in 1657.[8] In his will, proved in 1690/91 in the Prerogative Court of Canterbury, he described himself as a yeoman.[9]

William Bracher and his son were both tailors in 1727, when they leased a dwelling house in Topp Lane.[10] Thomas Landock of Wool (Dorset) served William as an apprentice from 1735.[11]

The parish also had its innkeepers, its alehouse keepers and its ale wives. Alexander Green, blacksmith of Long Lane, entered

1   WSHC 383/382, p.3.
2   Ditto. See also WSHC P2/T/545.
3   383/99, p.19.
4   See above, p.54; WSHC P2/H/1092.
5   WSHC 383/346.
6   WSHC A1/110/T1659, f.125.
7   WSHC P2/C/587.
8   WSHC 383/725.
9   TNA PROB11/39.
10 WSHC 383/382.
11 TNA IR1/14, f.98.

recognizances to obtain alehouse licences in 1615,,[1] 1616,,[2] and again in 1620,,[3] although in 1617 he was accused of selling ale without one.[4] By 1646, William Green had a licence[5]; he may have been Alexander's son, carrying on his father's business. In 1615 and 1616, Alexander also stood surety for another Stourton alehouse keeper, Robert Britten, who did the same for him. In 1617 and 1619, Julian Britten, probably a relative of Robert's, was accused of selling ale without a licence.[6] John Dean was accused with him. John Bradden stood surety for both Green and Britten. Francis Cuffe and Thomas Parry were both accused of selling beer without licence in 1654; their accuser was Emanuel Swetnam, the miller.[7] John Jupe was similarly accused by the Mere Hundred jury in 1656, although it is not clear whether his house was in Stourton.[8]

In 1686, two beds were available for travellers in Stourton, with stabling for two horses.[9] Charles Evil was identified as Stourton's 'innholder' when he was named as administrator of his son William's estate in 1749.[10] He, John White, and Dulce Trimby, widow, all entered recognizances in £5 or £10 in order to obtain ale licences in 1737.[11] In 1754 occurs the earliest mention of the New Inn, which was licenced by Thomas Spencer.[12] Spencer, described as an 'innholder', stood surety for Thomas Carter when he obtained a marriage licence in 1750 to marry a Stourton girl.[13] Carter was an innholder from Mere. The parish elite were also involved in the trade: Walter Barnes, one of Stourton's leading Catholics, owned an inn at Shaftesbury when he died in 1698/9,[14] but almost certainly leased it out.

1   TNA A1/110/T1615/48.
2   WSHC A1/110/T1616/25.
3   Williams, N.J., ed. *Tradesmen of early Stuart Wiltshire: a miscellany*. Wiltshire Archaeological & Natural History Society Records Branch 15. 1960, p.18.
4   WSHC A1/110/T1617/130.
5   WSHC A1/110/T1646.
6   WSCH A1/110/T1617/130, /T1619/172-3.
7   WSHC A1/110/T1654, 102.
8   WSHC A1/110/T1656, 83.
9   Chandler, John. 'Accommodation and travel in pre-turnpike Wiltshire', *Wiltshire Archaeological and Natural History Magazine*, 84, 1991, p.87.
10 WSHC P2/E/340
11 WSHC A1/325/1.
12 WSHC A1/325/12.
13 Sarum Marriage Licence Bonds **www.findmypast.co.uk**
14 TNA PROB11/451/253.

Ale wives probably made their own ale, but there were also a few maltsters who brewed it for the more substantial innkeepers. William Jefferies, who 'spoiled the highwaie' at Longland in 1640, was a maltster; did he build his malthouse on the highway?[1]

Stourton also provided employment for a number of professionals. The church provided employment for several people: the rector, sometimes a curate, the parish clerk, and, in 1722, an architect. The rectors will be discussed in chapter 10. They were all outsiders. Most had attended university, several having been fellows; most were also drawn from clerical families, and some were very well-connected in the wider church.

The village school, established by the Hoare family, was run by schoolmasters and mistresses. In 1722, Henry Hoare agreed with the Rector, John Drew, to fit up four rooms in the Parsonage House 'for the teaching of children to read & write & sum'. The premises were assigned to John Drew, the Rector's son (then aged 18) who was presumably to act as schoolmaster. Subsequently, the schoolmistress had a seat in the parish church, although we are not given her name. The 'schoolgirls' also had their seat, as did 'the boys in the schools of the said inhabitants'.[2] Whether the plural indicates that there was more than one school is not clear.

Hoare's school was not the first to operate in Stourton. In 1584, the churchwardens presented that 'Mr Bonnam hath a scholem' in his house & doth teache children but they knoweth not by whome he is licensed and authorized so to do' . One wonders if this was a Roman Catholic attempt to educate their children. Unfortunately, we have no further information. Two centuries later, however, in 1783, the Catholics had 'a woman's school for children'.[3] It is worth adding that Lord and Lady Stourton were still supporting a school teaching 32 pupils in 1845.[4]

Evidence for only one medic practising in Stourton has been found. He was John Drew, who was described in the 1712 will of his father-in-law, Edward Cornelius, as a 'Doctor of Physick', and 'of Sturton'.[5] He

1   WSHC A1/110/T1640/76.
2   WSHC 383/928. See also Hurley, Beryl, ed. *Wiltshire pew lists.* Wiltshire Family History Society, 1994, p.40.
3   Ransome, Mary, ed. *Wiltshire returns to the bishop's visitation queries 1783.* Wiltshire Record Society 27. 1972, p.205.
4   'Catholic Schools *c.*1845', *Catholic Ancestor* 9(6), 2003, p.237.
5   TNA PROB11/526/12.

may have been related to the two Drew rectors, but this has not been established.

No evidence for other medical professionals actually working in the parish has been discovered, although we have already seen that one member of a prominent local family served his apprenticeship as a surgeon. After completing his term, Walter Barnes practiced in Shaftesbury, where he was described as an apothecary in 1734 and 1739[1]; in 1746, he took William Snook as an apprentice surgeon.[2] He outlived three wives, dying in 1776, and was described by Hutchins as 'an eminent surgeon of this town'.[3]

A few other local medics have been identified, but none of them were based in Stourton. William Paynter, surgeon, witnessed the will of Lord Stourton in 1548; however, this will was probably written at Newhaven, not Stourton.[4] Richard Morris, 'chyrurgion', of Zeals, was cited to appear at Quarter Sessions in 1658, accused of recusancy.[5] Christopher Alford, who died in 1699, was a barber surgeon, based in Mere, not Stourton.[6] Osmund Hill, the father of John Hill, the rector, was a 'barber' from Mere, who probably took a standing at Whitesheet Fair in 1726.[7] One wonders whether the rector absorbed any of his knowledge; clergy were frequently expected to provide remedies for the ills of their parishioners. Walter Barnes' aunt Dorothy's deed of gift in 1726/7 named an apothecary, Thomas Tatum, as one of her 'beneficiaries', that is, trustees, but he was of Mere, not Stourton.[8] At the end of our period, John Gapper was practising as a surgeon in Mere.[9] Local medics were based in small towns, rather than in country parishes like Stourton.

The legal profession was represented by the stewards employed by the lords of the manor, although many of them were non-resident; indeed, at least one was based in London. Stewards were well recompensed; one witness in a Chancery case said that the 12th Lord's steward, William Knipe, had a salary of £20 per annum, and made

1   WSHC 383/719 & 383/747.
2   Dorset History Centre D-GIM/K/29/2.
3   Hutchins, John. *History and antiquities of the County of Dorset.* 3rd ed. John Bowyer & Nichols, 1868, P.47.
4   TNA PROB 11/32/258
5   WSHC A1/110/T1658, 113.
6   TNA PROB 11/449/388.
7   See p.211.
8   WSHC P1/B/939.
9   Dodd, op cit, p.269.

at least another £40 from fees and other charges. A different witness in the same Chancery case said the fees and perquisites were worth £100 per annum.[1] These figures were roughly in line with the financial rewards available to stewards on other estates.[2] There was usually a steward responsible for the whole of the estate, which included not just the manor of Stourton, but also Stourton Caundle, Ower Moigne, East Chelborough, Kingston juxta Yeovil, and various other property in Wiltshire, Dorset and Somerset. However, some were merely stewards of particular manorial courts, with much fewer responsibilities.

The earliest steward whose name we know was William Hartgill, steward to the seventh Lord Stourton. He served as Member of Parliament for Westbury in 1545, and was a Justice of the Peace for Somerset and Wiltshire in 1547, but was murdered by the eighth Lord in 1556.[3] John Budden of Shaftesbury was serving as steward in 1600; he was also steward of the Duchy of Lancaster estate at Blandford, and served as Member of Parliament for Shaftesbury in 1601 and 1604.[4] In 1633, William Hussey and Robert Byfleet (of a Bratton Seymour Catholic family)[5] both became stewards, and undertook a survey of the manor together.[6] During the Interregnum, in 1649, Hussey joined with Walter Barnes (see below) to purchase and compound for William Stourton's estate in Monkton Farleigh.[7] The Hussey family was again mentioned

1   TNA C22/708/55
2   Hainsworth, D.R. *Stewards, Lords, and People: the estate steward and his world in later Stuart England.* Cambridge University Press, 1992, p.30-31.
3   The murder is discussed by Jackson, J.E. 'Charles, Lord Stourton and the murder of the Hartgills', *Wiltshire Archaeological and Natural History Magazine* 8, 1864, p.243-341. For Hartgill's biography, see History of Parliament Trust **www.historyofparliamentonline.org**. For his dubious activities as steward, see Mowbray, op cit, p.344-5.
4   History of Parliament Trust **www.historyofparliamentonline.org**
5   See Raymond, Stuart A. 'Catholic Families of South-East Somerset and their connection to the Stourton (and Bonham) Mission, c.1550-1650', unpublished paper.
6   WSHC 4314/1.
7   Green, Mary Anne Everett, ed. *Calendar of the proceedings of the Committee for Compounding with Delinquents &c., 1643-1660 ... cases 1647-1650.* HMSO, 1890, p.2056. The two also both witnessed a lease of Lord Stourton's property at Buckhorn Weston in 1648; cf. Mayo, Charles Henry, ed. *The Municipal Records of the Borough of Dorchester, Dorset.* William Pollard & Co., 1908, p.371-2. Hussey seems to have lived in Shaftesbury; he was assessed there on five hearths in 1662; cf. Meekings, C.A.F., ed. *Dorset Hearth Tax*

in 1670, when George Hussey of Coombe Hay, Somerset, was named as trustee of a Stourton family settlement concerning the manor of Bonham.[1] In 1672 Hussey was named as one of 11th Lord Stourton's joint executors.

Walter Barnes (sometimes described as 'of Shaftesbury') and his brother Charles, long-term servants of the Stourton family, and also fellow Catholics, both served as stewards during the dark days of the Interregnum. Lord Stourton also employed 'the said Walter Barnes as his attorney & solicitor in all his lawe suites & transactions of his estate'.[2] It has already been noted that Parliament permitted Barnes to hold Lord Stourton's courts when his property was confiscated in 1650, and that he became the yearly tenant of the confiscated estate – probably for Lord Stourton's benefit. He also 'purchased' two of Thomas Stourton's houses in London, and sought to compound for them, presumably on behalf of the future Lord Stourton.[3] He also represented a number of other 'delinquents' whose estates were sequestered, purchasing and renting a number of their confiscated estates in order to restore them to their 'delinquent' owners.[4] For example, he acted as steward to Lord Petre, and joined with Humphry Weld and William Hurman to purchase some of Lord Arundel's manors.[5] Similarly, he purchased estates at Norrington and Baverstock on behalf of their Catholic owner, Thomas Gawen.[6] He died in 1657.[7] Subsequently, his son Walter was described as a 'menial servant' of Lord Stourton in 1677.

A Mr Gore served Lord Stourton as steward in 1688, but it is likely that he concerned himself primarily with the family's estates in Somerset,

assessments 1662-1664. Dorchester: Friary Press, 1951, p.22.

1 WSHC 383/380.
2 TNA C9/384/33.
3 Green, Mary Anne Everett, ed. *Calendar of the proceedings of the Committee for Compounding with Delinquents &c., 1647-1660 ... cases 1643-1646*. HMSO, 1891, p.2508. Ditto, *cases July 1650-Dec. 1653*. HMSO, 1892, p.2447.
4 Green, Mary Anne Everett, ed. *Calendar of the proceedings of the Committee for Compounding with Delinquents &c., 1643-1660 ... cases 1643-1646*. HMSO, 1890, p.1222-4. Mayo, Charles Herbert, ed. *The Minute Books of the Dorset Standing Committee, 23rd September 1646 to 8th May 1650*. Exeter: William Pollard & Co., 1902, p.380 & 424.
5 TNA C5/42/17. Mayo, *Minute books*, op cit, p.365.
6 Waylen, James. 'The Wiltshire compounders', *Wiltshire Archaeological and Natural History Magazine*, 24, 1888, p.72.
7 TNA C6/303/26.

not with Stourton. He purchased various Somerset Hundreds from Lord Stourton in 1688, but his name has not otherwise been traced.[1]

Various members of the Roman Catholic Knipe family of Semley[2] acted as stewards in the later seventeenth century. They were related to the Barnes family in some way; when Robert Barnes died in 1672, he described George Knipe as 'my kinsman', and asked him to act as a trustee.[3] George also acted as a witness when Charles Barnes's possession of Topp was challenged by his sisters in a 1674 Chancery case.[4] The connection with the Barnes family continued into the eighteenth century; in 1738, Walter Barnes appointed John Knipe as arbitrator in a dispute with Henry Hoare.[5]

The Knipes descended from a Westmorland family; William Knipe attended Grays Inn in 1635, and was admitted again in 1640.[6] Lord Arundel employed him as a land agent in the 1630s and 1640s, and he suffered sequestration of his estate for recusancy under the Parliamentary regime.[7] He served William, the 11th Lord Stourton, from the death of the 10th Lord in 1633, until his Lord's own death in 1672.[8] The family's earliest mention in the Stourhead archives was in 1658, immediately after Walter Barnes's death, when H. Knipe witnessed some entries in Lord Stourton's entry book.[9] He and George Knipe witnessed Lord Stourton's lease of a tenement to Robert Gapper in 1663.[10]

William Knipe, as steward, was instructed to act as trustee for income from recently enclosed commons near Stourton Park when William Lord Stourton made his will in 1670.[11] He was also named as his

1   Mowbray, op cit, p.535.
2   For this family, see Williams, J. Anthony. 'The decline of a recusant family: the Knipes of Semley', *Wiltshire Archaeological magazine* 59, 1964, p.170-80. See also Raymond, Stuart A. 'The Knipes: a footnote', *Wiltshire Archaeological & Natural History Magazine*, forthcoming.
3   TNA PROB11/341/162.
4   TNA C5/484/53.
5   TNA C11/2072/19.
6   Foster. Joseph, ed. *The register of admissions to Gray's inn, 1521-1889, together with the register of marriages in Gray's inn chapel, 1695-1754*. Hansard Publishing Union, 1889, p.209 & 226.
7   Williams, op cit, p.171.
8   According to the deposition of George Hussey, c.1695-6; cf. TNA C22/663/21.
9   WSHC 383/109, f.39.
10 WSHC 383/721.
11 TNA PROB11/339/297.

Lord's joint executor. In the same year, he was named as a trustee in a Stourton family settlement of the manor of Bonham. He probably died in 1672,[1] before he could actually undertake his executorship duties. His son, George, had been admitted to Grays Inn in 1660,[2] took over his stewardship, and became administrator of William Lord Stourton's estate. Various evidence of his activities as steward can be found amongst the Stourhead archives. For example, he witnessed a lease to William Jupe in 1677[3] and received a number of fines in 1683 and 1684.[4] His other activities included advising the Roman Catholic Secular Chapter's treasurer, William Byfleet, the son of Robert Byfleet mentioned above.[5]

The connection of the Knipes with the Lords Stourton ceased after the 13th Lord came of age. Like his predecessor, William Hartgill, over a century earlier, George Knipe fell out with his Lord. But he was not murdered. Rather, the heir dismissed him, and brought a 'vexatious suit' against him in Chancery, in 1693.[6] This was very unusual; dismissals of stewards were rare events. Hainsworth has likened such events to the dis-inheritance of an eldest son.[7]

Knipe appears to have been replaced as steward by William Morgan of Holborn, Middlesex, who deposed that he had been appointed as steward by the new Lord Stourton.[8] Morgan, together with John Bromley, took a new survey of the manor.[9] However, his name then disappears from view.

Samuel Rich was the steward when Sir Thomas Meres brought his 1707 case against Lord Stourton for defaulting on his mortgage.[10] Rich witnessed a number of transactions between 1699 and 1707,[11] and

1 Williams, 'Decline...', op cit, p.172.
2 Foster, op cit, p.289.
3 WSHC 383/721.
4 WSHC 383/352, p.5. The document refers to 'Mr Knipe; presumably this was William.
5 Williams, op cit, p.105 & 196-7.
6 TNA C6/303/26; C22/708/55. Knipe brought a related case against Lord Stourton two years later; cf TNA C22/663/21. For a discussion of the dispute, see Raymond, Stuart A. 'The Knipes: a footnote', *Wiltshire Archaeological & Natural History Magazine*, forthcoming.
7 Hainsworth, op cit, p.253.
8 TNA C22/708/55
9 WSHC 383/346.
10 WSHC 383/366.
11 WSHC 383/721 & 724.

his name is mentioned in a number of deeds abstracted by Mowbray.[1]

When Sir Thomas Meres purchased the manor, he appointed a Mr John Cheeke as his steward; he took the survey of 1717, preparatory to Henry Hoare's purchase.[2] Apparently, the new steward did not give satisfaction; one of the leases he wrote received 'so imperfect an entry' that it had to be 'perfected by another person more to the benefit and satisfaccon of the then Ld of the said mannor'.

After 1717, Henry Hoare brought in his own stewards and legal advisers. Elias Hosey presided at the manorial court from 1719 until 1741.[3] Joshua Cox was similarly long-serving. He was bequeathed £200 in Henry the Good's will in 1725 for 'an acknowledgement of his great Services to me desiring he will continue his good offices to my Dear Wife after my Death in the management of her Jointure Estate in Stourton'.[4] Cox was based at Bartlett's Buildings, Holborn, London, and undertook legal work in the capital. In 1743 he was nominated as steward in order to take a surrender in the capital.[5] He could also be found at Stourhead on occasion. In 1740, he was paid £8 7s for his work in 'levying a fine and inrolling Walter Barnes conveyance' of the property which Hoare flooded for his lake.[6] In 1742, he swore to the genuineness of Jane Hoare's will.[7] In 1748, he was asked to beat the bounds of the manor with the tenants in order to determine their respective common rights.[8] He did not, however, as far as is known, preside at the manorial court. From 1742 until 1746, that task was taken over by William Austen.[9] Samuel Cox, perhaps a relative of Joshua's, presided between 1747 and 1749, perhaps longer.

Thomas Hawkins was another London lawyer employed by the Hoares. In 1731, he appointed Thomas Hawkins of St Brides solely to take the surrender of Thomas Martin, one of the customary tenants of the manor.[10]

1   Mowbray, op cit, p.522, 523, 527, 528 & 535.
2   WSHC 383/348, p.4.
3   WSHC 383/353.
4   Dodd, Dudley, ed. *The letters of Henry Hoare 1760-1781*, Wiltshire Record Society 71, 2018, p.250.
5   WSHC 383/741.
6   WSHC 383/61.
7   TNA PROB11/719/352.
8   WSHC 386/353.
9   WSHC 383/353.
10 WSHC 383/345.

Francis Faugoin was also described as a 'steward', although he was not a lawyer. His responsibilities under the Hoares at and after the end of our period were primarily for the gardens.[1]

Stewards and lawyers were amongst the many servants of the Stourton family. Their other servants were employed in a wide variety of capacities. At least one, Mathew Stourton, who served the 11th Lord,[2] was a distant relative, descended from the 7th Lord. Others were leading figures in the parish, and were suitably rewarded with grants of land; others were merely labourers or household staff. A few were executed with Charles, 8th Lord Stourton, for the murder of William Hartgill in 1556/7.[3] These included John Symes, whose gallows were set up on Whitesheet Hill; they are mentioned in a perambulation of the bounds of Norton Ferris manor.[4] Another, John Davies, was described as a yeoman and personal servant of his lord.[5]

Thomas Cabill, who 'servid the [10th] Lord Storton', refused the oath of allegiance, was interrogated about his Catholicism by Elizabeth's minions, and was imprisoned.[6] William Holmes, the servant of Lady Stourton (the 8th Lord's widow), betrayed a Roman Catholic priest, William Cornelius, when he was staying at Chideock in 1594; Cornelius was executed.[7] Edward 10th Lord Stourton's 1632 will[8] divided his servants between those who attended on his person 'at London or in the countrye', and 'all my other household servants. The former were bequeathed a whole year's wages, the latter six months. Some of them were named in a codicil. Richard Dean, 'my kitchen boy' was given 'the worst suite and cloake of al my apparrell'; the rest of the testator's clothing was to be divided between Joseph Quynton, Philip Atkins, Edward Walewright, Timothy Skreen and John Evil. These were presumably his servants at Stourton, as he made a separate bequest to un-named 'servants here at London'.

1   Dodd, op cit, p.261-3.
2   TNA C22/663/21.
3   Mowbray, op cit, p.393
4   WSHC 383/198.
5   Mowbray, op cit, p.393.
6   Petti, Anthony G., ed. *Recusant documents from the Ellesmere manuscripts.* Catholic Record Society 60. 1968, p.89. It is not clear whether he served the family in Stourton or elsewhere.
7   Foley, Henry. *Records of the English Province of the Society of Jesus.* Burns & Oates, 1878. Vol.3. p.457.
8   TNA PROB11/163/663.

We have already met the Barnes family, who served the Stourtons throughout the sixteenth and seventeenth centuries. The family, as we have seen, were prominent Roman Catholics. In 1613, Robert Barnes was said to have been the chief keeper of Stourton Park and warren for many years.[1] He had servants of his own. John Stile and Richard Bayley both described Robert Barnes as their master when they were examined in the Court of Star Chamber in 1613.[2]

A number of other servants of the Stourton family can be identified. William Holmes was described as 'late servant to Lady Stourton' when he was examined regarding Catholic priests visiting the Arundel family (whom he had also served) in 1594.[3] Agnes Jacob was a servant of Mr Stourton of Bonham House when she died in 1611; the word 'stranger' is deleted in the parish register entry, suggesting that she was not a local person. Cicely Messalin was a servant when she died in 1612; only one other person of this surname is mentioned in the parish register, suggesting that she too was not local. A number of others who were presented for recusancy are identified in chapter 10; they include two 'gentleman' servants. In the 1690s, Charles Davies, probably a relative of the servant who was executed over a century earlier, was paid 'for nourseing or boarding' William Stourton, the brother of Edward Lord Stourton, who died in infancy.[4] In 1703, John Rodway was granted a lease of Pool Close in return for a fine of ten shillings and 'the good service' he performed.[5] Joseph Turner was described as a servant of Thomas 14th Lord Stourton when he took a lease of Trench Cliff (in Bonham) from his master in 1743.[6]

When the Hoares succeeded the Stourton family, they continued to employ many servants. Thomas the butler was paid his wages of £2 10s in 1724.[7] He probably lived in. So did James Land, who made provision for his burial by Grace Applegate, his executrix, but only 'if my Mistress is not pleased to do it'.

---

1   TNA STAC8/73/13. See also WSHC 383/721 for a lease of 1634, which describes him as 'servant'.
2   TNA STAC8/73/13. See pp. 99, 195-6 for discussion of this case.
3   *Calendar of State Papers Domestic ... Elizabeth 1591-1594*. Longmans Green Reader & Dyer, 1867, p.488.
4   TNA C22/708/55; Mowbray, op cit, p.507.
5   WSHC 383/733.
6   WSHC 383/386.
7   WSHC 383/58.

Richard Edwards, a member of an old Stourton family, was described as 'Mrs Hoare's man' in 1728, when he was paid 7s 1d in 1727 for 'keeping puppies'; he was probably 'Richard the 'footman' whose bill of 7s was paid in 1728.[1] It seems likely that Charles Evil was a servant of the Hoare family, who occasionally slept at Stourhead; when he died in 1749/50 he had a bed there.[2] In 1727, Joshua Cox, as estate steward, paid 2s 6d to 'Mrs Barnes's boy' for bringing a horse from Shaftesbury.[3]

An important role on the estate was played by the gamekeeper. Reference has already been made to Robert Barnes' role as chief keeper in the 1610s, and to his servant Richard Bayley, who was seriously injured twice in confrontations with neighbouring keepers whilst carrying out his duties.[4] A century later, in 1724, a huntsman was paid £9 17s 11d by Henry Hoare,[5] who also appointed Joseph Reed as gamekeeper in the same year.[6] It is unlikely that he was a local man; gamekeepers' masters needed men they could rely on, and so avoided appointing men with local loyalties. Reed agreed to serve for a salary of £20 per annum, plus perks, although he was to pay rent if he tenanted one of Hoare's houses. He was to take 'care of the ponds ducks pidgeons and woods', and was to become the tenant of the intended warren when it was built. He was 'to mend or make any netts which herafter there may be occasion for to take fish connies or any other game', and to 'keep at his own cost all such dogs or ferritts as he shall have occasion for in his business. Five years later, the gamekeeper was 'Richard', who was paid £8 4s for eight months work on 16th November 1729. He was still keeper in 1732.[7]

Lords of the manor were not the only masters of servants. The minor gentry, some yeomen and tradesmen, and the clergy, also had need of them. In 1648, Edith Courtney, the servant of John Freake, came under suspicion of stealing his wife's gold ring and other items.[8] It seems likely she was dismissed; her name is not mentioned in other parish documents. By contrast, in 1657, Freake's brother-in-law, Walter

1   WSHC 383/59.
2   WSHC P2/B/11164.
3   WSHC 383/59.
4   TNA STAC8/256/26.
5   WSHC 383/58.
6   WSHC 383/114.
7   WSHC 383/59.
8   WSHC A1/110/T1648, 216.

Barnes named his servant George Moores as his executor.[1] When Richard Bayley, yeoman, died in 1694, he bequeathed 40s to Richard Hascoll, 'my man'. Joseph Lampard's 1744 lease of Stourton Farm made express provision for his servants to have house room, presumably at Stourhead.[2] Many young people entered service in their teens, living in their masters' houses and eating at their tables. Some continued in service throughout their lives. When Montague Barton, the rector in 1780, reported that there were 83 Papists in his parish, he also observed 'there are many more belonging to the parish who are out at service'.[3] That was probably the case throughout our period.

In 1665/6, Nathaniel Field, the rector, bequeathed twenty shillings to 'all my servants which shall be in my house at the time of my death'.[4] One of them was probably John Sturges, who had testified on behalf of his master in a 1662 Chancery suit.[5] At that time he had been employed by Field for some fourteen years (although he was described in his deposition as a husbandman); one of his duties had been to collect the rector's tithe. William Glide had similarly served Dr.King, Field's predecessor.[6] Three other servants of Nathaniel Field can be named: Mary Forward, the wife of a husbandman from Mere, served him in the 1650s, probably before she was married.[7] William Skreen of Zeals said that he had served Field for four years.[8] John Green, husbandman, had 'lived with him three years'. We have already met the Green family. The names of Field's other servants do not appear in any other Stourton documents. The Skreen surname, however, frequently appears in Mere parish register. Glide and Sturges presumably came from further afield.

Religious considerations could be involved in the employment of servants. Roman Catholics preferred to engage servants who shared their own beliefs. In March, 1638/9, the man servant (un-named) of Mr John Ewens was cited, with his master, to appear before the Archdeaconry Court, presumably accused of recusancy. In the following June, it was

1   TNA PROB11/273/261.
2   WSHC 383/721.
3   Cited by Williams, J. Anthony. *Catholic Recusancy in Wiltshire, 1660-1791.* Catholic Record Society, 1968, p.214.
4   WSHC P1/F/134.
5   TNA E134/14Chas2/Trin3.
6   TNA E134/23Chas2/Mich7.
7   TNA E134/14Chas2/Trin3.
8   TNA E134/23Chas2/Mich7.

the turn of his 'maide servant', Cicily. An un-named servant of John Warham was presented with his master as a recusant at Trinity Quarter Sessions 1658.[1] It is possible that Henry Miles, who received a bequest of £5 in the 1725 will of his master, William Cuffe,[2] was also a Catholic. As has been seen, at least some of the Cuffe family were Catholics.

An alternative to service was apprenticeship. The Statute of Artificers and Apprentice, 1563, required tradesmen to serve a seven year apprenticeship before they practised their trade. Private apprentices had to serve their masters for seven years, and to be totally obedient to them; sometimes their parents paid a premium to secure the apprenticeship. Masters were usually expected to provide food, clothing, and lodging, and to teach apprentices their trade. Apprenticeship indentures rarely survive, as they were private documents which did not have to be deposited with any official body (except in the case of paupers). The only private Stourton indenture known to have survived is that of Henry Edwards, who was apprenticed to Henry Shargall of Bowerchalke, carpenter, in 1736, paying a premium of £6 10s.[3] Indentures, however, are not the only source that can be used to identify apprentices. A variety of other sources reveal a number of Stourton boys who were apprenticed elsewhere, and a number who served their terms in Stourton. Perhaps the most prominent was the Catholic Walter Barnes, who in 1718 travelled to Dulverton (Somerset) to serve his term as an apprentice surgeon with Nathaniel Poole; he paid a premium of £30.[4]

His brother, Robert Barnes, was due to be apprenticed to Mr Gildon, 'a silk mercer who takes him gratis', in May 1723.[5] His father Walter owed Mrs Stourton £6 'for clothes for my son during his apprenticeship yet to come'.[6] This Mr Gildon was probably a relative of Joseph Gildon of Bonham, Walter Barnes's brother in law,[7] who owned houses in London, and whose son John had been apprenticed there in 1693.[8] Indeed, it may be that Joseph was the intended master. In the event, Barnes was

1   WSHC A1/110/T1658, 107.
2   WSHC P2/C/1076.
3   WSHC 1240/42.
4   TNA IR1/7, f.45.
5   WSHC 383/740.
6   WSHC 383/740.
7   Raymond, Stuart A. 'Barnes: a Catholic Family on the Borders of Wiltshire and Somerset, c.1548-c.1750', *Genealogists Magazine* 32(9), 2018, p.342.
8   TNA PROB11/407/176; London Apprenticeship Abstracts 1442-1850 **www.findmypast.co.uk**

actually apprenticed to John Abrams, a London painter stainer, who took a premium of £16.[1] He was described as a gilder in his 1728 will, and was probably employed on the work at Stourhead.[2]

Thomas 14th Lord Stourton, in his 1743/4 will, left £50 to John Nelson, 'whom I put out apprentice to Mr Villeneuf in London'.[3] Thomas Stone, the grandchild of John Jupe, was an apprentice when Jupe died in 1638/9, leaving him ten shillings, 'to be payd when hee shalbe out of his apprentishipp'.[4] Charles Davies's family paid £15 to send him to Covent Garden to learn the trade of a cordwainer from Mr Marmaduke Jackson.[5] Five other Stourton boys are known to have been apprenticed with London livery companies in our period. James Bennett was apprenticed to a cutler in 1595, Edward Gibbs to a currier in 1653, John Shepherd to a tyler in 1674, John Gildon to a tallow chandler in 1693, and George Janninson to a painter in 1704.[6] Charles Evil did not have to go quite that far in 1725 to learn to be a joiner: his master was John Jesope of Gillingham.[7]

Richard Atkins, unusually, was able to stay in his home parish: he was apprenticed to John White, one of Stourton's butcher, in 1724; the premium was £8.[8] White also took William, the son of Elizabeth Hole, in 1740, at the same premium.[9] Two years later, however, when Samuel Prout became his apprentice, White received a premium of £20.[10]

Samuel Edwards, who was named as a life in a lease by John Hill in 1743, when his age was estimated at 22, was probably the blacksmith's apprentice.[11] When he obtained a marriage licence in 1747, the bond

1   TNA IR1/9, f.113; London Apprenticeship Abstracts 1442-1850 **www. findmypast.co.uk**
2   WSHC P1/B/976.
3   TNA PROB11/733/155.
4   TNA PROB11/180/368.
5   TNA IR1/13, f.94.
6   London Apprenticeship Abstracts 1442-1850 **www.findmypast.co.uk**
7   TNA IR1/11, f.45. The duty was paid in London, and the clerk had a poor grasp of the geography of the South-West. He described Gillingham as being in Somerset!
8   TNA IR1/10, f.40.
9   TNA IR1/50, f.53.
10 Dale, Christobel, ed. *Wiltshire apprentices and their masters 1710-1760.* Wiltshire Archaeological and Natural History Society Recrods Branch 17. 1961, p.123; TNA IR1/50/152.
11 WSHC 383/353.

described him as a blacksmith.[1] No other relationship can be traced, and the blacksmith had no children.

Thomas Evil was apprenticed by his father to Richard Young, a wheelwright, of Hatchbury, but apparently deserted his master and enlisted in 'His Majesty's service', only to return to Stourton claiming poor relief in 1752.[2]

Several boys from other parishes are known to have served their apprenticeship in Stourton. Samuel Prout of Dorset was another of John White's apprentices; his indentures were dated 1742.[3] Thomas Landock came from Wool, Dorset, to learn the trade of a tailor from William Bracher in 1735, paying a £10 premium.[4] It is likely that there were many others of whom we do not have record.

There were also many pauper apprentices. The terms of apprenticeship were much harder for paupers. They could be apprenticed when they were much younger than private apprentices, and they had to serve for much longer – until they attained the age of twenty-four. And their parents had no say in their apprenticeship. Nevertheless, at least one Stourton apprentice served a master who had also taken private apprentices. John White, the butcher, accepted James Arnold as a pauper apprentice in 1737. He received no premium, but the boy would have served him for much longer than his private apprentices. Assuming that all his apprentices served out their terms, three of his apprentices would have been working together for him for a number of years in the 1740s.

The indentures of ten pauper apprentices (including two girls) from between 1729 and 1737 can be found amongst Stourton's parish records.[5] In view of the dominance of agriculture and the cloth industry in Stourton, it is not surprising that three of the boys were apprenticed locally to husbandry, and expected to become agricultural labourers. Four (including three of the Friths) were apprenticed to broad weaving, and sent to serve masters in Mells. Others found masters nearer to

1   Sarum Marriage Licence Bonds **www.findmypast.co.uk**. His age then was stated to be 30. He was actually baptised 2nd February 1718/19.

2   WSHC 1240/21.

3   Dale, Christobel, ed. *Wiltshire apprentices and their masters 1710-1760*. Wiltshire Archaeological and Natural History Society Records Branch, 17. 1961, p.192. I have been unable to find the relevant entry in TNA IR1.

4   TNA IR1/ 14, f.98.

5   WSHC 1240/19.

home. Both the Arnold children were apprenticed to Stourton masters. George Frith was apprenticed to a cordwainer in Castle Cary. Mary Barnett and John Markey both went to Kilmington, the latter (probably) to a relative; Henry Owen was sent to Zeals. The two girls were to learn 'housewifery'.

Four of the boys were from the Frith family, although it is not clear whether they were siblings; only James and John, the children of William and Edith Frith, appear in the parish register. James was twelve when he was apprenticed, John ten. Two other children appear in the parish register, Jane and Shadrach; no other evidence concerning them survives, and it is not possible to construct pedigrees for the family. Similarly, the baptisms of the two Arnold children are not recorded, although the indentures indicate that they were siblings. They were presumably born before their parents, James and Frances Arnold, moved to Stourton; five younger children are recorded in the parish register.

Another opening for paupers was soldiering. As discussed in chapter 4, constables were responsible for the recruitment of the Militia, and a number of Stourton parishioners were selected to serve – although we have few details. We know almost nothing about Stourton soldiers who fought in the Civil War, although some certainly did. George Phillips was granted a pension of £2 from the maimed soldiers' fund in 1663, although it was reduced to £1 in 1670 – possibly because he was a Roman Catholic.[1] He was, presumably, disabled, but did not die until 1st January 1693/4, perhaps fifty years after sustaining his injuries.

Another maimed soldier granted a pension was Thomas Stone of Gasper. He had served for three years under 'Lord Hoppen', presumably Lord Hopton, the royalist commander, but was 'by severall wounds disabled to perform this service'. He had 'lay lame for the space of two years and upwards', and was 'by reason of his old age unfitt to labour'.[2] His children, John, Francis, and Mary were baptised between 1641 and 1645. He probably served as parish clerk,[3] and signed the terrier in 1662.[4] It seems that he took a long time to petition for a pension. As he lived in Gasper, on the Somerset side of the border, his petition was

1 WSHC A1/160/2 Midsummer sessions; A1/160/3 Christmas Sessions. He was cited to appear before the Archdeaconry Court on several occasions in the late 1660s; WSHC D2/5/1/8.
2 WSHC A1/110/T1682, 81; A1/160/4.
3 Hobbs, op cit, p.225.
4 WSHC D/1/24/193/4.

addressed to the Somerset bench, despite the fact that it found its way to Wiltshire Quarter Sessions. The names of those signing his petition are interesting – not only the rector, churchwardens, and overseers, but also three leading Catholics, including William Lord Stourton, Mathew Stourton, and William Moores. The latter, curiously, signed the petition on 3rd July 1675, although it does not seem to have been presented until 1682. Stone was granted a pension of two pounds per annum. His pension was not granted until July 1682.

The only other evidence for military activity we have is the 1747 will of George Drew, who was then serving as a 'marine soldier' on board HMS Namure under the command of Brigadier General Pawlett.[1] He was probably the grandson of the rector, John Drew, and would probably have been an officer.

---

1 TNA PROB11/776/410.

9
Living Conditions:
Houses, Food, and Possessions

THE WAY IN which people ate, slept, dressed and relaxed, is central to our understanding of how they lived. Shelter, food, and clothing are all essential to human life. One could get by without furniture, but its possession and use tell us a lot about our ancestors, and about the social differences between the wealthy and the poor. Other possessions tell us what early modern Stourtonians did in their leisure time. Their weapons tell us both about hunting, and about fighting.

Houses

In most English parishes, some of our evidence for housing would consist of bricks and mortar, or perhaps timber and lathe. In Stourton, most houses on the Hoare family's estate were demolished and rebuilt anew. Whether that included the 'two very good new stone built farme houses with all proper outhouses', which had fallen in hand in 1704, and were said to be worth £1200, is not clear.[1] In 1812, 'a lot of cottages that stood very disadvantageously between the church and gardens' were pulled down. On the estate now owned by the National Trust, only the farmhouse at Coldcot, and a house on Stourton Lane, pre-date the Hoare era.[2] The fourteenth-century house at Bonham is also still standing; it was added to in the sixteenth century, becoming a Roman Catholic chapel and priest's house with, apparently, a tunnel for the priest to escape through.

Houses built for the poor were not built to last. Unfortunately, we have very little evidence relating to them. Cottages erected without permission on the common were likely to be insubstantial – a mere

1 WSHC 383/255.
2 Wiltshire Buildings Record B22 pt.2.

wooden frame covered with whatever material came to hand to keep out the weather. They could, however, last for some years; before 1692, John Jupe built such a cottage. His daughter, Mary Hartnall, was still living there in 1717.[1] There were five similar cottages on the waste of the manor of Bonham in 1717.[2] Cottages for the poor built by manorial lords may have been more substantial; in 1625, Edmund Leversedge and Sir Thomas Thynne, of neighbouring Longleat, were prosecuted for building sixty cottages just over the parish boundary, on the waste in Selwood Forest. They were occupied by cottagers who despoiled the King's woods.[3]

Normally, we could also expect evidence for housing from the hearth tax returns of the later Stuart era. Unfortunately, the returns for Wiltshire have mostly been lost. However, we do have the Somerset returns for 1664-5, which cover the tithing of Brook, that is, Gasper.[4] These indicate the number of houses in the tithing, and the number of hearths on which tax was paid for each house. There were 39 houses; three of the taxpayers paid tax on two houses, so there were only 36 taxpayers. There were fourteen houses with one hearth, nineteen with two, five with three, and one with four. Various explanations as to why tax should be reduced are given. One of Thomas Hunt's hearths was a 'private oven' (was he a baker?), which was exempt. Similarly, one of the three 'hearths' belonging to James Stroud, was 'only a furnace and noe hearth'; Stroud was a tanner. John Presley, Robert Shepherd and William Chinnock had all 'pulled downe' one of their hearths, presumably in order to escape the tax. One of Anne Open's hearths was in 'a small cottage in the possession of her daughter who is very poore'. One of the two hearths in William Poor's Lower House was 'a small cottage not worth 20s per annum in the possession of a poore person'. The poor were, of course, exempt. Thomas Stile had 'returned one too many by mistake'; by contrast, John Lamb had 'returned one short'.

For 1670, we do not have a list of those who paid the hearth tax, but we do have a list of 25 residents in the tithing of Brook (Gasper) who

---

1   WSHC 383/348, p.2.
2   Somerset Heritage Centre Q/RRp/1.
3   Sharp, Buchanan. *In Contempt of all Authority: rural artisans and riot in the West of England 1586-1660.* Universityof California Press, 1980, p.160-61.
4   TNA E179/256/16, pt.18. This has been edited by Holworthy, R., ed. *Dwelly's national records, vol.1. Hearth tax returns for Somerset 1664-5.* Fleet: E. Dwelly, 1916, p.95-7.

were exempt.[1] Most presumably only had one hearth, although three had two. Some of the exempt had paid tax in 1664-5.

Most of our evidence for housing derives from descriptions of houses in wills and probate inventories. This can be supplemented by the less detailed evidence of deeds and leases. Probate inventories sometimes, usefully, list decedents' goods room by room. This enables us to see how particular rooms, such as the 'chamber over the kitchen', or the 'parlour', were used. Wills sometimes identify the rooms in which particular items being bequeathed were kept. Probate records cannot, however, be relied on to enumerate all the rooms in a house; references in wills are only incidental, and inventories only identify the rooms in which the decedents' goods were kept. It is always possible that there were other rooms that were empty, or that there were other occupants living elsewhere in the house. Dual occupation is sometimes mentioned in wills, as we will see. Not all inventories mention specific rooms. In some cases, that may be due to the fact that there was only one room.

The basic pattern of most houses described in the probate records seems to have been two ground floor rooms, perhaps with a cross passage (although this is rarely mentioned), and another two rooms upstairs. The ground-floor rooms were the hall or parlour, and the kitchen, with chambers (bedrooms) over both. Visitors would be met in the hall, which was likely to be equipped with seating and tables, and also with a hearth. The kitchen, where food was prepared, was also on the ground floor, with another hearth. Chambers were frequently described as being 'over' one of these rooms, on the first floor; they were generally reserved for particular individuals, and served as bedrooms – although beds could also, on occasion, be found in the hall or the kitchen. There were variations to this pattern. In 1728/9, for example, Joan Target had a 'room over the entry' which she appears to have used as her bedroom.[2]

Larger properties might have another parlour and/or a buttery, again, with chambers above. The buttery was generally located close to the kitchen, as it was used for storage of food and other goods. A variety of other rooms, such as lofts and garrets, could also be found. The backside was probably a lean-to at the rear of the house, used for the

1   TNA E179/343. Certificates of exemption; cf. Dwelly, E., ed. *Dwelly's national records, vol.2. Directory of Somerset*. E.Dwelly, 1929, p.286-7.
2   WSHC P1/T/345.

storage of firewood and other items. In 1697/8 Charles Davies stored his fuel in a woodhouse.[1] Wealthier residents might have outhouses such as stables, barns, milk-houses or dairies, and boulting houses (used for sifting and storing flour). Walter Barnes had a milkhouse in 1698/9.[2] Tradesmen such as Robert Green, the blacksmith,[3] had their 'shops', that is, workshops, probably attached to the house. Green's shop housed 'ye new anvills & bellows and some hammers'. In 1711, John Hill of Gasper was using his 'shop' to carry on business as a mercer; it housed all his trade goods, such as linen, bottles, thread, lace, soap and candles. He also had two small casks of brandy 'in the stayre head'.[4]

A survey of 1703 indicates that the outhouses at Stourton Castle included coach houses, barns, stables, and oxen house; there were also three gardens, an orchard, two courts, and three out-courts.[5] Many of the dwelling houses and cottages leased out by the estate also had their own gardens and orchards.

Inventories frequently identify the goods found in particular rooms, enabling us to see how rooms were used. The 'hall' (sometimes called the 'howse') was likely to contain tables and seating. So was the inner 'parlour', which was likely to be a more private room, or perhaps another bedroom. A feather bed and other bedding was in Francis Jupe's parlour when he died in 1666.[6] Chambers were usually bedrooms. John Porter's 1608 will mentions three chambers, all of which contained beds and bedding.[7] The function of the kitchen was the same as it is today: the preparation of food, as evidenced by the numerous pots, pans, pot-hangings, and other kitchen equipment described in inventories. In some houses, there might be a buttery for the storage of food. The presence of fire places and chimneys in some rooms may be indicated by the presence of fire-side equipment. John Jupe in 1637/8 was more explicit; he bequeathed "all my spitts andirons & other iron ware which belongeth unto ye hall chimnye' to his daughter Mary, who was also given the beds and bedding 'in my owne chamber'.[8]

1 WSHC P2/D/414.
2 TNA PROB4/3909.
3 WSHC P2/G/518.
4 WSHC P2/H/1092.
5 WSHC 383/253.
6 WSHC P2/IJ/143.
7 WSHC P2/P/163.
8 TNA PROB11/180/368.

Ideally, we would be able to identify houses assessed to hearth tax with houses whose rooms are listed in inventories. Unfortunately, that cannot be done for any of the houses in Gasper for which returns survive. However, two of these houses are mentioned in wills.

John Presley had two hearths in 1664-5. His 1671 will[1] shows that the house descended to his son Thomas, but he was instructed to allow his sister Elizabeth the use of an 'uper chamber'. This was presumably the room 'which shee doth commonly ley in', which contained her bed and bedding, together with 'a coffer and a box and a little brase crocke', all of which were included in her legacy. Elizabeth's brother John was also mentioned in the will; he was to live in 'the kichinge ende of my dwellinge house', and was also to occupy 'the plote of garden ground which he now injoyeth'. It became his responsibility to 'keepe that part of the house in repairation at his own cost and he to alowe [Thomas] a way to com to the oven to bake without any denial'. Thomas Presley was to live in the rest of the house, which evidently had more than the two rooms occupied by his siblings. He probably had a hall, which would have had the second hearth. He may, conceivably have had a separate chamber, or he may have slept in his hall. The oven in the kitchen indicates that his brother also had a hearth. There was no hearth for his sister.

In 1664/5, William Poor also had two hearths. When he died in 1682, his son John and his daughter Mary Feltham were occupying separate parts of the house, presumably with their respective spouses (John's wife Joan was mentioned in this context in William's will, but Mary's husband Robert was not). William and his wife Mary presumably also occupied a separate part of the house. William's will directed that his children were to continue their occupancy for their lives; they were also to continue using their respective plots in the garden, and John was to 'have liberty to make use of the oven without any denial'.

Wills provide a number of other examples of houses being divided up by testators. William Barnard in 1652 left his wife 'the hall with the chamber over the same, and also the chamber within the said chamber', but left his son Thomas 'all the residue of my dwellinge house, with all the barnes and other outhouses thereon to belonginge'.[2] Roger Open (1656),[3] gave his son in law, John Trimby, 'libertie to live in my house att Stourton, hee allowinge my wife the hal and chamber over the same to

1   WSHC P2/P/476.
2   TNA PROB11/223/594.
3   TNA PROB11/259/615.

and for her use dureing her life, provided that he repaire the said house as it shall be needeful'.

Other examples of houses divided up between several occupants can be found in leases. We have already seen that the cottage leased by George Green in 1719 was substantial enough to double as a court house, and as the place where the churchwardens prepared for church ales.[1]

We do not get a full description of the cottage purchased by John Coake of Iwerne Courtney from Robert Tabor in 1717. When he assigned the remainder of his lease to Philip Tabor of South Brewham in 1723 he noted that 'two lower ground rooms and the chamber ... just over them being at the west end of the said cottage' were occupied by Thomas Tabor, the son of the purchaser – and presumably a relative of the original lessee.[2]

It is likely that it was this cottage which Henry Miles leased in 1744. His lease stated that it had previously been tenanted by Thomas Tabor, and one of its conditions was that Tabor could continue to occupy 'two lower or ground rooms ye chamber or chambers over ye same at ye west end of ye said cottage'. Again, we do not have a description of the east end of the cottage, but it was probably similar to the west end, and was typical of other cottages in the parish. Miles only paid a fine of £5, and a rent of 1s 4d.[3]

These examples suggest that many houses in Stourton were divided up between adult members of the same family, rendering small houses even more cramped for space. The wills of both Presley and Poor emphasised the need for those occupants who did not have an oven in their own rooms to be given access to one by the other occupants. Both also indicate the importance attached to the fact that they had their own gardens.

Overcrowding was probably exacerbated by the fact that many cottagers took in 'inmates' to lodge with them. This practice was deplored by all those above them in the social scale. In 1628, a number of the tenants of neighbouring Mere deposed in the Exchequer that the erection of new cottages, and the division and subletting of existing tenements, had greatly increased the numbers of the poor.[4]

1   WSHC 383/99. p.23. See also above, pp. 81-2
2   WSHC 383/726.
3   WSHC 383/353.
4   Sharp, Buchanan. *In contempt of all authority: rural artisans and riot in the West of England, 1586-1660.* University of California Press, 1980, p.160.

Fuller descriptions of houses are given in probate inventories. The earliest Stourton house described in an inventory is that of Thomas Jennens in 1558/9.[1] He had a 'howse' containing a 'board' (a table), a form, two stools, and an old 'coberd', which presumably contained his pewter vessels and his chaffing dish. He kept his money (amounting to 6d!) in his chamber, which he evidently used as a bed-room, as it contained 'ii floke bedes ii bolsters ii pyllowes on peyre of blanketts iii peyre of shetts ii coverletts ii tabell clothes ii towelles ii pyllowes', together worth one guinea. There were also two coffers. The only other room in the house was his 'kychine', where he kept a variety of pans, pot hooks, a 'fryyinge pane', and other kitchen equipment, as well as a hatchet. Outside he had a barn. His inventory was valued at a mere £21.

The house of Mathew Combes, who died in 1671, was typical of houses occupied by small husbandmen. On the lower floor, he had a hall, with its table board and its chairs, and a kitchen, with crocks, pans, pothooks, and other kitchen equipment. Ascending the stairs, he found room for 'I old dust bed & bedsteed' at their head. There were chambers above both the kitchen and the hall, the latter termed 'parlour chamber'. Both contained beds and bedding. Combes' inventory was valued at just £28 11s 3d.[2]

William Moores' estate was valued at just over £43 in 1698. Unlike Combes, he described himself as a yeoman,[3] but his house was very similar. Moores' tables and chairs were in the hall. No kitchen was mentioned, but his buttery probably fulfilled the same function; it contained all his 'pewter and brasse', together with 'two halfe hoggsheads and two quarter barrles with other lumber'. There were chambers above both rooms, both containing beds and bedding.

Sometimes houses of the relatively wealthy were quite small. John Humphreys's estate in 1673 was valued at just over £93, but his inventory only mentions a hall and a chamber, as though they were the only rooms in the house.[4] Both rooms were full of his goods. In his hall he had tables and chairs, fireside implements, an hour glass (a hint of luxury), three flitches of bacon, probably hanging from a beam, and a vast array of crockery. His chamber was full of beds and bedding. There were also various chests, coffers, and cupboards, and six books.

1   WSHC P2/3Reg/94D & P2/G/5.
2   WSHC P2/C/630.
3   WSHC P2/M/770.
4   WSHC P2/H/706.

John Riall's house in 1607/8 was slightly larger; it had a parlour and a kitchen, with two chambers above them. In the kitchen, there were only tables and benches, but there was also an 'old kitchen' where he kept his crockery, pot hooks, and other kitchen equipment. In his buttery there was a cupboard, together with five barrels, and other wooden vessels. Unfortunately their contents are not indicated. He also had a boulting house, where he kept his four sieves for sifting grain. His cheese press, and his 'turne' (for spinning) were also there. His inventory was valued at just over £47.[1]

Inventories also describe a few houses of minor gentry. Walter Barnes's 1699 inventory is badly damaged,[2] but it still enables us to see inside the house of one of Stourton's leading Catholics. He probably had both a hall and a parlour (although the inventory is damaged where it should say 'hall'). He certainly had a hall chamber and a parlour chamber, both of them bedrooms. There was also a kitchen and a kitchen chamber, together with a 'high garret chamber and a 'great garet chamber'. All the chambers contained bed and bedding. In the 'passage chamber' there was a chest, and there was probably a bedstead at the top of the stairs. There were also outhouses. The washhouse contained 'three tubbs six houdles four pails two wooden horses and one chees prese'. In the milkhouse there were probably eight cheeses, with a trough, butter churns, 'three hames', and 'other things of small value'. There was 'horse furnityre' for the appraisers to value in the stables, as one might expect.

The most extensive inventory in our period was that of Nathaniel Field, the rector, who died in 1665/6.[3] He was a relatively wealthy man; his appraisers assessed the value of his goods at just over £726. The Rectory was probably larger than any of the other houses in the parish, except for (at that date) Stourton Castle. It had a kitchen, a dairy, a 'smale drinke buttery', a well house, a duck house, a hall, a buttery, a parlour, a parlour chamber, a hall chamber, a kitchen chamber, a maids' chamber, a men's chamber, and a garret. There was also 'ye backside and barne', where wheat, rye, and oats valued at £60 were stored.

Field probably always resided, except when he was thrown out by the Parliamentary forces. His successors did not always do so. John Drew, the pluralist, who had been instituted as rector of Kingston

1   WSHC P2/R100.
2   TNA PROB4/3909.
3   WSHC P1/F/134.

Deverill in 1706, resided there rather than in Stourton. As we have seen, a wing had been renovated in order to be used as a schoolroom in 1722. However, by 1726, the rest of the Rectory and its outbuildings were 'much out of repaire'.[1] The Chancellor of the Diocese being informed, he issued a commission to view the house and to obtain estimates for repairs. Drew must have been unpleasantly surprised when John Farr, the apparitor, delivered the letter informing him of the commission, and suggesting that 'if you think proper you or your agent may appear at the execution and returne of such commission to see the ... dilapidations fairly valued otherwise to make your objections'. Farr had to certify that the letter had been delivered. The estimates for the work needed give us a picture of the rectory as it was then. Like most of the other houses in the parish, the property was thatched; George Howell, the thatcher, estimated that it required seventy 'reed sheefs', which, with other materials and 'workmanship' would cost £2 11s. Plastering needed inside would cost £1 9s 6d, according to the plasterers, Francis Cartwright and Timothy Coney, who seem to have been working with two masons, Andrew Smith and Mathew King; they also stated that one of the barns would cost 1s 6d to repair. It was the oast barn which required most expenditure; two carpenters, Thomas Spinks and Richard Young, costed repairs at £22 11s. Further expenditure was also required outside: Jos Charleton put the cost of work on gates, hedges, and stiles at just over £4.

It is not clear whether the proposed repairs were carried out. The description of the house in the terrier of c.1785 does not seem to tally with the description in Nathaniel Field's inventory. Did Drew react to the commission by having the house re-built? If so, his new house lasted for barely a century; the rectory was rebuilt again in 1820.[2]

Most houses were probably built of timber, although stone was used.[3] Stourton Castle and its Gatehouse were built of stone, although both have long since been demolished. Stourhead was built beside the site of the Castle between 1721 and 1724, and the present Gatehouse is a replica of c.1800. The fourteenth-century house at Bonham may originally have been built of stone, but its sixteenth-century western range is partially timber-framed. Cottages at Long Lane End, built in

---

1   The following paragraph is based on WSHC D/1/61/1/37.
2   Wiltshire Buildings Record B22, pt.2.
3   Much of the information in the following paragraph is from British Listed Buildings Online **www.britishlistedbuildings.co.uk**

the seventeenth century, are also timber framed, although they have been partially rebuilt in stone. The Old Laundry was probably erected in the mid-seventeenth century as a stone cottage. Heath Hill farmhouse is of limestone and brick. Its 1680 datestone is probably a twentieth century replacement, but it was built in the late seventeenth century. The farmhouse at Gasper is built of stone rubble and brick, with a tiled roof; it has a 1718 datestone. In Farmer Lampard's 1744 lease of Stourton Farm, he promised to erect 'another commodious and convenient barn' at Search. A 'great stone barn' was already there, although its demolition was under consideration.[1] Stone was also used for the barn at Stourton Farm whose demolition was being considered in 1744.[2] By 1783, the Rectory was stone under a tiled roof – but it was probably newly built; in 1726, as noted above, it had been thatched.[3]

The use of timber for building ceased when the Hoare's purchased their estate. Stone was readily available in the parish.[4] Greensand could be had from quarries at Bonham and Tucking Mill. Chert was available on the edge of the chalk. Sandstone was quarried at Search. Henry Hoare established a brick kiln at Road Green in 1743, which presumably provided bricks for building work throughout the parish, as well as at Stourhead.[5] The Hoares used tiles when they built new houses, but most of the properties they purchased were thatched – and thatch continued to be renewed throughout our period. That is clear from presentments made in the manorial court.[6] For example, in 1723, Mr Edmund Wadlow was ordered to 'repair his dwelling house by putting some new rafters therein & thatching the same'. In the same court, Mr Edward Bennett's barn was said to be 'much in decay', and he was ordered to repair 'the roof thereof in timber and thatching'. Roger Helliker and Charles Eveleigh were both ordered to repair their dwelling houses 'by thatching ye same' in 1731. Henry Cooper's house was 'very much out of repair for want of thatching' in 1737. When Joseph Lampard's house at Stourton Farm needed repair, he was to pay for 'straw and reed for thatching the dwelling'.[7]

1   WSHC 383/721.
2   WSHC 383/721.
3   WSHC D1/24/193/6; D/1/61/1/37.
4   Wiltshire Buildings Record B22, part 2.
5   WSHC 383/98, p.10; 383/99, p.37.
6   WSHC 383/353.
7   WSHC 383/721.

Water was supplied to most houses by wells; Joseph Lampard had the use of one at Stourton Farm.[1] There are many references to well buckets, ropes, and chains in the inventories. Nathaniel Field, the rector, as noted above, went one better: he had a well house.[2] Water was also available from the River Stour. We have already seen how Henry Hoare agreed to create watering places for cattle at the edge of the pond he was converting into a lake in 1739.[3] John Hill's 1711 will instructed his sons to share access to the 'close through which the water runeth to dip take and carry away water'.[4]

Furniture

Furniture in seventeenth-century houses was sparse. Indeed, in the previous century William Harrison had remarked on 'the great (although not general) amendment of lodging' that had taken place in living memory. 'Our fathers (yea and we ourselves also), have lien full oft upon straw pallets, on rough mats covered only with a sheet, under coverlets made of dagswain or hap harlots ... and a good round log under their heads instead of a bolster or pillow'.[5]

Beds were generally the most important pieces of furniture in our period. Most people had them, although few would have had more than enough for the number of people living in their house. The terminology used to describe them differed from current usage. The bed was merely the mattress, which might be filled with flock (that is, wool dust) or with the probably more comfortable feathers. Both forms of stuffing were cheaply and easily available. The bedstead was the frame on which the bed was placed. The two together formed the 'bed performed', that is, fully set up. The 'bed tye' (mattress case) is occasionally mentioned separately in inventories; it was likely to be made of 'ticking', that is, hard linen.

Bedding included blankets, coverlets (sometimes termed rugs), pillows, bolsters filled with feathers or 'dust', and sheets. Apart from the bolster filling, the materials from which these were made are rarely mentioned. Blankets were probably woollen. 'Pillow tyes', that is, pillow

1   WSHC 383/721.
2   WSHC P1/F/134.
3   See p. 122.
4   WSHC P2/H/1092.
5   Harrison, William. *The Description of England*, ed. Georges Edelen. Ithaca: Cornell University Press, 1968, p.201.

cases, were probably made from a fine linen cloth knowns as Holland, although this is explicitly stated in only a few instances.[1] Pillows were usually filled with feathers. Sheets of linen were probably common. The actual word is not used in the context of bedding, but there were several linen weavers in the parish.[2] In her 1726 'private instructions', Dorothy Barnes gave her 'best holland sheet' to her grandson Walter.[3] Sheets of canvas are also mentioned; canvas was coarse, unbleached cloth made from hemp or flax, and frequently used for supporting mattresses, although it is only mentioned in a few inventories. Agnes Newman was given 'a feather bed with a feather bolster and a feather pillowe a paire of canvas sheetes and a coverlett' in her father's 1632 will.[4] Bolsters were common; like the bed tye, it might be stuffed with feathers, dust, or flock.

There were two main types of bedstead. The standing bedstead, in which the head of the household probably slept, was solidly built. In wealthier households, it might be a four-poster, with curtains and valence around the canopy. Nathaniel Field, the rector, perhaps slept in the 'bedsteed with curtaines & vallains' recorded in his 'hall chamber , and valued at £3 in his inventory.[5] Standing beds might have space underneath for storing the low 'truckle' bedstead, on which servants and children slept. Field had one of these too, in the same room as his own bed. There were also two feather beds, that is, mattresses, two feather bolsters, a pair of 'down pillowes , three pairs of blankets, a rug, and a coverlet, together worth £4 15s. A garrett, perhaps used by another member of the family, contained a standing bed, with a truckle bed, valence, and bedding, together worth £7 18s 4d. Similar bedding, worth no less than £9 15s, was also found in the 'kitchen chamber'.

Field's servants also had decent beds. In the 'Men's Chamber' there were two bedsteads, a flock bed, and a dust bed, together with bolsters, blankets, rugs and a coverlet. The maid's chamber provided female servants with 'one feather bedd one feather boulster one rugg & six paire of blanketts', together worth £4.

1   See, for example, the will of Anthony Newman, 1632, TNA PROB11/178/44; and the inventory of Mathew Combes, 1671; WSHC P2/C/630.
2   For example, Richard Green of Gasper, who died in 1603; cf.WSHC P1/G/333.
3   WSHC P1/B/939.
4   TNA PROB11/178/44.
5   WSHC P1/F/134.

The appraisers of Field's successor, John Derby, did not enumerate his goods room by room when he died in 1671.[1] They simply stated that he had 'seaven feather beds and flock beds with rugs blanketts and coverletts and three shutes of curtaines and vallance , together worth £20.

Francis Jupe was another member of the parish elite, with an inventory valued at £387 6s.[2] In his 'kitching chamber', he had a 'joined' bedstead, that is, it had been made by a joiner with mortice and tenon, and fixed with pegs and dowels rather than nails. It must have been a four-poster, as he also had a valence. In the same room, he also had a truckle bed; beds and bedding together were worth £9 10s. In addition, there was a feather bed (a mattress) with bedding in the parlour. By 1666, when Jupe died, it is probable that his children had left home, so the truckle bed and the feather bed might have been used by servants.

Thomas Barnard, who died in 1681, was another wealthy yeoman. We can deduce that he had two four poster beds, as he had valences in both his hall chamber, and in his chamber within the hall. He also had another 'two half heded bedsteeds'. These had short corner posts, with either no canopy, or one covering only the head of the bed. In 'the Chamber over the Kitchin' he also had 'one flock bed and bedsteed with what beloung to it', although its value is not clear, as it was valued together with 'about seven hundred of cheese' and other items. Walter Barnes[3] had three valences in separate rooms.

When his appraisers valued Thomas Stourton's inventory in 1669, they were very concise.[4] It seems likely that he was living in the house of his brother, Lord Stourton. He had 'one feather bed and bolster' valued at £10, but no bedstead, although we may assume that the very high value included bedding. The bedstead was probably his brother's.

There is no inventory for Charles Evil, but the importance he attached to beds is evident in his will. Beds or valences were bequeathed to six of his children. William received 'the bed & all belonging thereto, except the curtains & valians in the room where I now lie'; the curtains and valence were given to Ann.

The poorer inhabitants also usually had beds, although they were unlikely to be four-posters. In 1558, Thomas Jennens had no bedstead,

1   TNA PROB4/21045.
2   WSHC P2/IJ/143.
3   TNA PROB4/3909.
4   TNA PROB4/6892.

but presumably lay his 'ii floke bedes ii bolsters ii pyllowes on peyre of blanketts iii peyre of shetts ii coverletts ii tabell clothes ii towelles ii pyllowes', valued at one guinea, on the floor. The total value of his goods was £21. In 1667/8, Thomas Sandle had two bedsteads, two dustbeds, and bedding, together with four coffers and a box, worth £2 14s.[1] His goods were valued at £37 8s 2d.

We have already met Mathew Combes, husbandman, whose goods were valued at just over £28 in 1671.[2] He was quite well off for beds. In the 'Parlour Chamber' were '2 flock beds ii feather boulsters iiii feather pillowes ii paire of old blancketts & iiii old coverleds; in the 'kitchinge chamber,' he had 'one old flock bed one old bedsteede one paire of old blancketts ii old coverleds'; at the 'staire head there was another 'old dust bed & bedsteed'.

Even the poorest were able to make provision for sleeping. When Rachel Cheanen died in 1672 she did not have a bedstead, but she did have 'one coverled', 'three paire of old sheets', 'to pellows and one bolster', and 'three pellities' (pillow ties). Together, they were worth 34s 6d. She did not have any other furniture. The rest of her inventory only recorded a few kitchen utensils, plus £3 in cash, perhaps the wages due to her at death if she had been in service. Her total inventory was valued at almost £7.[3]

Tables and seating were generally less prominent than beds in seventeenth century inventories. Most householders, however, had a 'table board', that is, a board with trestles or a frame to support it. They were generally used for dining, although the two 'desks' that Richard Culliford, gent., had may have been used for studying.[4] Householders were also likely to have forms, stools, benches, or chairs to sit at table. As early as 1558/9, Thomas Genyns had 'in the howse on borde a forme ii stooles', together worth a mere 6d.[5] In 1687, John Welch's '1 table board 2 formes 4 cheares' were worth rather more than those owned by Genyns, being valued at 6s.[6] Some decedents had more than one table: in the kitchen of John Hill, yeoman, for example, could be found a 'long table', a 'little table', and a 'dressing table', as well as two forms and five

1   WSHC P2/S/706.
2   WSHC P2/C/630.
3   WSHC P2/C/629.
4   WSHC P1/C/409.
5   WSHC P2/G/5.
6   WSHC P2/W/670.

chairs.[1] In a few houses, benches could also be found; they were long forms with a backrest. In 1607/8 John Riall, husbandman, had one in his parlour, and two in his kitchen.[2] Mary Poor[3] probably inherited her bench from her husband William, who died in 1682.[4]

Chairs were as common as forms, although they could be more expensive. Those owned by wealthier decedents could be fairly elaborate; one rector, Thomas Derby, who died in 1671, had 'fower leather russia chaires one of wrought cloth with two little stooles [footstools?] answerable'. He also had another 'wrought chaire with two low stooles'. Together with other 'lumber', his seating was worth £3.[5] His wealthier predecessor, Nathaniel Field in 1666, had in his parlour 'eight leather framed chaiers and foure stooles', valued at £2 10s, together with two table boards & frames' worth £2.[6] Upstairs, in the parlour chamber, there were another 'five chaires three stooles and one couch worth £2 10s. The hall chamber had a table board, plus 'one couch and two chaires'.

Chairs could be seen as status symbols. Charles Chandler's 'great chair in the hall' which he bequeathed to his son Robert in 1611, was probably reserved for his use. Curiously, Robert was also left 'a new table bord in the loft'.[7] There is no inventory, so we don't know what other furniture Chandler had, but the loft seems to be an odd place for eating in.

Stools were relatively common. They were frequently 'joined stools', that is, they were made by a joiner using mortice and tenon joints, and fixed with pegs and dowels, rather than with nails. In 1608/9, Margaret Porter, widow, had no less than ten joined stools, together with two table boards, a chair, a form, and 'fower cushings'. Robert Jupe had even more; thirteen 'ioynt stools' were listed in his 1675 inventory, which was valued at a modest almost £35.[8] More modestly, John Bradden had '2 tabel boards on forme 3 joyned stooles' together worth £1. The

1   WSHC P2/H/1092.
2   WSHC P2/R100.
3   WSHC P2/P/565.
4   WSHC P2/P/560.
5   TNA PROB11/340/490 & PROB4/21045 .
6   WSHC P1/F/134.
7   WSHC P2/8Reg/168B.
8   WSHC P2/IJ/164.

total value of his 1643/4 inventory was just over £20.[1] Forms, stools, and benches were well within reach of the poorer decedents. Cushions and table cloths were rather less common, although even husbandmen might own the latter. John Genyns, husbandman, had a table cloth worth 1s as early as 1579 .[2] By contrast, Nathaniel Field, the rector, had 'table linnen sheetes and other linnen valued at £55.[3] Table cloths are frequently valued with other linen. John Derby, Field's successor, had 'sixteene paire of sheets six table cloathes and other table linen valued at £5,[4] some of which he bequeathed to his grand-daughter. Napkins were also frequently valued with table cloths; Richard Jupe had '3 tablecloths 1 dozen of napkins and 2 pare of sheets' when he died in 1675.[5] Cushions, by contrast, were only found in a few houses of the wealthier parishioners. Nathaniel Field had a dozen cushions worth £1.[6] But for most of his parishioners, comfort was not a priority.

A variety of other furniture is mentioned in the probate records. William Kenison[7] in 1611 had 'one chest one coffer & one box' woth 6s 8d, together with a 'cubbord'. These were fairly standard items of storage furniture. Thomas Barnard's 1681 inventory[8] noted a 'cheast to cabenets of drawers three boxes one cofer' in his hall chamber. John Hill in 1711 had a trunk in his chamber over the buttery, and two more in his chamber over the kitchen.[9] These storage items were probably used to store clothes, and also valuable items such as deeds, leases, silver spoons, the peeces of gold valued at £34 18s in the 1668 will of John Derby, the rector,[10] and the 'silver plate and gold ring' valued at £10, recorded in Walter Barnes' 1699 inventory.[11]

A few luxury items (in seventeenth century terms!) are mentioned in the probate records. Most curtains were for four-poster beds, to keep the drafts out at night. Window curtains were only found in two houses. Nathaniel Field had them in his parlour chamber (probably where he

1 WHSC P1/B/354.
2 WSHC P2/G/32.
3 WSHC P1/F/134.
4 TNA PROB11/340/490; TNA PROB4/21045.
5 WSHC P2/IJ/164.
6 WSHC P1/F/134.
7 WSHC P2/K/94.
8 WSHC P2/B/990.
9 WSHC P2/H/1092.
10 TNA PROB11/340/490.
11 TNA PROB4/3909.

slept), but his inventory does not mention them in any of the other rooms of the Rectory.[1] Walter Barnes, gent.,[2] one of Stourton's leading Catholics, had a pair of window curtains in one of his rooms in 1699. They did not become common until much later.

Time keeping instruments were another luxury item found in a few Stourton homes. The hour glass mentioned in John Humphreys's inventory has already been mentioned. In 1626, Richard Britten also had one.[3] Although their value was fairly small, only these two were mentioned in inventories. Clocks were much more expensive, another luxury item. The earliest mention of a clock was in Nathaniel Field's 1666 inventory[4]; it was worth £2 5s. Richard Cuffe, yeoman, also had one in 1688/9.[5] So did John Hill, yeoman, in 1711.[6] In 1721, William Maidment left his clock and its case worth £3, along with a variety of other goods, to his son Robert.[7] These men were all members of the parish elite.

Similarly, looking glasses were only found in the homes of the elite. Walter Barnes, gent., had one in his parlour, and another in his parlour chamber – the same room in which he had his window curtains.[8] Nathaniel Field also had one in his parlour chamber, similarly in the same room as his window curtains.[9] There was also one in his hall chamber. In 1681, Thomas Barnard, yeoman, had one in his 'chamber within the hall'.[10] In 1688, Richard Culliford, gent., had two looking glasses.[11]

Lighting, Heating, and the Kitchen

Lighting was provided by light from the fire, and by candles. There are many references to candlesticks in the probate records, although, curiously, they do not mention the tallow which they burnt. The candlesticks were mostly made from brass, copper or pewter. It may

1   WSHC P1/F/134.
2   TNA PROB4/3909.
3   WSHC P2/B/469.
4   WSHC P1/F/134.
5   TNA PROB4/25439.
6   WSHC P2/H/1092.
7   WSHC P2/M/925.
8   TNA PROB4/3909.
9   WSHC P1/F/134.
10 WSHC P2/B/990.
11 WSHC P1/C/409.

be that poorer parishioners relied on rushlights, made from the pith of meadow rushes, and dipped in fat.[1] These cost nothing, so would not have been listed in inventories.

Heating was usually by wood fire. Much of the parish was woodland, so plenty of wood was available. Many inventories refer to 'wood about the house', which in John Baken's case was valued at 6s 8d in 1641.[2] Robert Jupe in 1675 had wood in ye backside worth £3.[3] In 1681, Thomas Barnard, yeoman, had two loads of firewood in his 'backside'.[4] Richard Culliford, yeoman, in 1689 had 'a fagot pile hardwood and cole' valued at £2 6s 8d.[5] John Hill, yeoman, not only had '14 load of wood' in his 'lane and backside'; he also owned part of two wood piles at Pen worth £6.[6] Wood had commercial value, as John Derby recognised when he sued William Sparrow for tithe on faggots in 1671.[7]

There was minimal need for coal to be purchased, although it was probably used by the blacksmiths. We have already seen it mentioned in Richard Culliford's inventory. It is also mentioned in Francis Jupe's 1666 inventory; he had 'wood & coales' in his barton[8]', together with 'boards & other things', valued at £2 10s.

Furse was widely available for the gathering in Stourton, but its value was low, and it was only once recorded in the probate records, although it was probably much used for fuel. 'Wood & furses' valued at £2 were listed in Richard Cuffe's 1688/9 inventory.[9]

The hearth was a focal point in every house, both for heating and for cooking. It was surrounded by fireside implements, and by cooking utensils. The fuel rested on andirons and grates, and the fire was encouraged by bellows. Various pots and other utensils, frequently made of brass, could be hung from the pot-hangings in the chimney, or stood above the fire. Kettles appear in many inventories; they were open cooking pots with handles which could be suspended in the chimney. The skillet was also common; it was a three legged cooking pot with a

1   For these, see Jekyll, Gertrude. *Old English Household Life: some account of cottage objects and country folk.* 1925, p.19-25.
2   WSHC P2/B/673.
3   WSHC P2/IJ/164.
4   WSHC P2/B/990.
5   WSHC P1/C/409.
6   WSHC P2/H/1092.
7   TNA E134/23Chas2/Mich7.
8   WSHC P2/IJ/143.
9   TNA PROB4/25439.

long handle which could be stood above the embers. The cauldron was a larger version with a lid. Brandises and spits were used for griddling and roasting. Dripping pans might be placed under the meat to catch the drips. Chaffing dishes held hot embers, and were used to warm food. Tongs and forks were used to manipulate food above the fire. Cleavers were used to chop up meat. Food was served on platters made of wood or pewter, and eaten with the hands. There was no cutlery in the modern sense. Porringers were bowls, frequently with covers and ear-shaped handles, used for porridge, soup, and similar dishes. At the beginning of our period, many dishes, pots, jugs, porringers, cups, tankards, and similar items were made from wood (sometimes referred to as treen); by its end, most were made from pewter. Wood, however, continued to be used for making the barrels in which parishioners stored their small beer and other alcoholic beverages. Where decedents had a buttery, they were found there rather than in the kitchen.

Food

Only a small amount of information on food can be derived from probate inventories. Appraisers did not list perishable food kept for domestic consumption. They did, however, list food kept for sale, and also mention some of the implements used in food preparation. Inventories also list livestock and arable crops, some of which was destined for the tables of Stourton people. The discussion of agricultural practices in chapter 7 also provides some hints on the availability of food.

An interesting description of provisions in the house can be found in Anthony Newman's 1632 will.[1] He bequeathed to his widow, Anne, 'halfe of all such provision of victuell as oatemeal and other graines, beefe, bacon, butter and cheese, and other dead victual as I shall have at the tyme of my decease'. This is a good summary of the food that most people ate.

Bread was a staple part of the diet, although it is only directly mentioned once in the probate records, when 5s 4d was laid out for it at the funeral of Walter Hill.[2] Stourton's bakers and corn mills have already been discussed,[3] and it is evident that at least some Stourtonians baked their own bread.

1   TNA PROB11/178/44.
2   WSHC P1/H/214.
3   See above, pp. 147-9

Hill's funeral also saw 7s 'layde out for beere', which would have been brewed from malt made with barley. Beer and ale were important parts of the diet in our period, in the absence of clean water. Hill's executors also laid out 17s 2d for 'meete', although it is not specified whether this was pork, mutton, or beef.

Hill's executors also laid out 10d for 'frute'. That quite possibly meant apples, many of which would have been grown in the orchards on the estate. The inventories do mention that Nathaniel Field had an apple roaster, and there is also reference to an 'apple mill & sider presse' worth £2 in William Maidment's 1724 inventory.[1] He, and probably others, were brewing cyder. The mention of 'mault and hoppes' in the 1615 inventory of Thomasine Chandler makes it clear that she too was brewing, probably ale or small beer,[2] which was drunk in preference to water. We have already discussed the alehouses in the parish. Brewers may have been supplied with hops from the hop yard at the Rectory.[3]

There is also mention of 'a garden of cabbeges' in Peter Pitnie's 1612 inventory.[4] Vegetables are almost invisible to the historian. Apart from this mention, the only evidence for them in Stourton is provided by the numerous mentions of gardens in deeds and leases. The importance attached to gardens has already been emphasised; they must have supplied an important part of parishioners' diets.

We have already seen that this was a dairying region. Milk was perishable, and was not listed by appraisers, although it must have been drunk. Much of it was turned into cheese and butter. These were also perishable, but were frequently made for sale, so should have been listed. In 1602, William Tovey's appraisers seem to have been uncertain whether to mention his butter and cheese worth £6; the entry was made, but subsequently scored out.[5] Some other appraisers were not so hesitant. Large quantities of cheese and butter are frequently mentioned; so are cheese presses and butter churns (or barrels). Some examples can be given. Francis Jupe, yeoman, had 'halfe C of cheese' worth £1 10s.[6]

1   WSHC P2/M/925.
2   WSHC P2/C/279.
3   Hobbs, Steven, ed. *Wiltshire glebe terriers 1588-1827*. Wiltshire Record Society 56. 2003, p.406-7.
4   WSHC P2/P/191.
5   WSHC P2/T/58.
6   WSHC P2/IJ/143.

Similarly, in 1711, John Hill, yeoman,[1] had 'halfe one hundred of cheese'. Richard Smart in 1701 had 'two pailes [and] a cheese presse'. He also had 'a parcel of cheese' valued at £2 5s.[2] . In 1667/8, Thomas Sandle had 'chease and baken' worth 10s.[3]

Margaret Porter, widow,[4] was evidently an experienced dairy woman; she had no less than seven cheese vats, as well as a cheese press. In 1641, John Baken had cheese and butter worth 9s.[5] John Bradden had a cheese press and a 'butter horne' in 1680.[6] In 1688, Robert Green, blacksmith,,[7] had 'an old cheese presse', and a 'butter barrell', as well as milk pans. The rectory was well supplied: Nathaniel Field had 'one cheese steand' worth no less than 10s, as well as two butter dishes, three butter tubs, and a butter churn.[8] Walter Barnes, gent., had a butter churn in his milkhouse.[9] In 1692, Richard Charlton had 'an old cheess steen' and 'a butter barrell'.[10]

Poultry and pigs, as already noted, were kept by many householders for domestic consumption. The value of poultry was minimal, so it is likely that many were omitted from inventories. Eggs would have formed a staple part of the diet. Pigs were the main source of meat. Robert Davies' 1622 inventory, valued at £40 4s, included 'on fliche of porke' worth 5s.[11] In 1608/9, Margaret Porter, widow,[12] had four 'flytches of bacon' worth £1 6s 8d. In 1615, Thomasine Chandler[13] had 'bacon and cheeses worth 26s. At the Rectory, Nathaniel Field[14] had no less than 'one bacon racke & 6 flitches of bacon'. Robert Davies's '2 fleches of bacon' were worth 13s 4d. In previous centuries, it is likely that bacon was frequently found hanging from the rafters, to keep it out of the way of vermin. However, in the sixteenth century the more sophisticated bacon

1   WSHC P2/H/1092.
2   WSHC P1/S/666.
3   WSHC P2/S/706.
4   WSHC P2/P/164.
5   WSHC P2/B/673.
6   WSHC P2/B/959.
7   WSHC P2/G/518.
8   WSHC P1/F/134.
9   TNA PROB4/3909.
10 WSHC P1/C/424.
11 WSHC P2/D/133.
12 WSHC P2/P/164.
13 WSHC P2/C/279.
14 WSHC P1/F/134.

rack was increasingly coming into vogue. The wealthy rector, Nathaniel Field, owned one. Walter Barnes, gent., had 'one bacon racke with bacon theron', worth c.£2[1] But ownership was not restricted to the wealthy. Richard Charlton,[2] whose inventory was valued at a mere £28 2s 8d in 1692, also had one. So did Robert Green in 1687,[3] and John Hill in 1711.[4] They were both blacksmiths, so had probably made them themselves.

The wealthier might also eat beef. We have already seen that Anthony Newman bequeathed beef to his widow. Beef does not recur as frequently in the inventories as bacon, but it is mentioned. Robert Green's 'baken & beef' were valued together at £1 6s 8d.[5] Robert Jupe[6] and John Hill[7] both had beef forks, presumably used to eat beef. Mutton was also available from the numerous sheep kept by Stourton's farmers, although they were kept primarily for their wool. Mutton is not mentioned in inventories, perhaps because the value of a flitch was too low. The four quarters of mutton alleged to have been stolen by Robert Smart in 1741 were valued at 3s 3d.[8]

For the parish elite (and indeed for poachers), venison was readily available. Stourton Park was well stocked with fallow deer – so well stocked that in 1546 the seventh Lord Stourton had been able to accuse a new keeper appointed by his steward, William Hartgill, of losing 100 of them.[9] In 1549, Hartgill, writing to Sir John Thynne, counter-charged that Lord Stourton's men 'make the King's Forest to be my Lord Stourton's purlewe'.[10] In 1613 Robert Barnes, gent., was accused in Star Chamber of illegal hunting in Selwood Forest.[11] The charge may have been trumped up by Sir Maurice Berkeley in retaliation for a previous Star Chamber case brought by Lord Stourton

1 TNA PROB4/3909.
2 WSHC P1/C/424.
3 WSHC P2/G/518.
4 WSHC P2/H/1092.
5 WSHC P2/G/518.
6 WSHC P2/IJ/164.
7 WSHC P2/H/1092.
8 WSHC A1/150/19
9 Mowbray, Baron. *The History of the Noble House of Stourton, of Stourton, in the County of Wilts*. 1899. p.307.
10 Jackson, J.E. 'Charles, Lord Stourton and the murder of the Hartgills', *Wiltshire Archaeological and Natural History Magazine* 8, 1864, p.292.
11 TNA STAC 8/73/13.

against his own servants.[1] Barnes claimed to be keeper of Stourton Park, and as such, entitled to hunt there. The Park, as already noted, had been enlarged by John, the 9th Lord. A deer leap had been devised which enabled deer from Selwood Forest to enter, but not to escape back into the Forest.[2]

The lords of Stourton also maintained a warren, as has already been seen. Rabbits would have featured frequently on the table at Stourhead

The elite – and probably others – also had access to fish. Medieval lords had created a series of fishponds in Six Wells Bottom, and the Hoare's development of the lake at the end of our period is likely to have resulted in the availability of more fish.

It has already been noted that the lords of the manor claimed fishing rights for the whole length of the River Stour, from Stourton to the sea. One wonders whether the 5s 3d spent on 'fish sent to Stourton' in 1722/3 was actually spent on purchasing fish, or whether it related to the fish caught when Henry Hoare formally exercised his right to fish at Sturminster Newton in that year.[3]

All these elite foods would probably also have been found on the tables of many local poachers! Reference has already been made to a number of cases in Chancery which concerned, inter alia, the 'poaching' of rabbits. In 1685, when John Welch was examined, presumably on suspicion of poaching, he reported the mysterious regular disappearance of his nag: 'last night his nag was taken out of his ground and in the next morning put into his ground againe'. Such disappearances (if that is what they were!) had occurred on several previous occasions. 'He doth suppose it was some hunters that did it!'[4] A little over a century later, the 'justicing book' kept by Sir Richard Colt Hoare contains many references to poaching, and it is unlikely that its incidence had changed much in the intervening half century.[5]

Clothing

Clothing was obviously important to Stourtonians, but unfortunately it is not possible to say much about it from local evidence.

1   TNA STAC8/256/26.
2   TNA STAC8/256/26.
3   WSHC 383/58; 383/97.
4   Somerset Heritage Centre Q/SR/161/13.
5   WSHC 383/955 .

Most inventories simply refer to 'wearing apparell', occasionally describing it as made from wool or linen, and generally valuing it at under £3 (although sometimes its value is not clear because it was valued with 'money in his purse'). Richard Green's 'wearing apparill' was valued at £10 in 1704, but he was a linen weaver, so perhaps kept some clothes for sale.[1] The £30 at which the rector Nathaniel Field's 'wearing apparrell' were valued in 1666 was exceptional, but, as we have seen, so was his wealth.[2] Amongst his clothes was a 'suit of damaske' which he gave to his daughter Elizabeth. Damask was a rich silk fabric, woven with an elaborate design. The value of his clothes was only exceeded by those owned by his aristocratic contemporary, Thomas Stourton,[3] valued at £40 in 1669.

In a few inventories there is a little more information. In 1579, John Genyns,[4] husbandman, bequeathed his 'brone hollen dublette and my beste stockens' to his father, and his 'leather dublette my russett jerkings a payer of breeches, two payer of stockinges and my best shoes' to Gasper Smart. The doublet was the typical male dress, a close fitting garment, perhaps with detachable sleeves, and worn with hose, that is, breeches and stockings forming a single garment reaching from waist to toe. The jerkin was a short jacket, perhaps made of leather. His 'wearing apparrell' are not mentioned in Genyns' inventory, so its value is not known.

In his 1589 inventory, John Bradden's appraisers listed 'one cote too dublets to pere of hoise and a hate a peer of showes', all valued at 3s.[5] Bradden was one of the poorest decedents, with an inventory valued at just over £3.

In 1591 Edmund Davies[6] had 'ii gownes ii pettecords & a wastcote' worth £1, plus 'a cloake a hatt a paire of hose & shoes' valued at 5s. His 'pettecords' were probably small waistcoats worn under an outer garment.

Alicia Green,,[7] who died in 1700, was the only woman whose apparel was described in the probate records. She left 'one petticoate with

1 WSHC P1/G/333.
2 WSHC P1/F/134.
3 TNA PROB4/6892.
4 WSHC P2/G/32.
5 WSHC P2/B/115.
6 WSHC P2/D/41.
7 TNA PROB11/458/186.

a blue pockett ... my longest holland apron and one bonelace napkin that is my best' to her daughter Jane. Her grand-daughter, Hannah, received 'one black serge gowne and one redd petticoate with redd and blew lace', and 'a couple of my best changes and one suite of my lynnen and one great white whittle and one holland apron'. Her 'petticoates' were skirts worn externally. 'Changes' were fabrics of changeable colours, possibly silk. The 'whittle' was a cloak.

Weapons

The inhabitants of early modern Stourton lived in a violent age. We have already seen how the retainers of Lord Stourton and Sir Maurice Berkeley clashed in the Forest of Selwood, and how Richard Bayley, one of Lord Stourton's keepers, suffered several injuries in consequence, one by the thrust of a pike.[1] Many years later, Mr John King's eye was 'struck out ... with a cudgel' on the road between Silton and Gasper in 1707.[2]

The retainers of Sir Maurice Berkeley were accused of carrying swords, daggers, long pikes, bows and arrows, 'and other unlawfull weapons' in a Star Chamber bill.[3] It may be supposed that such weapons were common in Stourton, although they are rarely mentioned in our documentation. We know that John Kerbey had 'a wepon called holie water springes' in 1603.[4] Quite what that was is not clear. John Rose had a 'bowe' worth three shillings in 1619.[5] Almost a century later, in 1711, John Hill had two guns.[6] In 1748/9, William Evil bequeathed 'a bras of pistols & all belong there unto' in 1748/9; he also had a 'short gun'.[7] These weapons were probably primarily intended for hunting, although, as we have seen, they could also be used for affray. Such weapons would also have been useful during the Civil War. We have seen that Stourton Castle was besieged and made uninhabitable in 1644[8]; its occupants would have had weapons to defend themselves. Weapons and armour

1 TNA STAC8/256/26; STAC8/73/13.
2 Somerset Heritage Centre Q/SR/244/5.
3 TNA STAC8/256/26.
4 WSHC P2/K/72.
5 WSHC P2/R/144.
6 WSHC P2/H/1092.
7 WSHC P2/E/340.
8 Firth, C.H., ed. *The Memoirs of Edmund Ludlow, Lieutenant General of the Horse in the Army of the Commonwealth of England, 1625-1672.* Clarendon Press, 1898. Vol.1, p.97.

would also have been needed for Stourton's participation in the irregular musters which took place whenever the country was threatened by war. The constable would have had charge of the parish armour, although minimal evidence relating to this survives. All we know is that Richard Rogers had a hauberk, that is, a coat of mail, in 1602.[1] That was a useful piece of armour to take to musters.

Leisure

Not much is known of how Stourtonians enjoyed their leisure in our period. Most of them probably had little leisure, although the annual church ale at Pentecost was a highlight of the year. We have already seen that the tenant of the Court House was required to allow the churchwardens access to 'brew and bake' for this event. Another annual event was the fair at Whitesheet Hill. It ran for three days. In 1726 seventeen of the stallholders agreed to pay 2s 6d each to fund 'some diversions', such as 'cudgiling or a plate to be run for'.[2]

Other sports engaged in by parishioners included tennis and bowling, both of which were probably for the parish elite rather than the lower orders. Tennis was presumably played on the 'tennice court' which adjoined the Court House in the late seventeenth century'.[3] There was a bowling green for the Lord of the manor at Stourton House at the beginning of the eighteenth century.[4] The only other sport mentioned in the records is football: in June 1648, Walter Tabor 'went unto a football match'.[5]

Leisure time could also be occupied by playing games at table. Margaret Porter in 1609 had 'a payre of playinge tables'. These were presumably for playing cards or some similar pursuit.

Music was another minority interest. In 1600, John Kerbey had 'two basse viols & a treble' worth 6s 8d.[6] He may have been part of a village band accompanying church services.

Books rarely feature in inventories. The major exception to this rule was Nathaniel Field, the rector, who possessed an extensive library

1   WSHC P2/R/77.
2   WSHC 383/903.
3   WSHC 383/97, f.17.
4   WSHC 383/737.
5   WSHC A1/110/T1648, 116.
6   WSHC P2/K/72.

when he died in 1666.[1] He used his books to write a biography of his father, as we shall see in the next chapter. His successor, John Derby, gave 'all my bookes notes and papers of my studdy except some English bookes' to Mathew Derby in return for acting as overseer of his will, but they were valued, together with his 'weareing cloathes' and 'some other small things in his studdy', at a mere £10. It is reasonable to assume that there were also books in Stourton House, and in other gentlemen's houses. It has already been noted that Francis Faugoin, the steward at Stourhead, purchased a copy of Jean de Quintinye's *Compleat Gard'ner* in 1736.[2]

Few below the rank of the gentry owned books, although the fact that most of the probate records were written by local people makes it obvious that many Stourtonians were literate. The only books recorded in the probate records were those owned by Richard Rogers, gent., in 1602, which were worth 4s,[3] those listed in John Rose's 1620 inventory, worth 2s,[4] and the six owned by John Humphrey in 1673,[5] which had no great value; they were lumped together with a variety of other goods and furniture together valued at £1 13s 5d. Parishioners were much more likely to use their literacy in business transactions than in reading; for example, Thomas Barnard,[6] yeoman, had 'book debts' amounting to 10s when he died in 1681. Similarly, Robert Sandle, cordwainer, in 1686 had 'mony due upon booke lying in desperit debts' amounting to £11.[7] Both presumably recorded their debts in a 'book'. Robert Green, the blacksmith, was also keeping a 'shop book' when he died in 1687.[8] Thirty years later, in 1711, the 'mortgages bonds bills and book debts' of John Hill, yeoman, were valued at over £135.[9]

The only books which most parishioners were likely to read were the *Bible* and the *Book of Common Prayer*. Mary Poor, widow, had both when she died in 1681; her copies were worth 2s 6d.[10] John Stroud, tanner, owned two bibles, 'my best bible', and 'my little bible', both

1   WSHC P1/F/134.
2   http://catalogue.swanngalleries.com/ (search 'Quintinye')
3   WSHC P2/R/77.
4   WSHC P2/R/144.
5   WSHC P2/H/706.
6   WSHC P2/B/990.
7   WSHC P2/S/932.
8   WSHC P2/G/518.
9   WSHC P2/H/1092.
10 WSHC P2/P/565.

of which he bequeathed in 1685.[1] These were not mentioned in his inventory, but one of them may have been the bible mentioned in the inventory of his executor, his brother James; it was worth 4s.[2] It is likely that many others also had their own bibles and prayer books, but their value was low, and appraisers may not have bothered to list them. It is likely, too, that many parishioners bought chap-books from pedlars at their door, but these were ephemeral, and almost certainly not worth listing.

Conclusion

Probate inventories are the prime source for information on the material goods of Stourton's inhabitants in our period. However, when John Coake purchased Robert Tabor's cottage in 1717, he also purchased its contents.[3] The list of items sold included 'two beds and bedsteds and all furniture thereunto belonging'; there were also a variety of kitchen utensils such as pewter dishes, brass kettles, and a chaffing dish, together with storage furniture such as a chest and a trunk. The furniture included a table board, three chairs, and three 'joyned stools'. Comfort was provided by 'one brass warming pan'. The entire contents cost him 5s. These goods were probably typical of what might be found in all the cottages in Stourton in the early eighteenth century

1 WSHC P2/S/939.
2 WSHC P2/S/960.
3 WSHC 383/726

10
Religious Life in Stourton: Anglicans and Catholics

RELIGION DIVIDED STOURTON in our period. The Stourton family were patrons of the living until they sold up, and were devout Catholics. In the early years of the sixteenth century, they executed an ambitious building programme in the church, probably erecting the porch, raising the roof to install clerestory windows, creating a chantry chapel, and extending the chancel.[1] However, after the Reformation, their devotion to the old religion probably caused them to neglect their parish church – although they were still buried there. According to Jane Hoare, writing in 1736/7, 'the service of God [was] sadly neglected when dear Mr Hoare [Jane's husband] first came hither'.[2] That was in 1717. Hoare was a devout Anglican; his widow said that he 'used his utmost endeavours to have it performed with that regard as it ought to be'. He spent much money on renovating the church, and Jane thought it 'my duty to follow his example and to perpetuate the method of worship we are in at present'. As we shall see, her will founded a charity to effectuate that purpose.

Meanwhile, the Stourton family continued to provide the facilities needed for Roman Catholic worship to continue in the parish. At the same time as Lord Stourton sold the manor of Stourton, his brother Thomas built a chapel at Bonham, and his heirs continued to support a priest there until the mid-twentieth century.[3]

1   Calland, Gary. *St. Peter's Stourton: a tour and history of the church.* Henry Cadogan Hoare, 2010, p.53.
2   Stourhead House Research Room folder C.1.
3   For a useful account of the Stourton mission, see WANHS mss 1370. Bernadette, Sister. *Some aspects of Catholic Life in Wiltshire 1660-1850, with particular reference to the family and village of Stourton.* B.Ed dissertation, 1976.

The Reformation was not appreciated by the people of Stourton.[1] The chantry founded by William, 5th Lord Stourton in the north aisle (referred to as the chapel of the Blessed Virgin Mary in his 1522 will) was closed down,[2] and the chaplain appointed to pray for his soul dismissed. The property at Maiden Bradley and Yarnfield which funded it was sold by the Crown, with other chantry property, to Edward Dyer in 1585.[3] The chantry chapel became the north aisle. In 1552, the Edwardian Commissioners removed four bells from the church.[4] In 1553, as the reign of Edward VI drew to a close, the churchwardens presented that 'the body of the church is in decay. They had no service this half year. They have no carpet for the Lord's table, or napkins for the bread. The churchyard is in decay. They have no church stock'.[5] This presumably meant that Edwardian injunctions to remove idols and whitewash walls had been implemented, although it was left to Henry Hoare to remove the rood screen, which was still there when he purchased the manor in 1717.

The Edwardian rector, William Walsh, presumably felt unable to conduct Cranmer's services – so he refused to conduct any services at all. The people of the parish took their lead from the attitude of the 8th Lord Stourton, who was an ardent Catholic, and, indeed, the author of two theological treatises. He was much more in tune with the approach Queen Mary was to take – and with popular attitudes. On Mary's accession, he was rewarded with the Lord Lieutenancy of three counties – but, sadly, threw away his promising prospects by murdering his late father's steward, and suffered execution.

The course of the Reformation in Stourton can be followed to a limited extent in the religious preambles used by testators in their wills. In 1522, William Lord Stourton left his soul 'to the Allmighty Father, the Blessed Mary, and all her saints'.[6] In his will of 1551/2 – under the Edwardian Protestant regime – Augustine Bassyngay omitted mention

1   For another discussion of the Reformation in Stourton, see Calland, op cit, p.54-61.
2   In his will he asked to be buried there; cf. TNA PROB11/21/319..
3   Neal, Simon R. *Calendar of patent rolls 28 Elizabeth I, 1585-86. C66/1271-1285.* List & Index Society 294. 2002, p.104 & 113.
4   TNA E315/514, f.25.
5   Calland, op cit, p.57.
6   TNA PROB11/21/319.

of Mary and the saints.[1] But in 1557 Edward Parott, writing during Queen Mary's Catholic reign, mentioned 'the whole company of heaven'.[2] Bequests of the soul mentioning the Virgin Mary, the saints, and the 'whole company of heaven' are indicative of Catholic beliefs. So are bequests such as Thomas Parett's 1557 gift of 'one wether shepe' to 'the sepulcre light in my parishe churche of Stowrton'.[3] Thomas Jennen's 1557/8 will was the last Stourton will to mention 'our blessed Lady Seynt Mary and ... the holy company of heaven'.[4] Henceforth, bequests of the soul usually follow the standard protestant formulation seen in William Britten's 1562/3 will: 'My soule to Almightie God my maker and redemer'. The abandonment of the old formulation, however, did not necessarily mean the abandonment of Catholic doctrine. When John, 9th Lord Stourton, died in 1588, he used the new formulation,[5] but, as we will see, his sympathies were with the old religion.

In 1558, in neighbouring Mere, the accession of Elizabeth, and the expectation of some 'alteracon of some pte of Relygyon', caused 'some varyannce and contencon' amongst the parishioners, an inability to elect new churchwardens, and an unwillingness to hold 'ales' or other fund raising. Stourton parishioners would have shared these concerns, although they may not have followed Mere's example in purchasing an English bible, with 'a boke of the comunyon, iii books of the psalter, and too other bokes to syng the suyce yn', during the following year. The Mere churchwardens' accounts also record 'the takyng downe' of the altar and the rood loft in 1559.[6] Stourton's rood loft, as already noted, stayed put for another century and a half.

John, 9th Lord Stourton was an infant when his father was executed in 1557. He was brought up as a Roman Catholic, but was stopped when, at the age of 22, he tried to flee the country. He was confined to Lambeth Palace, under the watchful eye of Archbishop Parker, for re-education in Protestantism. In 1575, he reluctantly agreed to conform, and took up his seat in the House of Lords. In 1584, he gave 12d to Mere church 'for a peale' to be rung. In 1590, his heir gave Mere church a further

1   WSHC P2/2Reg/167d.
2   WSHC P2/3Reg/15C.
3   WSHC P2/3Reg/24C.
4   WSHC P2/3Reg/94D
5   TNA PROB11/73/395.
6   Baker, T.H. 'The churchwardens' accounts of Mere', *Wiltshire Archaeological and Natural History Magazine* 35(110), 1908, p.29-31.

3s 4d.[1] His name – and those of 'his brethren' - are included on a list of supporters drawn up on behalf of Mary Queen of Scots in 1574 and 1582.[2] But he was forced to be one of the Commissioners for her 1586 trial.

Despite his use of a protestant will formulation, the 9th Lord's will craved pardon 'for his great offences'. He is said to have expressed great remorse at being unable to receive the rites of the Roman church when he died, as there was no priest available to shrive him. Indeed, when Father Cornelius was saying mass for his soul, the recusant priest was said to have seen a vision of him in purgatory, desiring his prayers, and asking his mother to have prayers said for him.[3]

His successor, as far as we know, had no such regrets. It is unclear how the 10th Lord Stourton continued to foster Catholicism in an era when harbouring a Catholic priest was a capital felony, and when failure to attend church could result in a fine of £20 per month. No records were kept. But we do know that a relative, William Stourton (perhaps the son of the seventh Lord), accused of recusancy, was thought to be in hiding in Somerset in 1592.[4]

When records do commence, we find that Stourton had a flourishing Catholic community. Edward, 10th Lord Stourton was determined to maintain as safe a haven for his faith as he could. His mother, the widow of the executed Lord, who had re-married Lord Arundel, hosted the martyr Father Cornelius in London, and subsequently in Chideock, for over a decade before he was discovered and executed in 1594.[5] Edward was his mother's son in this respect. Father Cornelius had conducted mass daily at Chideock, and Edward had been a regular attender.[6]

It is likely that Father Cornelius visited Stourton. Other priests certainly did. We know that the 9th Lord Stourton was maintaining two

1   Ibid, p.76 & 213-4.
2   Wainewright, J.Bannerman, ed. 'Two lists of Influential Persons, apparently prepared in the interests of Mary Queen of Scots, 1574 and 1582', *Miscellanea 8*. Catholic Record Society, 13. 1913, p.90 & 139.
3   Challoner, Bishop. *Memoirs of missionary priests and other Catholics of both sexes that have suffered death in England on religious accounts, from the year 1577 to 1684*. Philadelphia: John T.Green, 1839, p.184.
4   Mowbray, Baron. *The History of the Noble House of Stourton, of Stourton, in the County of Wilts*. 1899, v.i, p.321.
5   Foley, Henry. *Records of the English Province of the Society of Jesus*. Burns & Oates, 1878. Vol.3. p.450-51.
6   Foley, op cit, vol.3, p.458.

priests in 1588, although neither was present when he died. A few years after Cornelius's execution, Richard Bray converted Edward's nephew, John Rogers, who was serving another Lady Stourton (a daughter of the Catholic Treshams of Northamptonshire) as tutor to her children. It may be that their chance meeting occurred at Stourton. Rogers entered the English College at Rome in 1604, and had a long career as a Jesuit priest.[1] Bray may also have been responsible for the conversion of the son of the Stourton family's neighbour at Godminster, Edward Cottington.[2]

Despite leadership from the Stourtons, the Church of England gradually attracted the loyalty of many parishioners. The troubles of the Reformation resulted in a rapid turnover of rectors.[3] William Stacy was presented by William Lord Stourton, and served as rector from 1541 to 1551. He probably did not know how to respond to the Reformation. His successor, Walter Walsh, presented by Sir William Fauntleroy (acting on behalf of the late Lord Stourton) lasted from 1551 until the end of 1555, when he resigned. Richard Williamson was presented by Lord Stourton, and instituted immediately, but nothing more is known of him. Nor is anything known of the 'Sir Edmund', described as 'now curatt at Stowrton' in the 1560/61 will of Alexander Davies.[4]

After the accession of Elizabeth, and throughout the seventeenth century, the Stourtons continued to own the advowson; in 1705 the rector stated that 'the Lord Stourton was 'the undoubted patron'.[5] It was said to be worth £600 in 1704.[6] The penal laws prohibited Roman

1   Kenny, Anthony, ed. *The Responsa Scholarum of the English College at Rome, part 1: 1598-1621.* Catholic Record Society 54. 1962, p.148; Foley, Henry. *Records of the English Province of the Society of Jesus.*Burns & Oates, 1878. Vol.4, p.419; Anstruther, Godfrey, *The Seminary Priests: a Dictionary of the Secular Clergy of England and Wales. II. Early Stuart 1603-1659.* Great Wakering: Mayhew-McCrimmon, 1975, p.269.

2   Kenny, Anthony, ed. *The Responsa Scholarum of the English College at Rome, part 1: 1598-1621.* Catholic Record Society 54. 1962, p.65-6; Raymond, Stuart A. 'Catholic Families of South-East Somerset and their connection to Stourton, c.1550-1650'. Unpublished paper.

3   For the succession of rectors, see the Clergy of the Church of England Database **http://theclergydatabase.org.uk**.

4   WSHC P2/4Reg/70C.

5   WSHC 413/450. The Papist return of 1706 made the same comment; cf. D1/9/1/2.

6   WSHC 383/255.

Catholics from presenting clergy, but it may be that Lord Stourton still had influence; at any rate, it was noted in the 1704 valuation that 'the next turne be granted'.

Late sixteenth-century presentments were made by the Crown. Roger Audley was presented by the Crown, and instituted in 1560.[1] He was deprived by the arch-protestant, Bishop Jewell, in 1566, and succeeded by John King. Thus began the century long incumbency of a clerical dynasty.

The first John King[2] was from a Norfolk family; he became a fellow of his Cambridge college in 1556.[3] After 1567 he held Stourton in plurality with Taplow, Buckinghamshire,[4] and became a canon of Windsor in 1580. King was particularly well connected with the Protestant establishment; one of the overseers of his will was Richard Field. Field was sufficiently eminent to be mentioned in the *Oxford Dictionary of National Biography*. His second wife was Archbishop Cranmer's great-niece. He attended the Hampton Court conference, which led to the production of the Authorised version of the Bible. His son Nathaniel, whom we have already met, subsequently became rector of Stourton.

We do not know a great deal about what John King did in Stourton, but it is probable that he was the man initially responsible for propagating protestant doctrine in the parish. Bishop Jewell realised that he needed someone of standing in the parish, in view of the Catholic proclivities of its lords.

King may have disappointed Jewell. In 1584, the churchwardens presented him because he 'hath made but ii sermons wth us this yeare'.[5] The only substantial evidence we have of King's activities is the parish register, which he began to keep in 1570. This does show that, whilst many families withdrew from participating in Anglican baptisms and marriages, more preferred to continue frequenting their parish church. The fact that these routine celebrations took place in the parish

1 Only his name is given in Cambridge Corpus Christi College Parker Mss 097.
2 Morrison, George Austin. 'Richard King 1616-1668', *Notes & Queries for Somerset & Dorset*, 12, 1911, p.261-2 & 293-6. Morrison provides the basis for many of the following biographical details.
3 *Alumni Cantabrigiensis*
4 He was granted a dispensation to hold the two benefices in plurality in 1595, 'not withstanding insufficient qualification'; cf *Calendar of state papers domestic, Elizabeth 1595-1597*. H.M.S.O., 1869, p.5.
5 WSHC D1/43/5.

church gave the rector the advantage. And for burials, Catholics had no alternative to the parish graveyard.

The rector died childless in 1607, and was buried at Windsor. As well as naming Dr. Field as his overseer, he named his cousin, another John King, as executor. This cousin was also bequeathed his books and sermons, and succeeded him as rector of Stourton.

Born in 1576, this second John King was a fellow of Merton College Oxford, and tutor to the Earl of Essex.[1] He was presented to Stourton by James I,[2] subsequently becoming a canon of Westminster in 1613, and of Windsor in 1615.[3] His first wife, Elizabeth Foxcroft, presented him with seven children baptised at Stourton. Two died in infancy; another in his early twenties. The eldest, John, graduated from Christ Church, Oxford, as a Master of Arts in 1632.[4] In 1649, he was bequeathed 1,000 pieces of eight in his brother Nicholas's will, but nothing more is known of him. Nicholas was a wealthy merchant living in Seville, who also bequeathed a substantial amount to the poor of Stourton.[5] Richard, another brother, also became wealthy. He was apprenticed to Gilbert Kynder, a London mercer, in 1634,[6] and served as sheriff of London for part of 1657.[7]

Rachel was the only daughter of John King to survive to adulthood. She married Nathaniel Field, the son of the overseer of the first John King's will. On their marriage (probably in 1631), Rachel's father secured appointment for himself to the rectory of Islip (Oxfordshire). He also acquired the right to present to his former rectory, and presented his new son-in-law to succeed him at Stourton.[8] That was a suitable dowry for a clerical family.

Nathaniel Field was born in 1600, probably brought up at Burghclere (Hampshire), graduated from New College Oxford in 1621,

1   Foster, Joseph. *Alumni Oxoniensis ... 1500-1714*. James Parker & Co., 1891, vol.2, p.852.
2   Calland, op cit, p.66.
3   According to the *Alumni Cantabrigiensis*, he was also rector of Whitford in Flintshire. However, this is not confirmed by the Clergy of the Church of England Database **http://theclergydatabase.org.uk**.
4   Foster, op cit, vol.2, p.852.
5   TNA PROB11/209/163.
6   Records of London's Livery Companies Online **www.londonroll.org**
7   Stow, John. *A Survey of the Cities of London and Westminster, Borough of Southwark, and parts adjacent*. Vol 2 (book 4). J.Read, 1735, p.82.
8   Williams, Barrie, ed. *The subscription book of Bishops Tounson and Davenant, 1620-1640*. Wiltshire Record Society 32. 1977, p.54.

became a fellow in 1625, and was ordained deacon and priest at Oxford in 1628; he published a substantially revised second edition of his father's *Of the Church* in the same year. He became a canon of Chichester the year after he was instituted at Stourton. It was probably whilst he was rector of Stourton that he wrote his father's biography. The book was not published until 1716, long after Nathaniel's death.[1]

Field was presumably evicted from his incumbency at Stourton during the civil war, as his name appears in Matthews' biographical dictionary of 'sufferers'.[2] He evidently recovered, at least financially, after the Restoration: his probate inventory was valued at £726 in 1665/6.[3] His brother-in-law's legacy to his wife of 500 pieces of eight would have helped him to get through the Interregnum, and perhaps contributed to this valuation.

Three children, John, Elizabeth, and Richard were baptised in Stourton between 1636 and 1648. John presumably pre-deceased his father; when Nathaniel made his will, he only mentioned Elizabeth and Richard. Curiously, Elizabeth obtained a marriage licence in 1664 to marry Richard Batt of the Inner Temple (and also of East Chinnock, Somerset).[4] However, her father's will gives her maiden name. The marriage evidently did not proceed, since she subsequently married John Abington of Over Compton (Dorset)[5] Another daughter, whose name we do not know, was neither baptised at Stourton, nor mentioned directly in the will. Presumably, she too died before her father. She had married a Grenewell; Nathaniel gave substantial bequests to her children, Rachel, Anne, and Nathaniel Grenewell.

Richard, Nathaniel's son, was granted a 21 year lease of land in East Enbourne, Berkshire, by the Dean and Canon of St. George's Chapel, Windsor, in 1661.[6] That demonstrates his father's connections. He became a Cambridge don, and was appointed a fellow by charter of

1   *Some Short Memorials Concerning the Life of that Reverend Divine Doctor Richard Field.* 1716.
2   Matthews, A.G. *Walker revised, being a revision of John Walker's sufferings of the clergy during the Grand Rebellion, 1642-60.* Clarendon Press, 1948, p.362.
3   WSHC P1/F/134.
4   Sarum Marriage Licence Bonds **www.findmypast.co.uk**; Inner Temple Admissions Database **www.innertemplearchives.org.uk/detail.asp?id=14101**
5   The parish of her husband is given in the marriage licence bond.
6   Dalton, John Neale, ed. *The manuscripts of St George's Chapel, Windsor Castle.* Dean & Chapter of St. George's Chapel, 1957, p.313.

James II in 1687.[1] Rachel Field was buried 4th April 1664, her husband, Nathaniel, on 22nd March 1665/6.

In the following century, there were only four rectors, two of them from the same family. John Derby was instituted in 1666, John Drew in 1671, his son, also John Drew, in 1714, and John Hill in 1727. Derby's incumbency was the shortest in our period, lasting a mere five years. He claimed to be an MA,[2] but there is no record of this in either of the two university biographical dictionaries. Derby was a local man, born in Yeovil, and brought up in Gillingham; he left twenty shillings to the poor of both places, as well as twenty shillings to the poor of Stourton 'where I hope to be buried'.[3] He was presented by a Gillingham yeoman, Thomas Phillips. The parish register records his burial on 28th December 1671, but does not otherwise mention his family. His will only mentions one daughter, Jane, who had married Thomas Ianns; she was named executor of his will, and her daughter Mary received a substantial legacy. His inventory was valued at £181 10s. Like Nathaniel Field, he too had books, but they were lumped together with 'weareing cloathes' and other small thinges in his studdy' valued altogether at £10.

Derby's successor, John Drew, came from Bruton, and took his BA at Oxford in 1661, aged 18[4] (although he was said to be aged 'abve 46 yeares of age' in c.1693[5]), ordained deacon in Wells Cathedral in 1665, and served as curate of Lamyat before his institution at Stourton, to which he was presented by Edward Morris in 1672. The bishop also granted him a licence to preach throughout the diocese.[6] He and his wife, Dorothy, had one son, John, baptised on 10th March 1673/4. Dorothy was buried 22nd December 1698.

It is not clear when Dorothy's husband died, but he was succeeded by his son (also John) in 1714.[7] The new rector had taken his BA at Oxford in 1694, and his MA at Cambridge in 1706. In that year, he became rector of Kingston Deverill,[8] and after 1714 held both rectories in plurality until he died in 1728. He had five children, one of whom died

1   *Alumni Cantabrigiensis*
2   WSHC D1/2/22.
3   TNA PROB11/340. For his inventory, see PROB4/21045.
4   *Alumni Oxoniensis*
5   WSHC 383/352.
6   WSHC D1/17/1.
7   Clergy of the Church of England database **http://theclergydatabase.org.uk**
8   *Alumni Cantabrigiensis*

in infancy. Another, George, was serving as a 'marine soldier' aboard HMS Namur when he made his will in 1747.[1]

The next rector was John Hill, the son of Osmund Hill of Mere.[2] John took his BA at Oxford in 1708 aged 22.[3] He served as schoolmaster at Mere from 1708, at a salary of £25 per annum,[4] becoming curate to John Drew in 1724. When Drew died, Hill was presented to Stourton by his father, and instituted in 1727. The right to next presentation had been purchased from Sir Thomas Meres before 1717, when the latter had been lord of the manor.[5] The deed described Osmund as a gentleman, but elsewhere we learn that he was a barber (probably a surgeon); he may have been the 'Mr Hill' who took a standing at White Sheet fair in 1726.[6]

The rector had seven sons and five daughters. The eldest, John, was baptised at Mere in 1714. Another, Henry, died as a baby in 1727. Thomas followed his father into the church; he took his BA at Cambridge in 1743/4,[7] and was serving his father as curate in 1749[8] and 1753[9] (possibly earlier; he witnessed a bastardy bond in 1745[10]). It may be that he was the Thomas Hill who served as vicar of Combe (Hampshire) between 1754 and his death in 1772, and also at Froxfield (Wiltshire) from 1766.[11] When the rector was invited to join in the grand party at Stourhead in 1751, there were six people in his household.[12]

The rector's daughter, Grace, who was named after her mother, married her father's namesake, another John Hill.[13] Before her marriage, Grace lived with Jane Hoare, Henry the Good's widow, presumably as a

1   TNA PROB11/776/410.
2   He served as high constable of Mere Hundred in 1690; cf WSHC A1/110/ T1690, 101.
3   *Alumni Oxoniensis*
4   See Hoare, Richard Colt, Sir. *The History of modern Wiltshire: Hundred of Mere.* John Nichols & Son, 1822, p.72.
5   Mowbray, op cit, v.1, p.534.
6   WSHC 383/906. For his status, see Stourton, Kilmington and Mere Genealogies **http://wiltshire.anu.edu.au.**
7   *Alumni Cantabrigiensis*
8   Clergy of the Church of England Database **http://theclergydatabase.org.uk/**
9   Dodd, op cit, p.279.
10 WSHC 1240/28.
11 Clergy of the Church of England Database **http://theclergydatabase.org.uk.**
12 WSHC 383/259
13 See p.54

servant; she was given £20 in Jane's will 'if living with me at the time of my death'.[1] Perhaps she was able to use that as her dowry.

None of her sisters is known to have married. At least three of them lived to a good age and were buried in Stourton. Did the rector lack funds for dowries? Marriage was also not for most of his sons. Only William is known to have had a wife; she bore five children, baptised in Stourton between 1747 and 1759.

The rector provided for his widow, Grace, and perhaps for other sons, by leasing a cottage in 1742 for her life, and for the lives of his sons Henry and John.[2] In 1744 he was paying an annual rent of 3s.[3] In 1736, the property was sub-let to Christopher Parsons, who was ordered by the manorial court to remove his sheep from the highways, or face a fine of 6s 8d if he kept them there.[4]

One wonders if there was any relationship between the rector of Stourton and the rector of neighbouring Kilmington, Samuel Hill. Samuel had sufficient status to be appointed to the Bench; in 1741 he examined Jane Miles as to the paternity of her bastard child.[5]

Henry Hoare, when he purchased the manor of Stourton in 1717, also purchased the advowson. However, it was not until 1755 that his son was able to present a new rector. Montague Barton's incumbency lasted for 35 years, but is outside of the scope of this book.

The rector depended for his income upon his glebe, his tithe, and offerings from his parishioners. The glebe[6] in the early seventeenth century was one of the larger farms in Stourton, consisting of eight fields covering over 90 acres. The land was primarily pasture and meadow, but also included a few acres of woodland, a garden, an orchard, and a 'recke yard'. Buildings included the parsonage house, a barn, and, in 1608, 'an old cottage' at Cribbes, which lay beside a mill pond. By 1662 this had become a hop yard, and in 1740 it was a nursery, rented by Henry Hoare,

1   TNA PROB11/719/352.
2   WSHC 383/98, p.11.
3   WSHC 383/345. The property is not described in our sources.
4   WSHC 383/353.
5   WSHC 1240/28.
6   The following paragraph is based on 17th and 18th c. glebe terriers, cf WSHC D1/24/193/1-5. These are abstracted in Hobbs, Steven, ed, *Wiltshire glebe terriers 1588-1827*. Wiltshire Record Society 56. 2003, p.406-9. For a map of the glebe when the rector exchanged lands with Sir Richard Colt Hoare in 1826, see WSHC D1/3/1/14.

the lord of the manor.[1] The manorial court regularly forbade the rector to keep sheep in the common, or the highways.[2] The rector, however, claimed the right to feed 200 sheep on Stourton Common.

It is not clear whether any of the rectors farmed their glebe themselves, but there is evidence that it or parts of it were let. In the early part of Elizabeth's reign, the parsonage was let to Roger Greaves.[3] A late sixteenth-century terrier reveals that Mathew Fewell was the tenant of 8 acres of pasture and meadow, and 10 acres of arable, James Burdele had 6 acres of pasture and meadow, Edmund Butler rented 7 acres of pasture and meadow, and 6 acres of arable; Richard Hayme rented 'a little house sometimes was lodging for the serving priest'.[4] Some rectors were pluralists, and lived elsewhere, letting their glebe.

Tithe was also important, although only limited information concerning it has survived. Henry Hoare paid Mr Hill his 'tyth of hay' in 1727, amounting to £6-04-06.[5] In 1750, a mistake was made, and Henry Hoare reclaimed £1-14-06 that had been overpaid.[6] Nathaniel Field sued Emanuel Swetnam, the miller, for tithes on corn and lambs in 1662, perhaps because he had been unable to collect them during the Interregnum.[7] He won his case, at least, as far as it concerned Stourton Mill.[8] A few years later, John Derby similarly sued William Sparrow for tithes on faggots of wood from a coppice on the boundary with Penselwood. He lost his case, as the land concerned was found to be in the parish of Penselwood, not Stourton.[9]

Some incumbents charged fees for conducting baptisms, marriages and burials. We do not know whether Stourton's rectors did so, but the parish register suggests that during John Hill's incumbency Stourton became a minor marriage centre for the surrounding area. For the seventeenth century, the places of residence of marriage partners are rarely recorded. However, during Hill's incumbency, the number of instances of couples with no apparent connection with Stourton

1 WSHC 383/61, f.6.
2 WSHC 383/353.
3 TNA C3/75/34.
4 Hobbs, *Glebe Terriers*, op cit, p.406.
5 WSHC 383/59.
6 WSHC 383/6.
7 TNA E134/14Chas2/Trin3.
8 TNA E 126/8/136. Judgement on the amount due for Swetnam's Mill was withheld.
9 TNA E134/23Chas2/Mich7.

marrying in St Peters grew considerably. In the 1710s, there were six, in the 1720s, four, in the 1730s, thirteen, and in the 1740s, no less than twenty-nine. Couples came from as far away as Salisbury and Norton St Philip to marry in Stourton. In some cases, both parties came from the same parish; for example, George Millard and Hannah Shepherd, both of Warminster, married in Stourton in 1745.

Technically, a marriage licence was required in order to marry away from the home parishes of both parties. Was this requirement being evaded? Did those who wanted to avoid the calling of banns or the obtaining of a marriage licence come to Stourton to be married? And was either the rector, John Hill, or the curate (perhaps his son Thomas) earning extra income by running an illegal marriage centre? It is difficult to see any other explanation for the high number of marriages of couples from other parishes in the 1740s. It might be added that there was an earlier example of a couple marrying with neither banns nor licence: John Shepherd and Mary Brickle did so in 1704, according to the bishops' transcript of the parish register.[1]

The living was said to be worth about £200 per annum in 1693,[2] and £160 in 1703.[3] The rector was sufficiently well-off to come second in the list of Stourton contributors to the £400,000 grant in 1642; Nathaniel Field paid £1 17s – three times as much as most other taxpayers, although far less than Lord Stourton.[4] He also contributed £3 5s towards the collection for the relief of Irish Protestants in 1648.[5] Field was a relatively wealthy man, and probably had a private income other than his living. One notable feature of the inventory, as already noted, is his 'bookes in ye library valued at £200.[6] As has already been seen, Field was a learned man, the son of a leading churchman, a Prebendary of Chichester, and author of a biography of his father. He put his books to good use.

The duties of rectors were many and various, although we know little about the way in which they were performed. They were responsible

1   Ellis, John Henry, ed. *The Registers of Stourton, County Wilts., from 1570 to 1800.* Harleian Society publications 12. 1887, p.53.
2   WSHC 383/352.
3   WSHC D1/3/5/3. In 1829, its value was estimated at £588 17s., cf. WSHC 130/76.
4   TNA E179/259/25. Pt.1., rot.2.
5   WSHC 413/29.
6   WSHC P1/F/134.

for the conduct of worship, and for the pastoral care of their people. Services were conducted in accordance with the *Book of Common Prayer*, in its various incarnations, except perhaps during the Interregnum when it was illegal. During that period, Parliament's *Directory* should have been used. The Interregnum also saw many 'fast dayes appointed and sett aparte for a publique fasting and humiliacion' ordered by the authorities. In 1652 recusants were accused of failing to attend them.[1]

Some members of the congregation had their own copies of the bible and the prayer book, which they could use to follow services. Mary Poor's 1683 inventory records 'one bible and one prayer booke' worth 2s 6d.[2] John Stroud, a tanner, had two bibles to bequeath in 1685.[3]

Others, as has already been noted, had their own musical instruments, and may have provided music for services. In 1603, John Kerbey had 'two basse viols & a treble', worth 10s,[4] perhaps used to accompany the singing of psalms. Hymn singing did not become common until the eighteenth century.

Sermons should have been regularly preached, although it was permissible to read a chapter from Bishop Jewell's *Book of Homilies* instead. In 1674, the churchwardens reported that they were in need of a copy.[5] But most incumbents were well qualified to preach, even if, like Mr King, they sometimes failed to do so. As will be seen, a charity established in 1737 provided for rectors to be paid if they preached regular sermons.

The churchwardens' accounts sometimes record the purchase of bread and wine, indicating that the sacrament of holy communion was regularly celebrated, at least during the final decades of our period.[6] That is made explicit in the entries for 1741, when 'wine for 12 sacraments' was purchased, and for 1747, when 2s was paid for 'bread for 12 sacraments'.[7] Celebration was evidently monthly, in these years at least.

By contrast, the service of confirmation was not frequent; indeed, it was rare, since it required the visit of a bishop. Yet partaking of holy communion was supposed to be restricted to those who had been

1   WSHC A1/110/T1652,
2   WSHC P2/P/565.
3   WSHC P2/S/939.
4   WSHC P2/K/72.
5   WSHC D1/54/6/5. They also lacked a book of canons.
6   Earlier accounts do not survive.
7   WSHC 497/6.

confirmed. One wonders if the rule was always obeyed. We only have records of two confirmation services at Stourton in our period.[1] In 1703, over 126 people were confirmed. Eight years later, in 1711, there were 62.[2] Both services were conducted by Gilbert Burnet, the Bishop of Salisbury, who was indefatigable in visiting his diocese. It may be suspected that the higher numbers in 1703 were due to the fact that the interval since the previous confirmation had been much longer. The names of confirmees were written into the parish register. Some may have come from other parishes to be confirmed whilst they had the opportunity, although most of the names seem to be those of Stourton families.

The rite of confirmation confirmed the confirmee's baptismal vows. It was considered important that those vows were clearly understood. Consequently, the parish youth (other than the Catholics) were almost certainly catechised by the Anglican clergy, who also had some involvement in Stourton's school. We have already seen that John Drew let part of his Parsonage to Henry Hoare as a school room in 1722, that his son probably served as schoolmaster, and that John Hill had been a schoolmaster at Mere before becoming a curate.

The rector also acted as trustee to a number of parish charities, distributing aid to the poor at Christmas and on other occasions. He certified the poverty of poor householders when the hearth tax was being assessed,[3] and witnessed apprenticeship indentures (both pauper and private), removal orders, and bastardy orders.[4] In 1611, John King petitioned Quarter Sessions on behalf of George Hilgrove, whose property had been destroyed by fire. He succeeded in securing five marks from the Bench.[5] John Hill received 10s 6d from Henry Hoare in 1746, 'to be given to John Jackson, son in law to Peter Gover to carry him and his family into Yorkshire' – presumably he was supervising a pauper removal.[6] Probate records reveal rectors witnessing wills, and taking the

---

1   Hobbs, Steven, ed. *Gleanings from Wiltshire parish registers*. Wiltshire Record Society 63. 2010, p.225. Some Stourton parishioners may, of course, have visited other parishes for confirmation.
2   In 1783 there were 52; ibid, p.226.
3   Dwelly, E., ed. *Directory of Somerset part 1*. Dwelly's national records 2. 1929, p.187.
4   WSHC 1240/19, 1240/28 & 1240/42.
5   WSHC A1/110/T1611, 111-12.
6   WSHC 383/61, f.6.

oaths of executors and administrators. One of the rectors, John Hill, acted as a surrogate for the Archdeacon when he granted probate of the will of James Land in 1741 (which he had also witnessed).[1] Rectors were evidently concerned about their Roman Catholic parishioners; some of them noted 'papists' in the parish register; others (notably Nathaniel Field in 1662[2]) presented them at ecclesiastical visitations.

Not all rectors resided on their cure. John Drew, for example, lived in his rectory at Kingston Deverill, and allowed his Stourton rectory to fall into dis-repair. In 1726, his neglect, as has been seen, came to the notice of the Chancellor of the Diocese.[3] We have already seen that the first John King was also a pluralist; we know he died at Windsor, so may not have resided at Stourton. Nathaniel Field's canonry probably took him to Chichester regularly. The absence of a rector frequently meant that a curate had to be appointed to undertake their duties.

A variety of other reasons might lie behind the appointment of a curate. At least one appointed his son, presumably to give him some experience. Other rectors may have suffered from illness or incapacity. A number of curates are listed in the Clergy of the Church of England database. It is rarely, however, apparent how long they served for, and at least three are missing from this database. John Scorse was the curate when the 1553 visitation was held,[4] but is not mentioned. Nor are 'Sir Edmund', curate, who was bequeathed 12d by Alexander Davies in 1560/61,,[5] or Roger Williams, described as curate of Stourton when he witnessed the will of John Blanford in 1574.[6]

John King appointed a succession of curates in the late sixteenth century: Thomas Mowpe, Walter Fewell, Richard Griffen, and John Merick.[7] More is known about their seventeenth-century successors.

1 WSHC P2/L/629.
2 WSHC D1/54/1/4. This presentment is printed in Grout, Diana, & McAbendrath, Liz., eds. *Churchwardens' Presentments for 40 parishes between Warminster Salisbury and Downton. Volume 4.* Wiltshire Family History Society, 2014, p.8-9, and also (in facsimile) in Calland, op cit, p.63.
3 WSHC D1/61/1/37. See also above, p.182.
4 WSHC D1/43/1.
5 WSHC P2/4Reg/70C.
6 WSHC P2/5Reg/216D
7 Clergy of the Church of England Database **http://theclergydatabase.org. uk.** Merick paid the clerical subsidy in 1595 (TNA E179/53), and witnessed the wills of John Kerbey (1600; cf.WHSC P2/K/72) and Rinold Jupe (1600; WSHC P2/IJ/37).

Roger Hewlett matriculated B.A. at University College Oxford in 1610, aged 17.[1] In 1616, he was licenced as a preacher throughout the dioceses of Gloucester, Salisbury, and Bath and Wells; between 1617 and 1622 he served as curate at Knook. The second John King employed him as curate at Stourton between 1623 and 1632. In the late 1630s, he was the curate at Downton, but does not seem to have become a parish priest. Four of his children were baptised at Stourton between 1623 and 1630; one was buried.

John Sampson received his ordination as deacon and priest in 1674 and 1675, whilst serving as curate at Stourton under John Drew. He was probably a local boy from Brewham; if this identification is correct, he matriculated from St Albans Hall, Oxford in 1669, and may have gone on to serve as curate at Charlton Horethorne in 1684, and as rector of North Cheriton in 1687.

Drew subsequently appointed Nathaniel Forster as curate in 1707 and again in 1710; he was cited to appear at visitation in 1708 and 1711.[2] He came from a clerical family; his father served as curate at Durrington. He had studied at Merchant Tailors School, and took his MA at Oxford in 1711. Subsequently, he served as rector of Misterton (1720), Stawley (1728), and Whitchurch Canonicorum (1732), and also as a minor canon of Winchester (1713-15).

Weare Yeamans was a Bristolian, although when he died his mother was 'of Wincanton', and was unwilling to administer his estate.[3] He had matriculated at Balliol College, Oxford, in 1699/7, taking his BA in 1706, and MA in 1708.[4] He was ordained by the Bishop of Bath and Wells in 1706, and named as a Stourton curate in 1714 and 1716. He probably served there until he died in 1724.

The rectors also nominated parish clerks.[5] It was the clerks' responsibility to lead the singing, keep the church swept and clean, perhaps write up the parish register, and undertake all the menial tasks involved in running the church. Sometimes, they also taught school, wrote parishioners' wills, and undertook various other duties. Thomas Trymell witnessed the will of Augustine Bassyngay in 1551/2, describing

1   *Alumni Oxoniensis.*
2   WSHC D1/47/1.
3   WSHC P2/Y/75.
4   *Alumni Oxoniensis.*
5   Hobbs, *Gleanings,* op cit, p.225.

himself as 'clerk'; it is likely that he was the parish clerk.[1] Francis Bacon described himself as parish clerk when he wrote the inventory of Peter Pitnie in 1602.[2] Two other will witnesses also described themselves as 'clerk', and were probably parish clerks. John Russell witnessed the will of Thomas Bacon in 1604[3]; Randulph Morgan witnessed the will of John Rose of Gasper in 1619.[4] Another clerk, Richard Milborne, died in office in 1610.[5]

The second John King nominated several parish clerks at short intervals in the early seventeenth century. In 1612, he appointed Edward Densham, in 1613, Francis Bacon (perhaps the same man who wrote Peter Pitnie's inventory), in 1615, Robert Britten, and in 1617, William Henry.[6] Thereafter, we have no information until John Sandle died in office, in 1645.[7] His successor, John Drew, nominated successively Thomas Stile, Thomas Stone, and William Evil, although only the date of the latter – 1691 – is known.[8]

In the 1730s and 1740s, the churchwardens' accounts record that the parish clerk was normally paid wages of £2 per annum, although sometimes he submitted an additional 'bill' for a few shillings, presumably for work done beyond the call of duty.[9] He was entitled to an annuity of ten shillings from Jane Hoare's charity (see below), but it is not clear whether this was paid through the churchwardens. Unfortunately, the accounts do not usually reveal the clerk's name, although 'Charles Evil's bill and wages' amounting to £2-16-10 was paid in 1747. One wonders whether Charles succeeded his father William in the role.

Many other day to day activities are recorded in churchwardens' accounts, which survive from 1734.[10] The ringers on Guy Fawkes day were paid 5s. Visitation costs had to be met; in 1734 the visitation was held at Salisbury, and cost the parish twenty-two shillings.

1 WSHC P2/2Reg/167d
2 WSHC P2/P/191.
3 WSHC P2/B/252.
4 WSHC P2/R/144
5 Ellis, op cit, p.65.
6 These details are taken from Hobbs, *Gleanings*, op cit, p.225. The dating of William Henry in this volume is incorrect; my thanks to Steve Hobbs for elucidating this point.
7 Ellis, op cit, p.67.
8 Hobbs, *Gleanings*, op cit, p.225.
9 WSHC 497/6.
10 WSHC 497/6.

Unfortunately, surviving accounts are too late to record the renovation of the church undertaken by Henry Hoare at the same time as he was building Stourhead. We have already seen how he secured the appointment of Nathaniel Ireson as churchwarden in 1722, in order to more effectively supervise the work. A plaque on the wall still records that the church was 'new paved and seated and beautefied' in 1722-3. The work involved the demolition of the rood screen and loft, the construction of a new altar and a burial vault for the Hoares, the erection of a gallery, the laying of new paving, and the installation of box pews.[1] Unfortunately, it is likely that many escutcheons of the Stourton family, which are known to have been in the church in the seventeenth century, were destroyed during the renovations[2].

The importance attached to social hierarchy meant that families had to be seated in church according to their place in the pecking order. A new seating plan was therefore essential. It is probable that Ireson himself compiled the church seating plan which survives amongst the Hoare family's archive.[3] It is undated, but cannot be later than August 1723, when Charles Barnes (who is named in it) died.

Seating was the responsibility of the churchwardens, and was fixed. The pews were numbered, presumably from front to back. Some were allocated 'for' particular properties; for example, Paul Charlton had a seat in pew 5 'for his freehold in Gasper'. The more substantial inhabitants sat at the front. Pew no 1 was allocated to the demesne farm and to Coldcot farm – probably the largest farms in the parish. Lord Stourton, however, was allocated pew no.11, towards the rear, reflecting the fact that, following his sale of the manor, he only held a small amount of property in the parish. It is probable that, given their Catholicism, the Stourton family never attended, and were therefore able to avoid the indignity of having to recognize their reduced status in church. The new lord of the manor, Henry Hoare, is not actually named in the pew plan, as his pew was quite separate from the rest of the congregation. It was in the south transept, and even had a fireplace, which can still be seen.[4]

Mostly, the men sat on one side, the women on the other. The only

1   Calland, op cit, p.20.
2   Ellis, op cit, p.viii.
3   WSHC 383/928, included in Hurley, Beryl, ed. *Wiltshire pew lists*. WIltshire Family History Society, 1994, p.39-40. It is partially reprinted in Calland, op cit, p.74-5. The pews were replaced in 1847, cf. Calland, p.93.
4   Illustrated on p. 264.

exceptions to this rule were in the front two pews, which seated some of the leading tenants. Towards the back were seats for women coming to be 'churched' after child-birth, together with seats for the schoolmistress and her charges. Pew no 28 was allocated to 'the Parsonage House'. It is likely that there were also seats at the back for the parish poor, although that is not specified. Certainly, when the church was re-pewed by Sir Hugh Richard Hoare c.1847, provision was made for the poor.[1]

Despite a number of empty seats on the plan, it seems clear that the pews could not accommodate the entire population of the parish. Just over 100 pew-holders were named. Of course, it is likely that the many Roman Catholics in the parish rarely attended – although provision was made for them. Mr Charles Barnes, for example, was allocated a seat in pew 3 for his leasehold, and a seat in pew 12 for The Street.

The involvement of Henry Hoare in the renovation of Stourton church was far from being the only reason why he was nick-named Henry 'the Good'. He was a noted philanthropist, involved in a variety of London and national charitable enterprises. When he purchased Stourton, the new lord of the manor took a close interest in the welfare of his tenants and their children. This extended to the provision of education. We have already discussed the provision he made for schooling in Stourton. He presumably paid for the schoolmistress. His 1725 will left a substantial amount for the building and support of charity schools.[2]

Hoare also left £30 to the 'poor householders of Stourton'.[3] His widow, Jane, emulated his example. In 1737, she established another Stourton charity.[4] She purchased an estate at East Knoyle from her son, in order to provide an annuity of £12 for the rector of the parish, provided that he 'shall reside constantly', that he 'publickly administer the Holy Sacrament of the Lord's Supper' on the first Sunday of each month, and that he preach 'a sermon every Sunday in the afternoon from Easter day to the Feast of St Michael', and on Good Friday morning. He was also to 'hear the children ... say the church catechism' every Sunday during Lent. An annuity of ten shillings was to be paid to the parish clerk, provided that he regularly swept and cleaned the church, paying particular attention to the monument to Henry Hoare. A further annuity

1   WSHC 497/7.
2   Oxford Dictionary of National Biography **www.oxforddnb.com**
3   Hoare, Richard Colt. *The Modern History of South Wiltshire*. John Bowyer Nichols & John Gough Nichols, 1822, p.57.
4   WSHC 497/6.

of £3 10s was to be divided between twenty poor housekeepers of the parish' who 'with all their family are of the communion of the Church of England', They were each to receive 'one twelve penny loaf and two shillings & six pence for ever'. The trustees were gentlemen and clergy from neighbouring parishes.

In addition to their formal charities, the Hoare family also distributed largesse. Jane Hoare s 1739 will (proved in 1742) left the enormous sum of £20 to be distributed to the poor householders of Stourton on the day of her funeral.[1] When Edward Edwards was seriously ill in November 1741, Jane's son Henry gave him 10s 6d.[2] In 1751, as we have seen, the Hoare family provided Christmas dinner for the whole parish.

A number of other parochial charities were founded by prominent parishioners. Nicholas King, the son of the former rector, who had become a wealthy merchant of London and Seville, gave £100 in 1651 (described in his will as '500 pieces of eight')[3] to purchase an annuity of £5, which was to be 'disposed and laid out for ... the clothing of five aged poor persons' resident in Stourton. He named eight local trustees, including the rector (who was his brother-in-law).[4] By 1723, only three of the original trustees survived; several more names were added, including that of Henry Hoare.[5] Edmund Wadlow likewise left £60 in trust in 1725; Henry Hoare was named as trustee, and was to distribute the interest on the capital between ten poor people of Stourton, and five of Gasper.[6] Wadlow also instructed his executor to erect a memorial stone in the church to record his gift.

The wills of other parishioners reveal much about their attitudes to charity, and to the church. Prior to the reformation, bequests to the church were usual. When William, 5th Lord Stourton died in 1523, he left 6s 8d to Salisbury Cathedral, and 10s to the 'Friars Preachers of Sarum'.[7] His successor, Edward, the 6th Lord, similarly bequeathed 10s to the Cathedral, but he also gave 20s to 'my parishe churche', and another

1   TNA PROB11/719/352.
2   WSHC 383/61.
3   Morrison, George Austin. 'Richard King, 1616-1668', *Notes & queries for Somerset & Dorset* 12(94), 1911, p.265.
4   WSHC 497/6.
5   WSHC 383/519.
6   TNA PROB 11/606/58; WSHC 497/6.
7   TNA PROB11/21/319.

20s to the parish church of Stourton Caundle. His 'chappelyns' were given a half year's wages; whether that meant his household chaplains, the chantry chaplain, or perhaps the rectors of Stourton and Stourton Caundle, is not clear.[1] However, the church was not mentioned in the will of William, 8th Lord Stourton in 1548.[2] He would have seen little point in making such bequests, given the dissolution of the monasteries, and the iconoclasm of Edward VI's reign.

Bequests for the church did, however, continue to be made. Most Elizabethan testators bequeathed money to Stourton church and/or to Salisbury Cathedral. In 1562/3, William Britten specified that he wanted to help pay for 'the reparations of the bells' at Stourton.[3] Two Elizabethan testators thought of the poor of Stourton. John Genyns gave them 12d in 1579.[4] Much more was expected from the lords of the manor, but in 1588 John, 9th Lord Stourton left it to his wife to decide the amount as she 'shall thincke convenient'.[5] Others remembered churches elsewhere. One, George Stile, left 4d to Wells Cathedral in 1592.[6] Another, George Kerbey, evidently had some connections with Gillingham and Mere, as he left both churches 2s. He also gave the ringers in both places 16d, presumably to ring his knells.[7] John Genyns' bequest of 4d to 'Coliton Haven' was more secular, but it reminds us that briefs inviting donations for a wide variety of purposes were regularly read in Stourton church. A printed brief for the repair of Colyton Haven (in Devon) was being widely circulated in 1579; the churchwardens of Ashburnham (Sussex) retained their copy in their parish chest.[8] In 1678 over thirty parishioners made a donation to the brief for the rebuilding of St Pauls Cathedral after the Great Fire.[9]

In the first half of the seventeenth century, testators placed greater emphasis on bequests to the poor. Lord Stourton gave £10 to be distributed amongst them 'att the discretion of my executors' in 1632.[10]

1   TNA PROB11/25/443.
2   TNA PROB11/32/258.
3   WSHC P2/4Reg/132B.
4   WSHC P2/G/32.
5   TNA PROB11/73/395.
6   TNA PROB11/80/364.
7   WSHC P2/K/72.
8   East Sussex Record Office PAR233/9/2/1.
9   London Metropolitan Archives MS 25565/25 f.84. The return is damaged so the amount they gave cannot be ascertained.
10 TNA PROB11/163/663.

More typical was Charles Chandler, who bequeathed 2s to the 'poore of this parish at my buriall'.[1] It was quite usual to distribute bequests to the poor at funerals. The church also continued to receive bequests, although the proportion of testators making them dwindled. There was only one bequest to Salisbury Cathedral in this period: Elizabeth Jupe gave 6d to 'Our Lady church of Sarum'.[2] Not all charitable donations, of course, were made by bequest. The bell inscribed 'RB', and hung in the church in 1624,[3] provides evidence that gifts to the church were being made; it is likely that many other gifts were unrecorded.

Some of those who made no charitable bequests were Roman Catholics, like Robert Barnes, gent., in 1646.[4] If they wished to give to their church, it was not a good idea to do so by bequest. Bequests for Catholic purposes were regarded as 'superstitious uses', and could render a will invalid in the opinion of the probate court.[5]

In the second half of the seventeenth century, the proportion of testators making charitable bequests fell dramatically. In 1652, William Barnard, yeoman, gave 10s each to the poor of Stourton and Mere, plus 5s to Stourton church.[6] Two successive rectors, Nathaniel Field and John Derby, both remembered the poor. Field, who was particularly well off, gave £5 to the Stourton poor, 'to be distributed at the day of y buriall'.[7] Derby gave 20s each to the poor of Yeovil, 'where I was borne', of Gillingham, 'where I was bred', and of Stourton, 'where I hope to be buried'.[8] When William, 11th Lord Stourton died in 1672, he left £10 to the Stourton poor, 'to be distributed amongst them by my executors … at my funerall or the next day after my interement'.[9] In 1674, Adam Cuffe was accused in a presentment of 'detaining a legacy' of 10s 'given to our church'.[10] He was the administrator of his father's estate, but waited

1   WSHC P2/8Reg/168B.
2   WSHC P2/IJ/68.
3   Walters, H.B. *The church bells of Wiltshire*. 1929 (reprinted Kingsmead Reprints, 1969), p.208.
4   TNA PROB 11/198/430.
5   For the way in which Dorothy Barnes got around this problem, see Raymond, Stuart A. 'Barnes: a Catholic family on the borders of Wiltshire and Somerset, c.1548- c.1750', *Genealogists magazine* 32(9), 2018, p.346.
6   TNA PROB11/223/594.
7   WSHC P1/F/134.
8   TNA PROB11/340/490.
9   TNA PROB11/339/297.
10 WSHC D1/54/6/5.

to obtain probate until after his mother had also died, over ten years later.[1] His tardiness caused him to be cited to appear in the Archdeaconry Court.[2]

Another interesting bequest was made by John Best in 1672. He bequethed £5 to the 'poore Roman Catholiques of Stowrton'.[3] That at least did not constitute 'superstitious uses', and thus fall foul of anti-Catholic legislation. Apart from these, only two or three late seventeenth-century wills remembered either the church or the poor. Indeed, eighteen wills were proved between 1678 and 1698, but none of them mentioned charity. We do, however, know that money was still being raised on briefs in this period; in 1670, one for the 'redemption of captives' in Algiers raised £5 1s.[4]

Between 1700 and 1750, the pattern remained the same. Apart from the substantial bequests of Edmund Wadlow and Jane Hoare, which have already been mentioned, there were very few bequests to the poor, and none to the church. The only other bequests to the poor in this period were made by a widow, Alice Green in 1707/8, who left £5,[5] and her son Alexander, who bequeathed two guineas in 1727.[6]

The will-making practices of Stourton testators clearly changed gradually during our period. The iconoclasm of the Reformation probably caused sixteenth-century parishioners to think twice before making bequests to the church. Those who became recusants obviously would not wish to do so. In the eighteenth century, the Hoare family's largesse perhaps persuaded testators that, given the renovations to the church in 1723/4, no more was needed – although it is worth noting that William Maidment junior gave a new bell to the church in 1728.[7] As for the poor, the Hoares almost certainly paid for the parish workhouse. But increasingly poor rates were being levied to support paupers. If rates were levied to provide poor relief, why give more?

Stourton was a hotbed of Roman Catholicism. It is one of the few places in England where a Catholic congregation survived without a

---

1   WSHC P2/C/587.
2   WSHC D2/5/1/8.
3   TNA PROB11/341/161.
4   WSHC D1/27/1/4/6.
5   TNA PROB11/506.
6   TNA PROB11/615/485.
7   Walters, op cit, p.208.

break from the mid-sixteenth century until the mid-twentieth century.[1] The Catholics depended upon the Stourton family for their chapel, and probably for their priest, at least in part.[2] Reference has already been made to their faith. One Lord Stourton was imprisoned in the Fleet in 1606.[3] Another suffered sequestration following the Civil War.[4] A successor was excluded from the House of Lords by an act of 1678.[5] After the 1688 revolution, the then Lord Stourton went into exile with his King. His brother Thomas erected a chapel with a priest's house on his manor of Bonham in 1714, when the manor of Stourton was sold.[6] The 1717 register of Papists estates valued Bonham at just over £74.[7] Even after Bonham was sold to Henry Hoare in 1785,[8] the family continued to support the chapel.

Most of our information regarding seventeenth century Catholics derives from the records of their persecution. There are many citations, presentments, and lists of excommunicants, naming Stourtonians, amongst the records of diocesan courts. The names of those heavily fined by Quarter Sessions or Assizes are listed on the recusant rolls[9]; a few late seventeenth-century indictments have also been discovered.[10] Recusants

1   For a list of priests, see Williams, J.Anthony. *Catholic recusancy in Wiltshire 1660-1791*. Catholic Record Society, 1968, p.245.
2   Many other gentle families probably also made contributions; cf. Raymond, 'Catholic Families', op cit.
3   Foley, Henry. *Records of the English Province of the Society of Jesus*, vol.I. Burns & Oates, 1877, p.65.
4   Green, Mary Anne Everett, ed. *Calendar of the Committee for Compounding &c. ...* H.M.S.O., 1890, vol.2, p.1583-4. For his negotiations with the Dorset County Committee, see Mayo, Charles Herbert, ed. *The Minute Books of the Dorset Standing Committee, 23rd September 1646 to 8th May 1650*. Exeter: William Pollard & Co., 1902, *passim*.
5   Foley, Henry. *Records of the English Province of the Society of Jesus*, vol.V. Burns & Oates, 1879, p.27.
6   Pugh, R.B., & Crittall, Elizabeth, eds. *A History of Wiltshire* vol.3. Oxford University Press, 1956, p.91.
7   Estcourt, Edgar E., & Payne, John Orlebar, eds. *The English Catholic Nonjurors of 1715*. Burns & Oates, [1885], p.228. Note that the date in the title of this book is misleading; the survey it abstracts was made in 1717.
8   Hoare, Richard Colt. *The Modern History of South Wiltshire*. John Bowyer Nichols & John Gough Nichols, 1822. Vol.1, p.89.
9   Stourton Catholics in the recusant rolls after 1660 are listed by Williams, J.Anthony. *Catholic recusancy in Wiltshire 1660-1791*. Catholic Record Society, 1968.
10 WSHC A1/165/2, f.6; A1/165/3, f.35.

sometimes had to pay double taxation, so can be identified on tax lists.

The Stourtons were in close contact with many other prominent Catholics nationally; for instance, the name of Humphry Weld of Lulworth can be seen on a number of their deeds.[1] He was a prominent London merchant, whose name also occurs in the deeds of many Yorkshire Catholic trusts, and who bought back many recusant estates seized during the Interregnum.[2]

A number of other prominent Catholic families lived nearby.[3] The numbers involved in the Mission were substantial. Twelve excommunicants were listed in 1624 – probably the tip of the iceberg. In the 1630s, it is possible to identify no less than 68 citations to attend the Archdeaconry Court of Salisbury which may be presumed to refer to Catholics; there were probably more.[4] The constables and juries of the Hundred of Mere made regular presentments of recusants between 1613 and 1680; in the 1630s there were usually fourteen or fifteen names on their list, and in 1658 no less than 45 were cited to appear. In 1641, nine recusants had to pay 8s poll tax, despite the fact that they were not liable to the subsidy of that year.[5] A year later, twenty-five recusants were assessed for the £400,000 grant; of these, only Lord Stourton had to pay on his lands. Twenty-four had insufficient land or goods to be liable, but nevertheless had to pay the poll-tax of 2s 8d imposed on recusants by the grant.[6]

In 1662, as has been seen, Nathaniel Field presented the names of 48 recusants who were 'conceaved to be Popishly affected'.[7] He was probably responding to Bishop Seth Ward's order to provide him with names after the 1662 Act of Uniformity.[8] The numbers presented at Quarter Sessions after the Restoration gradually fell, although in 1680

---

1   See, for example, WSHC 383/721 (1661).
2   Aveling, J.C.H. *The Handle and the Axe: the Catholic recusants in England from Reformation to Emancipation*. Blond & Briggs, 1978, p.171; Thirsk, Joan. 'The Sales of Royalist Land during the Interregnum', *Economic History Review* N.S., 5(2), 1952, p.194.
3   For the Mission's connections in Somerset, see Raymond, Stuart A. 'Catholic Families', op cit.
4   WSHC D1/5/3 & 5-7.
5   TNA E179/199/407, rot.4.
6   TNA E179/259/25, pt.1.
7   WSHC D54/1/4. The presentment is reproduced in Calland. op cit, p. 63.
8   Dauncy, Mary. 'Aspects of Salisbury's place in the Wiltshire cloth industry', *Hatcher Review* 3(28), 1989, p.388.

numbers increased to twenty. After that date, presentments ceased altogether.[1] Indeed, we have already seen that Richard Cuffe, who had previously been accused of recusancy, served twice as churchwarden, in 1695 and 1708.[2] Catholics were not, however, decreasing in numbers. Rather, they were not being presented. In 1676, 51 recusants were counted.[3] By 1767, that number had increased to 107.[4] Three years after the sale of Bonham, in 1788, Bishop Walmesley, the Vicar Apostolic of the Western District, reported to Rome that there were at least 150 worshippers in the congregation.[5]

Many Catholics from neighbouring parishes were attached to the Stourton Mission, and may occasionally have visited either Stourton Castle or Bonham to attend mass. There was strong support for the Stourton Mission from South East Somerset.[6] The Byfleets of Bratton Seymour, the Cottingtons of Godminster and Discove, the Ewens of Suddon and Stavordale, the Fitzjames's of Redlynch, and – further afield – the Muttlebury's of Ashill - were all powerful gentry families, some of whom were linked with the royal court. They also had many links with the Stourton family, and with each other. During the later Elizabethan era, the Fitzjames family in particular attracted considerable interest from the government; one of them had been suspected of involvement in the Babington plot,[7] and several had attracted suspicion of other traitorous activities. The conversion of some of the other Somerset families may have taken place a little later; for example, the Cottingtons probably took their lead from the conversion of Edward Cottington, who fled to Rome after studying at Oxford in 1600, and became a Jesuit.[8]

1   WSHC A1/110/T1613-T1680
2   WSHC D1/50/5; D1/54/21/4.
3   Whiteman, Anne, ed. *The Compton census of 1676: a critical edition.* Oxford University Press for the British Academy, 1986, p.125; WSHC D1/27/1/4/66. Also Simpson, Cecilia. 'A Census of Wilts in 1676', *Wiltshire notes & Queries* 3, 1899-1901, p.537.
4   WSHC D/1/9/1/3.
5   Deverill, Chris & Penny. 'St. Benedict's Bonham: the two earliest registers, 1767-1801, *South Western Catholic History* 10, 1992, p.2.
6   See Raymond, 'Catholic Families', op cit.
7   Green, Mary Anne Everett, ed. *State papers Domestic series of the reign of Elizabeth, 1591-1594 ... .* Longmans Green Reader & Dyer, 1867, p.100-101.
8   Kenny, Anthony, ed. *The Responsa Scholarum of the English College at Rome, part 1: 1598-1621.* Catholic Record Society 54. 1962, p.65-6; Foley,Henry. *Records of the English Province of the Society of Jesus.* Burns & Oates, 1878,

A number of other members of these families entered the priesthood; indeed, as we shall see, it is probable that Nicholas Fitzjames preceded Edward Byfleet as priest of the Stourton Mission. It is also possible that Francis Muttlebury, who was sent on the English Mission in 1642, went to assist the aged Fitzjames at Stourton.[1] These gentry could probably have sustained a Catholic Mission even without the Stourtons. They brought their servants with them: John Ewens' maid servant Cicily was cited in 1639[2]; so, in 1638, was his anonymous 'man servant'.[3] Bridget Popell of Discove's recusancy was presented at Somerset Quarter Sessions in 1632, together with that of the Cottington family; she was probably their servant.[4] John Muttlebury's servant, Margaret Dean, was repeatedly presented at Wiltshire Quarter Sessions between 1638 and 1641[5]; in 1639, she was said to have 'lately come into our parish'. Muttlebury himself was said to be 'dewling in Stourton' in 1637.[6]

Other Catholics came to Stourton from parishes in Dorset and Wiltshire. It is likely that Thomas Newman alias Evered, who was brought up at Salisbury and Mere at the end of the sixteenth century, and who became a Jesuit in 1693,[7] had at least some contact with the Stourton mission before he did so.[8] Timothy Skreen and his wife Mary also lived in Mere.[9] They were regularly presented at Quarter Sessions from 1633 onwards,[10] and cited in the archdeaconry court in 1639 and 1640.[11] Timothy was a servant, remembered in the 1632 will of his

vol.4, p.408-9; vol.7, p.175.

1   Birt, Henry Norbert, ed. *Obit book of the English Benedictines for 1600 to 1912, being the necrology of the English Congregation of the Order of St. Benedict from 1600 to 1883 compiled by Abbot Snow*. Privately Printed, 1913, p.65.

2   WSHC D2/5/1/7.

3   WSHC D2/5/1/6.

4   Somerset Heritage Centre Q/SR/67/278-279

5   WSHC A1/110/T1638/208, /T1639/123, /T1640/75, T1641/173.

6   WSHC A1/110/T1637/167.

7   Anstruther, Godfrey, *The Seminary Priests: a Dictionary of the Secular Clergy of England and Wales. I. Elizabethan, 1558-1603*. Ware: St. Edmunds College/ Durham: Ushaw College, 1968, p.112.

8   Kenny, Anthony, ed. *The Responsa Scholarum of the English College at Rome, part 1: 1598-1621*. Catholic Record Society 54. 1962, p.63.

9   WSHC A1/110/T1633/140.

10 WSHC A1/110. Presentments from the Mere Hundred juries and constables are in the rolls for Trinity Quarter Sessions.

11 WSHC D2/5/1/3, 6, & 7

master, Edward Lord Stourton.[1]

Many other servants of the Stourton family also followed the old religion. Some have already been mentioned in chapter 8. In 1623, Robert Draper was presented at Quarter Sessions for recusancy.[2] In 1626, and again in 1629 and 1630, Mr John Phillips was presented for recusancy; he was a [gentleman?] servant of Lord Stourton.[3] Also in 1626, Mr John Muttlebury was described as the 'man' of Mr Charles Stourton. He was presumably a scion of the recusant Muttlebury family of Ashill in Somerset; he and his wife Mary were regularly presented at Wiltshire Quarter Sessions throughout the 1630s and later.[4] It is probable that Joan Booth, another servant presented in 1626, was of lower status, as were Mary Cater and Joan Singer, presented for recusancy in 1629 and 1630,[5] and one 'Fillis', presented in 1636.[6] In 1644, after the sacking of Stourton Castle, the Mere Hundred jurors could not name any of Lord Stourton's servants who remained behind after their Lord had fled.[7]

After the Restoration, Thomas May, presented in 1662,[8] named on the 1678 recusant roll,[9] and presented again in 1683,[10] probably also served the Stourtons. It is likely that he was one of the witnesses who certified the manorial fishing rights for Henry Hoare in 1721. He made his mark on the certificate rather than signing.[11]

The Barnes family's social status, as has been seen, was slightly more exalted, although they had gained it by serving the Stourtons. They were one of the leading Catholic families with substantial property actually in Stourton.[12] In the 1630s, Mary Barnes and her children were

1   TNA PROB11/163/663.
2   TNA A1/110/T1623, 132.
3   WSHC A1/110/T1626/107, /T1629/117, & T1630/134.
4   WSHC A1/110/T1626/107. Presentments for other years are regularly found in the Quarter Sessions great rolls for Trinity sessions, in A1/110.
5   WSHC A1/110/T1629/117 & /T1630/134.
6   WSHC A1.110/T1636/134.
7   WSHC A1/110/T1644, 20.
8   WSHC D1/54/1/4.
9   Williams, op cit, p.324.
10 WSHC D1/54/10/5.
11 WSHC 383/113.
12 Raymond, Stuart A. 'Barnes: a Catholic family on the borders of Wiltshire and Somerset, c.1548- c.1750', *Genealogists Magazine*, 32(9), 2018, p.340-348. See also Raymond, Stuart A. 'Walter Barnes of Stourton (c.1680-1758): his Family, his Debts, and his Religion', *Notes & Queries for Somerset & Dorset*, 38(388), 2018, p.337-48. Some members of the family lived in Shaftesbury.

regularly presented as recusants at Quarter Sessions, although her husband Robert was not; he presumably sought to preserve his estate by attending the parish church. His children were baptised there, despite his evident Catholic sympathies.[1]

As has already been seen, two of Robert's children served Lord Stourton as stewards during the difficult days of the Interregnum. In the 1717 register of Papist estates the value of Walter Barnes' estate at Rode in Stourton was put at a mere 4s 6d; that of his mother Dorothy's Buckhorn Weston estate at £30. His sister Mary's house at Brewham was worth £20.[2]

The Barnes family also had their servants. It may be conjectured that the John Stile who, in 1613, had an altercation with the servants of Sir Maurice Berkeley whilst hunting with his master Robert Barnes,,[3] was the same John Stile, senior, who was excommunicated in 1624,,[4] and cited c.1635.[5]

The Barnes family also had their alliances within the faith. In the late seventeenth century, another Mary Barnes had married Richard Coffin, from the remote parish of Bradworthy (Devon).[6] Richard is mentioned in the recusant rolls of 1678-9, 1681-2 and 1683-4 .[7] One wonders whether Edward Coffin, who served as Catholic Vicar General of the Western District from at least 1661 until his death in 1678, was a relative.[8] When the oath of allegiance was tendered to Catholics in 1715, Mary Coffin was one of only two members of the Bonham congregation

1 WSHC A1/110, passim. The presentments were usually made at the mid-summer sessions.
2 Estcourt, Payne, & Orlebar, op cit, p.43 & 228.
3 TNA STAC8/73/13.
4 WSHC D2/5/2/2.
5 WSHC D2/5/1/3.
6 Richard Coffin is described as 'of Bradworthy' in his 1695 lease of seven acres at Shave; WSHC 383/723.
7 TNA E377/73, 76 &78. See Williams, J.A. 'Wiltshire Catholicism in the early eighteenth century: the diocesan returns of 1706', *Recusant history* 7, 1963, p.30.
8 Williams, J.Anthony. *Catholic Recusancy in Wiltshire 1660-1791*. Catholic Record Society, 1968, p.99 & 246. It is worth noting that his alias was Biddlecombe, and that Margaret Biddlecombe was presented as a recusant in Stourton in 1662; cf WHSC D1/54/1/4. See also Anstruther, Godfrey. *The Seminary Priests: a Dictionary of the Secular Clergy of England and Wales. II. Early Stuart 1603-1659*. Great Wakering: Mayhew-McCrimmon, 1975, p.24. Anstruther does not note that Biddlecombe was Vicar-General.

known to have refused it. The Justices probably did not bother with administering the oath to lesser fry. Her estate was then said to be worth just over £47; in the 1717 register of Papists' estates it was £50.[1]

The other Stourton refuser was Henry Wall, whose estate was valued at £50. But he was probably not a Stourton man; the 1717 register of Papists' estates records that his principal estate was at Rockhampton (Gloucestershire); he also owned a small property at Corfe Castle (Dorset), and a house at East Camel (Somerset).[2]

The Cuffes were another moderately well-off Catholic family. Richard Cuffe was the third son of John Cuffe, who may perhaps have been descended from the Somerset armigerous family.[3] He was described as a tailor in 1653,[4] but described himself as a yeoman when he made his will in 1688/9.[5] He paid the poll tax in 1642,,[6] was presented as a recusant at Quarter Sessions in 1667 and 1682, and (with his wife) was named on the recusant rolls in 1673 and 1678.[7] His wife, Selina, was sufficiently wealthy to leave the poor £5 in her 1698 will.[8]

The Stourton's tenantry were another important component of the Stourton Mission. William Moores, who was presented for recusancy in 1662,[9] renewed and expanded his lease of a farm at Stourton in 1678 for the considerable rent of £234 per annum.[10] This included a part of William Lord Stourton's 'newe inclosed common grounds lying neare Stourton Parke'.[11] Joan Moores, who was presented with him, was probably his wife.

There were many tenants of lesser status. Joan Adams, for example, cited in 1640,[12] tenanted an acre of arable in West Close.[13] George Butler had a cottage and twelve acres of land in Six Wells Bottom, re-

1   Estcourt, Payne, & Orlebar, op cit, p.286.
2   Estcourt, Payne, & Orlebar, op cit, p.43, 70 & 228.
3   Colby,Frederick Thomas, ed. *The Visitation of the County of Somerset in 1623.* Mitchell & Hughes, 1886, p.30.
4   WSHC 383/725.
5   TNA PROB11/398/16.
6   E179/259/25, pt.1.
7   Williams, op cit, p.296.
8   TNA PROB11/446.
9   WSHC D1/54/1/4.
10   WSHC 383/109, f.93.
11   TNA PROB11/339/297.
12   WSHC D2/5/1/3 & 7.
13   WSHC 383/97, f.4.

granted by Lord Stourton in 1658. He paid the poll tax in 1642[1]; he and his wife Judith were presented in 1662[2]; George was cited in 1667[3]; both appeared on the recusant roll in 1673.[4]

Richard Charlton, Mathew Combes, Christopher Windsor, and Roger Barton, were all husbandmen, and probably leased a few acres from Lord Stourton. Charlton was cited three times, in 1634,[5] 1640,[6] and 1641.[7] When he was buried in 1692, his inventory (assuming it relates to the same person)[8] was valued at just over £28. Combes was cited several times in 1636 and 1637.[9] His 1671/2 inventory[10] was appraised at £28 11s 3d. Christopher Windsor paid the poll tax in 1642.[11] He and his wife Mary were both presented by Nathaniel Field in 1662 [12]; they were also presented at Quarter Sessions in 1682 and 1683. Mary appears on the recusant roll in 1678,[13] Christopher in 1678 and 1683.[14] The baptisms of their children between 1649 and 1666 are interlined in the parish register, suggesting they were baptised by a Catholic priest. Christopher's 1691/2 inventory was valued at just over £30, including £20 cash.[15] He paid rent of 1s 4d per annum to Lord Stourton.[16]

Roger Barton paid the Catholic levies of 1641[17] and 1642.[18] He was a husbandman suspected of royalism in 1655,[19] and was presented as a recusant again in 1662.[20] Anne Barton, presented in 1662, was probably his wife.

1   TNA E179/259/25, pt.1.
2   TNA E179/199/407, rot.4; E179/259/25, pt.1.
3   WSHC D2/5/1/8.
4   Wiliams, op cit, p.287.
5   WSHC D2/5/1/5.
6   WSHC D2/5/1/3.
7   WSHC D2/5/1/7.
8   WSHC P1/C/424
9   WSHC D2/5/1/5.
10 WSHC P2/C/630.
11 TNA E179/259/25, pt.1.
12 TNA E179/199/407, rot.4; E179/259/25, pt.1.
13 Williams, op cit, p.349.
14 Williams, op cit, p.349.
15 WSHC P2/W/701.
16 WSHC 383/720. Indenture, 1693; 383/346; 383/352
17 TNA E179/199/407, rot 4.
18 TNA E179/259/25, pt.1.
19 British Library Add. Mss.34012.
20 TNA E179/199/407, rot.4; E179/259/25, pt.1.

Other Stourton Catholics were tradesmen. John Stile, mentioned above, may have been a tanner. Mary Alford, cited in 1640/1, was described as the daughter of a pedlar.[1] Documentation, however, is poor, and no information has been traced for many others named in citations or presentments. For example, who was Ann Hunnington, cited in 1640?[2] Or Captain Large, who paid the 1642 poll tax?[3] Or Thomas Mably, presented in 1662?[4] It is likely that at least some of the recipients of John Best's bequest to poor Catholics[5] were numbered amongst the untraced. They may have been labourers, poor tradesmen, or even paupers – although the latter could have expected short shrift from Anglican overseers. It is also likely that some of the untraced came from neighbouring parishes, and may have been of higher status. But it is evident that the recusants of the Stourton Mission came from a wide variety of backgrounds.

Originally, the Stourton family maintained a chapel in their house; it was recorded by John Aubrey in the late seventeenth century.[6] Catholic priests probably lodged with them before the chapel and priest's house at Bonham were established in 1714. They also provided financial support; in the late eighteenth century, and probably earlier, they were paying priests £50 per annum.[7]

The names of early priests at Stourton are not known: being a Roman Catholic priest was in itself treasonous. As we have seen, at least one of the priests probably known at Stourton – Father Cornelius – was executed for his faith. Large meetings for mass were dangerous in penal times. It is probable that the Stourton priest spent much of his time itinerating around his congregation, conducting mass in the houses of his flock.

Even when priests started to keep records, they had the confusing habit of adopting pseudonyms, frequently calling themselves by the names of related families. It is, however, possible to identify a few priests who were either in the vicinity of Stourton, or who served the Stourton

---

1   WSHC D2/5/1/3.
2   WSHC D2/5/1/7.
3   TNA E179/259/25, pt.1.
4   TNA E179/199/407, rot.4; E179/259/25, pt.1.
5   TNA PROB11/341/161.
6   Aubrey, John. *Wiltshire: the topographical collections*, ed. John Edward Jackson. Wiltshire Archaeological and Natural History Society, 1862, p.391.
7   Williams, *Catholic Recusancy*, op cit, p.115.

family, and who may therefore have been in charge of the Stourton Mission. We have already seen that Richard Bray was a 'very aged priest' with Stourton connections at the beginning of the seventeenth century, and identified perhaps two of his converts. Three decades later, in 1631, Thomas Martin, a secular priest, was in the Diocese of Bath and Wells, and may have served as Lord Stourton's chaplain.[1] The Stourton family may also have been served by David Codner, a Benedictine, who was living in Sir William Stourton's house (probably in London) in the early 1630s, but left c.1632.[2] Not much is known of him, but it is possible he had a connection to the Stourton Mission.[3]

The earliest priest definitely known to have been at Stourton was Nicholas Fitzjames, who died there in 1652.[4] He too was a Benedictine; it is likely that he served the Stourton Mission for many years, although there is no proof that he had charge of it.[5] He was a scion of the Fitzjames family who owned the nearby Redlynch estate.

Fitzjames's cousin, Edward Byfleet, was the first priest who can be proved to have served the Stourton Mission. He was the son of John Byfleet of Bratton, born in 1607. Robert Byfleet, who was named as a trustee in Lord Stourton's 1632 will, was probably a brother.[6] Edward (sometimes known as John) was professed as a Benedictine monk in

---

1   Questier, Michael C., ed. *Newsletters from the Caroline Court 1631-1638: Catholics and the politics of the personal rule.* Camden 5th series 16, 2005, p.113.

2   Questier, Michael C., ed. *Catholicism and community in early modern England: politics, aristocratic patronage, and religion, c.1550-1640.* Cambridge University Press, 2006, p.478.

3   Allanson, Athanasius. *Biography of the English Benedictines.* St. Laurence papers 4. Ampleforth Abbey Trustees, 1999, p.221.

4   Birt, Henry Norbert. *Obit book of the English Benedictines 1600-1912.* Edinburgh: Mercat Press, 1913. A list of Stourton and Bonham priests is given in Williams, *Catholic Recusancy*, op cit, p.170-174 & 245. See also Raymond, 'Catholic Families', op cit; the Monks In Motion database, **https://community.dur. ac.uk/monksinmotion**, and Dolan, D.Gilbert. 'Chapters in the History of the English Benedictine Mission', *Downside Review* 22, 1903, p.294.

5   It has been suggested that the Mission at Bonham was founded in 1640 (Mowbray, op cit, v.2, p.592), but this may be questioned. Firstly, the chapel at Bonham was only built in 1714; the Mission was originally based at Stourton Castle. Secondly, there is much evidence of Catholicism in Stourton before 1640, as has been seen. However, it may be that 1640 was the year in which Fitzjames was placed in charge of the Mission.

6   TNA PROB11/163/663.

1624, and served on the Cumberland mission from 1632. He was sent to Stourton in 1652, and remained there until his death in 1701. Like his Anglican counterpart, Nathaniel Field, he wrote a number of books whilst at Stourton.[1]

His brother, William Byfleet (a secular), who was serving as treasurer of the Catholic secular clergy's Old Chapter in 1682,[2] may have assisted him. William was said to be 'living with Mr Gildon near Shaftesbury' in 1684.[3] This may have been his brother-in-law.[4] In 1706, another priest was living in Stourton with Mrs Gildon.[5] The Gildons, incidentally, were also relatives of the Barnes and Coffin families of Stourton.[6] At least one of them, Mary Gildon, was a tenant of Lord Stourton in Dorset in 1649.[7]

Most of Byfleet's successors only stayed for a few years, and not all of their dates are known.[8] Until the mid-1720s, they were generally Benedictines, although Lord Stourton's tenants were being 'helped by a clergyman', that is, a secular priest, c.1705.[9] It has been suggested that this was one Mr Martin, who lived in Dorset, but who 'frequently visits and assists some familyes in Wiltshire'.[10] George (Placid) Robinson [alias

---

1   He was buried 11th December 1701, according to the parish register. See also Anstruther, Godfrey. *The Seminary priests: a dictionary of the secular clergy of England and Wales, 1538-1850. II. Early Stuart, 1603-1659*. Mayhew-McCrimmon, 1975, p.39-40, and the Monks in Motion database, **https://community.dur.ac.uk/monksinmotion**.

2   Williams, *Catholic Recusancy*, op cit, p.105.

3   Anstruther, Godfrey. *The seminary priests: a dictionary of the secular clergy of England and Wales 1558-1850, II. 1603-1659*. Great Wakering: Mayhew-McCrimmon, 1979, p.39-40.

4   Raymond, 'Catholic Families', op cit.

5   WSHC D/1/9/1/2.

6   Anstruther III, op cit, p.76.

7   Mayo, Charles Herbert, ed. *The Minute Books of the Dorset Standing Committee, 23rd September 1646 to 8th May 1650*. Exeter: William Pollard & Co., 1902, p.524 & 527-8.

8   For their succession, see Williams, *Catholic recusancy*, op cit, p.245. See also Dolan, D.Gilbert. 'Chapters in the History of the English Benedictine Mission', *Downside Review* 22, 1903, p.294-7. Some are noticed in the Monks in Motion database, **https://community.dur.ac.uk/monksinmotion**.

9   Williams, *Catholic recusancy*, op cit, p.171.

10 Stanfield, Raymund. 'Particulars of priests in England and Wales 1692', in *Miscellanea 7*. Catholic Record Society, 9. 1911, p.108. The suggestion was made by Williams, J.Anthony. 'Who was William Byfleet?', *Downside Review* 79, 1961, p.49.

Fairfax] served at some stage in this period, although we have no dates.[1] Placid Nelson, a Lancashire monk who had been prior of St. Edmunds in Paris, served for four years between between 1706 and 1711.[2] He was succeeded by Edward Salisbury, who had been born in Devon, and professed at Lamspringe.[3] John Rigmaiden, another Lancashire man professed at Dieulouard, served between 1712 and 1715,[4] and presumably supervised the move of the chapel from Stourton Castle to Bonham. Thomas Bruning, another Benedictine, followed in 1714. He had professed at Paris in 1696 during the Priorship there of Placid Nelson, one of his predecessors at Stourton. He died in 1719 as a result of a fall from his horse.[5]

Thereafter, the mission was served by Jesuits for the rest of our period. Between 1724 and 1727, the Mission was briefly served by Richard, the Jesuit son of the Jacobite Lord Caryll, many of whose relatives were priests, monks, and nuns.[6] William Beaumont, a newly ordained priest from Somerset, and another Jesuit, succeeded him in 1728; he may have remained in post until the end of our period.[7] Jesuits continued to serve the Mission until 1785.[8] None of Byfleet's successors in our period were local men.

Many members of the local gentry, however, did enter the Catholic priesthood.[9] The Stourton family in particular sent many of its members to join religious orders, or to be educated by them.[10] In 1638, Mary and Frances, the daughters of the 11th Lord Stourton, entered the nunnery of Cambrai aged fourteen and twelve respectively; however, they both

---

1 Birt, op cit, p.92. Monks in Motion database, op cit.
2 Birt, op cit, p.82.
3 Monks in Motion, op cit.
4 Allanson, Athanasius. *Biography of the English Benedictines*. St. Laurence papers 4. Ampleforth Abbey Trustees, 1999, p.191.
5 Monks in Motion, op cit. He was probably the son of Edmund Bruning of Winchester, whose name is included in the register of Papists' estates; cf. Estcourt, Payne, & Orlebar, op cit, p.238 & 284.
6 Foley, op cit, v.3, p.534-40. For Lord Caryll, see *Oxford Dictionary of National Biography* **www.oxforddnb.com**
7 Foley, op cit, v.7, p.44.
8 Holt, Geoffrey. 'The chaplains at Bonham: the Jesuits, 1720-1785', *South Western Catholic History* 13, 1995, p.7-14.
9 For the Somerset gentry, see Raymond, 'Catholic Families', op cit.
10 Much of what follows is based on Williams, J.Anthony. *Catholic recusancy in Wiltshire 1660-1791*. Catholic Record Society, 1968, p.262.

'went away', presumably when they had completed their education.[1] Mary married Sir John Weld, and died shortly afterwards. However, Frances returned to the nunnery and died as a nun of Cambrai in 1646.[2] In 1658, Thomas Stourton, the 11th Lord's brother, was accused of being 'a popish priest or Jesuit'.[3] Thomas, son of the 11th Baron, was educated at St. Gregory's, professed at Douai in 1645, and died in Paris in 1684.[4] William, 12th Lord Stourton, was 'a considerable benefactor' to St Gregory's at Douai. At least four of his sons were educated there in the 1680s and 1690s.[5] One of them, John, professed as a Benedictine monk in 1693, was ordained 1699, elected prior of St. Gregory's in 1717, subsequently served in the Northern Province, and became titular Cathedral Prior of Bath in 1729. He died at Antwerp in 1748.[6] Between 1705 and 1717, he had served as chaplain to the nuns at Cambrai, and was possibly responsible for encouraging other members of the family to join him there. In 1714 Mary, aged thirteen, grand-daughter of the 12th Lord Stourton, arrived at Cambrai; she was recorded as 'gone away' in 1718. Her sisters Catherine and Jane followed her in 1719. All of these girls probably went to Cambrai in order to receive a Catholic education, rather than to become nuns.[7] However, two more sisters, Catherine and Elizabeth, who entered the convent at Liege in 1726 and 1730, were still there when they died, in 1777 and 1741 respectively.[8]

Other members of the family exhibited their Catholicism in other

1   Gillow, Joseph, ed. 'Records of the Abbey of Our Lady of Consolation at Cambrai, 1620-1793', in *Miscellanea* 8. Catholic Record Society 13, 1913, p.45
2   Mowbray, op cit, v.1, p.499.
3   Mowbray, op cit, v.1, p.455.
4   Mowbray, op cit, v.1, p.498; Monks in Motion database **https://community. dur.ac.uk/monksinmotion**; Allanson, Athanasius. *Biography of the English Benedictines.* St. Laurence papers 4. Ampleforth Abbey Trustees, 1999, p.100.
5   Mowbray, op cit, v.2, p.1088.
6   Allanson, op cit, p.183; Oliver, George. *Collections illustrating the history of the Catholic religion in in the counties of Cornwall, Devon, Dorset, Somerset, Wilts., and Gloucester.* Charles Dolman, 1857, p.416; Bellenger, Dominic Aidan. *English and Welsh Priests 1558-1800.* Downside Abbey, 1984, p.194. See also Monks in Motion database, **https://community.dur.ac.uk/monksinmotion**.
7   Gillow, Joseph, ed. 'Records of the Abbey of Our Lady of Consolation at Cambrai, 1620-1793', in *Miscellanea* 8. Catholic Record Society 13, 1913, p.45, 64 & 69. See also Mowbray, op cit, v.1, p.511.
8   Mowbray,op cit, v.1, p.510.

ways. A Charles Stourton was at Douai in 1582.[1] Lord Stourton's house (it is not clear whether this was Stourton Castle, or his London house) was searched for Catholic priests in 1632, and one man was taken – although not the priest who was the subject of the search.[2] The family had close connections with the Bath Benedictines: William Stourton helped to finance their home at Belltree House, and Botolph Stourton was living there in 1715.[3]

Several children of Stourton stewards also entered religion. The Byfleet family has already been mentioned. The two Byfleet priests mentioned above were relatives of Robert Byfleet, who had been a Stourton steward. William Knipe, son of William Knipe, steward to the eleventh baron, was at Douai in 1661, and was sent to Paris in 1661 to succeed Mr John Gildon. The latter was himself descended from Walter Barnes, who has already been encountered as one of the Interregnum stewards of the Stourton estate.[4] Knipe was ordained in 1667.[5] When his father died in 1673, he left £100 to 'my friend Mr Dowaie', that is, to his son's College at Douai. He was obviously seeking a way to avoid the prohibition on making bequests to 'superstitious' uses.[6]

The Stourton Mission flourished during our period. The same cannot be said of Protestant dissent in Stourton. There was no meeting house in the parish.[7] No dissenters were returned in 1669, and only three in 1676.[8] Perhaps the latter resorted to the house of Francis Hartgill

1   Knox, Thomas Francis, ed. *The First and Second Diaries of the English College, Douay*. David Nutt, 1878, p.189.
2   Mowbray, op cit, v.1, p.453.
3   Williams, J.Anthony, ed. *Post-Reformation Catholicism in Bath, vol.1*. Catholic Record Society publications (record series 65. 1975, p.62 & 55.
4   Anstruther, Godfrey. *The seminary priests: a dictionary of the secular clergy of England and Wales 1558-1850, III. 1660-1750*. Great Wakering: Mayhew-McCrimmon, 1976, p.76-7 & 125. See also above, pp. 160-3.
5   Bellenger, Domini Aidan. *English and Welsh Priests 1558-1800*. Downside Abbey, 1984, p.194.
6   Williams, J.Anthony. *Catholic Recusancy in Wiltshire, 1660-1791*. Catholic Record Society, 1968, p.200.
7   Chandler, John, ed. *Wiltshire Dissenters' meeting house certificates and registrations, 1689-1852*. Wiltshire Record Society 40. 1985, p.xxviii.
8   Turner, G.Lyon. *Original records of early nonconformity, vol.3*, p.816; Simpson, Cecilia. 'A census of Wiltshire in 1676', Wiltshire notes & Queries 3, 1899-1901, p.537; Whiteman, Anne, ed. *The Compton census of 1676: a critical edition*. Oxford University Press for the British Academy, 1986, p.125; WSHC D1/27/1/4/66.

of Kilmington, which had been licenced by Robert Cox for Anabaptist worship under the Declaration of Indulgence in 1672[1] In 1777, Mary Smart of Kilmington bequeathed an annuity of 40s, to be paid from 12 acres of land in Gasper, to the dissenting minister of Horningsham.[2] In 1783, it was reported to the Bishop that there were two Presbyterians in Stourton.[3]

There were also echoes of a much older religion. It is not clear whether Margery and Thomas Symons lived in Mere or Stourton. In 1624, the Mere Hundred jury presented them as 'notable wytches'.[4] Two decades later, when John Freke's gold ring was stolen, his servant Edith Courtney consulted Thomas Temple as to its whereabouts, 'he having the repute of a cunning man'.[5] It is clear that what we would call superstition was widespread.

The evidence for 'magic' specifically related to Stourton is minimal. However, there is plenty of evidence from neighbouring parishes.[6] Indeed, in 1665, it was claimed that a witches' coven consisting of ten women and one man had met at Hussey's Ground in neighbouring Brewham.[7] It has been conjectured that Hussey's Ground was close to Alfred's Tower. If so, it may have been on Stourton's boundary. The coven included several members of the Green family, who may have been related to the Greens of Stourton. In the same year, a 'young maid' from Kilmington was said to have been 'bewitched by an apple', resulting in her death.[8]

Unfortunately, the evidence for demonology is very limited. It usually only survives when accusations of witchcraft were made. Similarly, as we have seen, our knowledge of Roman Catholicism,

1   Bate, F. *The declaration of indulgence: a study in the rise of organized dissent.* Liverpool, 1908, p.xlvi.
2   WSHC 383/535.
3   Ransome, Mary, ed. *Wiltshire returns to the bishops visitation queries, 1783.* Wiltshire Record Society 27. 1972, p.205.
4   WSHC A1/110/T1624/127.
5   WSHC A1/110/T1648, 216.
6   For an overview, see Pickering, Andrew. *The Witches of Selwood Forest: witchcraft and demonology in the West of England, 1625-1700.* Cambridge Scholars, 2017.
7   Pickering, Andrew, ed. *The Hellish knot: Witches and Demons in Seventeenth Century Somerset.* Ape or Eden Books, 2013, p.120-2. See also Pickering, *Witches,* op cit, p.81-2.
8   Pickering, *Witches,* op cit, p.60.

and, indeed of nonconformity, in this period is largely dependent on accusations of recusancy against their adherents. Even for those who attended the ministrations of the Anglican clergy, it is not possible to probe deeply into their true beliefs. We rarely have evidence which comes directly from the man in the pew. It has been possible to place the religious beliefs and activities of Stourton people in their institutional and social context. To go beyond that is to enter the realms of conjecture.

Stourton Bibliography

T HE FOOTNOTES GIVE details of the sources used in the text. Works which deal primarily with Stourton are listed here. A few of these are outside of our period, but are nevertheless important for the parish's history. There are of course many other works dealing specifically with Stourhead, but these are not listed.

Bernadette, Sister. *Some aspects of Catholic Life in Wiltshire 1660-1850, with particular reference to the family and village of Stourton*. B.Ed dissertation, 1976. WANHS mss 1370.

Bonham, Carol. 'Notes on the manors of Discove and Bonham on the Wiltshire-Somerset border from the 12th century', *Hatcher Review* 2(15),1983, p.228-32.

Calland, Gary. *St Peter's Stourton: a tour and history of the church*. Henry Cadogan Hoare, 2010.

Day, Cathy. *Wiltshire marriage patterns 1754-1914: geographical mobility, cousin marriage and illegitimacy*. Cambridge Scholars Publishing, 2013.

Deverill, Chris & Penny. 'St. Benedict's Bonham: the two earliest registers, 1767-1801', *South Western Catholic History* 10, 1992.

Dodd, Dudley, ed. *The Letters of Henry Hoare, 1760-1781*. Wiltshire Record Society, 71. 2018

Ellis, John Henry, ed. *The Registers of Stourton, County Wilts., from 1570 to 1800*. Harleian Society publications 12. 1887.

Hoare, Richard Colt. *The Modern History of South Wiltshire*. John Bowyer Nichols & John Gough Nichols, 1822.

Holt, Geoffrey. 'The Chaplains at Bonham: the Jesuits, *c.*1720-1785', *South Western Catholic History* 13, 1995, p.7-14.

Hutchings, V. *Messrs Hoare, bankers: a history of the Hoare banking dynasty*. Constable, 2005.

Jackson, J.E. 'Charles, Lord Stourton and the murder of the Hartgills', *Wiltshire Archaeological and Natural History Magazine* 8, 1864, p.243-341.

McGarvie, Michael. *The Bounds of Selwood: an examination.* Frome Society for Local Study, 1978.

McKewan, Colin. *Stourhead Lake Project 2005: Survey and Excavation of the Lakes at Stourhead House.* Nautical Archaeological Society, 2006. Online at **https://nauticalarchaeologysociety.org/sites/default/files/u9/NAS%20Stourhead%20Master%20composite%20Report-01_sml.pdf**

Mowbray, Lord. *The history of the noble house of Stourton.* 2 vols. Elliot Stock, 1899.

Raymond, Stuart A. 'Barnes: a Catholic family on the borders of Wiltshire and Somerset, *c.*1548- *c.*1750', *Genealogists magazine,* 32(9), 2018, p.340-48.

Raymond, Stuart A. 'Catholic families of South-East Somerset and their connection to Stourton, c. 1550-1650', unpublished paper.

Raymond, Stuart A. 'The Knipes: a footnote', *Wiltshire Archaeological and Natural History Magazine,* forthcoming

Raymond, Stuart A. 'Walter Barnes of Stourton (*c.*1680-1758): his Family, his Debts, and his Religion', *Notes & Queries for Somerset & Dorset,* 38(388), 2018, p.337-48.

Stourton Kilmington & Mere Genealogies **http://wiltshire.anu.edu.au**

Williams, J. Anthony. *Catholic recusancy in Wiltshire 1660-1791.* Catholic Record Society, 1968.

Woodbridge, Kenneth. *Landscape and antiquity: aspects of English culture at Stourhead 1718 to 1838.* Clarendon Press, 1970.

Place Name Index

Note that places with no county designation are either in Wiltshire, or overseas.

Subject Index

Personal Name Index

Note that the spellings of some names have been standardised

Stourton Church

Rear view of Stourton Church, showing the table tombs of some of the parishioners. Curiously, these are omitted from John Britton's engraving (see the front cover).

Monument to Henry Hoare, the Good

Stourton Castle, based on a drawing by John Aubrey

Fireplace in the Hoare family pew in Stourton Church

The Gatehouse

Bonham House and Chapel in the 19th century

Interior view of Bonham Chapel in the 19th century

Henry Hoare (the Good), by
Michael Dahl

Henry Hoare (the Magnificent),
by William Hoare (courtesy of
Getty Open Source)

Stourhead

The field known as Paradise is under the lake

Lightning Source UK Ltd.
Milton Keynes UK
UKHW021527110221
378627UK00005B/1353

9 781906 978686